The Great Get Out

The Great GET OUT

How to Build the Life You Want

JL ORR

OBOL HOUSE
PUBLISHING COMPANY

An imprint of Huntsville Independent Press

2112 Morningside Drive NW, Huntsville, AL, 35810

Obol House can bring authors to your live event.
For more information or to book an event, contact Obol House Publishing Company at +1 (256) 678-0411 or visit our website at: www.ObolHouse.com

Cover design by Chris Treccani - 3 Dog Creative
Interior design by Chris Treccani - 3 Dog Creative

The text for this book was set in Adobe Garamond Pro.

Manufactured in the United States of America
First Obol House paperback edition December 2025

12345678910

The Library of Congress has cataloged the hardcover edition as follows:

Names: JL Orr, author.

Title: The Great Get Out

LCCN (Pending)
Identifiers: ISBN 979-8-9934325-0-2 (pbk)
979-8-9934325-1-9 (hcv)

Table of Contents

Note From the Author

This book is dedicated to my immediate family, and husband, Kendrick Orr. Without your dedication to me as a wife, and constant hard work as a provider, I would not have had the time and opportunity to sit down and finish this book. Kendrick, whom I affectionately refer to as KO: you absolutely are an amazing man that doesn't nearly receive the recognition he should for being such a great man, a true leader, and legend ahead of his time in music and entrepreneurship! Thank you for offering to spend forever with me.

Our unique friendship and union has stood up to some remarkable trials that have proven to me this union is God ordained. Even though some days we drive each other crazy in all the best ways, I wouldn't have it any other way! You have my heart, and I promise to take good care of yours. Proverbs 27:17 says iron sharpens iron, and we are truly better together. Thank you for motivating me to finish this project and for producing the Mere Motivation podcast. Thank you for Builders R Us, LLC and building a future together with me. May all of our hopes and dreams come true. Thank you for being you! It's true what they say: God saved the best for last!

To my 3 sons Colin, Carson and Rasheed. Thank you for becoming such amazing young men. I have so much pride and respect for who you've become. You have given my heart so much joy. I am very grateful that I have you to love, and for the love and respect you give in return. I love being your mother.

To my daughter, Haley. Thank you for being the solid rock that you are, and for my 2 grandsons. You all bring me such joy!

To my daughter / baby cousin, Tyesha. You don't know how truly proud I am of you. Keep going!

To my siblings Chanel, Eric, Michelle, Michael, and Tashira. Keep making the world a better place.

To Auntie Valerie (Tiny) on my biological father's side. Thank you for your continual love and support.

To my mother, Shadiyah. Thank you for giving your life to Christ and becoming brand new.

To my Dad, Quinn. Thank you for stepping up to the plate and becoming the amazing father I never had. I love you all more than you will ever know. You are all the wind beneath my wings!

A special thanks to Catherine L. Cotton, may she rest in peace, and Thomas E. Cotton—the Matriarch and Patriarch of our family, without whom I would have never survived my childhood. Thank you for lighting the way!

Psalm 23

1 The Lord is my shepherd; I shall not want.
2 He maketh me to lie down in green pastures: he leadeth me beside the still waters.
3 He restoreth my soul: he leadeth me in the paths of righteousness for his name's sake.
4 Yea, though I walk through the valley of the shadow of death, I will fear no evil: for thou art with me; thy rod and thy staff they comfort me.
5 Thou preparest a table before me in the presence of mine enemies: thou anointest my head with oil; my cup runneth over.
6 Surely goodness and mercy shall follow me all the days of my life: and I will dwell in the house of the Lord for ever.

Foreword
By Melinda Ward

———————■———————

This memoir is not a story of tragedy, but of transcendence. It is the record of a soul that walked through fire and found light on the other side—not in spite of the pain, but because of what it revealed.

For years, silence and control were the air Jerri Orr breathed. There was abuse in many forms—some visible, others hidden behind vows and expectations. Maltreatment stripped away her sense of safety, self-worth and, at times, even her connection to God. Yet somewhere, deep within, a quiet whisper refused to die. It reminded her that she was more than what had been done to her. That whisper became a voice and that voice became a force that carried her out of darkness.

Healing did not arrive all at once. It came in layers—through tears, sometimes isolation, though truth, through rediscovering her own sacred connection to spirit and self. She learned that faith is not blind obedience; it is the courage to see clearly and s ll choose love—especially for oneself.

This memoir is not about revenge or regret. It is about reclamation. It is about what happens when you stop surviving and start living—when you realize that God never leaves, even when you feel the most forsaken.

To those still finding their way out of control, fear or shame: You are not alone. These pages remind you that healing is holy, freedom is possible, and that your story—no matter how broken it feels—can become a testament to the Lord's enduring grace.

Introduction
How did we get here?

———

"You better figure out how you like your eggs." If you recognize that line, you know my favorite Julia Roberts movie, *The Runaway Bride*. The concept has almost nothing to do with eggs except to point out there are many ways to do the same thing, so it's best you know yourself to live in your truth to the fullest. Like finding your center, it keeps you from just going along to get along. If you do not, you will never develop as a person.

The crazy thing is that the people who usually run away from their lives to find themselves are the people pleasers who have adapted to using fight or flight as skills for survival in a world where friendly people are bullied into putting others before themselves. Most people run away from their problems because firstly, they do not know how to set boundaries to keep others invading their personal space, physically and spiritually, and secondly, because they have not matured fully enough yet to know they can close the door and have the final say over themselves. It is about finding their voice and learning how to use it!

Take myself for example, this is the third time I have sat down to write this book, each time from a different perspective and at various stages of my life and it wasn't until I stopped running that I was able to write it.

Life unfolds in stages, and when I understood this better, I began to demand more of myself in maturity and accountability. The same 3-year-old crying and fighting sleep at 8 pm because I did not want to go to bed is easier to accept than if I, a 30-year-old, was still crying and fighting to stay up all hours of the night. At some point, as an adult, I had to be accountable to myself and say okay; as much as I would like to take the position, I was too old to act in a way that looked irresponsible.

On the other hand, as a 30-year-old people-pleaser, when I had to choose between adequately setting boundaries for myself or choosing to do what is best for others, I had the false impression that doing what was best for others was more important. That putting myself first was selfish, even if it meant doing the opposite of what was best for me.

My lack of healthy boundaries stunted my personal growth so much that I found myself continually self-sabotaging. I did not understand that always putting others first kept me from living to my full potential and succeeding! The irony of the phrase, "practice what you preach," means to take the advice you keep giving others. I was good at helping others and sucked at helping myself. I was stuck in the mentality of false humility, where I could give a compliment but not receive one. I know you feel me if you have that same quality. I was the woman who could tell another woman she looked good in the same dress I told myself I looked fat in! Why is that?

I grew up believing I was not worthy because I had more compassion for others than I did for myself. Not realizing that I needed to "get out" of the mentality that other people came before me. That it somehow made me a nice person because I allowed people to walk all over me—a learned behavior I did not know how to cross off my to-do list. I was programmed to have a servant's mentality, and that saying no was not an option for me. I was taught that prioritizing the needs of others before myself was the higher good, and that quality made me stronger, just like the old saying "what doesn't kill you makes you stronger." That is false teaching at its finest!

The first step towards change for me was realizing that I had a problem. Learning that my greatest strength was also my greatest weakness. That was a hard truth to accept when you get joy out of serving, but also understand that some people will use you up if you let them because that is what takers do. They drain you until there is nothing left and demand more, resorting to abuse when you are at your weakest.

Only a few years ago did the reality of what I was doing become clear to me. Unknowingly, operating out of my love for serving others had mixed me up with an unhealthy codependency for pleasing people. I was trying to build a platform for a healthy life out of it, and wondering why the bottom kept falling out. I did not understand the psychology behind it. I did not understand that a people pleaser should not partner up with someone that is very assertive or domineering, because you will never have room to grow outside of their expectations.

I prayed for the Lord to rebuild me into someone healthy and happy, a woman that had the courage and tenacity to speak up for myself. My prayer was, Lord, reset my mind mentally to a place before any abuse ever happened to me, and rebuild my mind so I can receive the life you have for me, to keep me from living in these dead cycles of self-sabotage.

At that time, I had been married thrice, and it took me a long time to accept the truth about myself after the fact that it was time to stop running and learn how to live. Thankfully my third husband was the chosen one that God would use to help me grow and to teach me that our relationship was more than a marriage but a friendship between two people that wanted the best for each other. He helped me to understand love was not one sided!

In the movie *Runaway Bride* she was engaged three times. The third and last guy was the guy she traded in her running shoes to, only after she figured out how she liked her eggs. The eggs were a metaphor for how she wanted to live her life. She finally found the person she saw herself in the most, the man she saw herself growing old with.

My name is Jerri Lynn, not Julia, and I have divorce papers for two marriages that I entered because they were the catch, and not I. That's right, you heard me. I was the bride that said yes even after having second thoughts, stuck in the mentality of unworthiness, with nowhere to go, because in my mind, I was still a runaway looking for shelter and safety. In reality, by the time I moved to Alabama, I had grown into a beautiful young woman that had an honest job working in the medical field, my own apartment and a car doing well as a young woman that by the age of 22 had survived more than I gave myself credit for. If I had a clear picture of that before the first marriage, I would have known he was not right for me.

Instead, I was looking for a protector and not a partner, stability and not someone to build a foundation with. I was more than a conqueror with a defeated mindset and didn't know it. I was not a runaway anymore, it's just that my mind had not caught up to my reality. However, I still had not truly found a place to call home. I invited toxicity into my life because I had no peace of mind. In the heart of silence, all I could see were all the bad things that happened to me were happening again in the silence, and I didn't want to be alone. I grew up on the run and I did not even see that I had grown up!

It took me so long to find a happy place that after a while I settled on just being a wife, because I knew if nothing else, I could serve well, since at the time that's all there was to my identity. By the time I had given birth to my first son I figured I'd be good at two things, becoming a loving mom to my children, the kind of mom I did not have growing up, and I would be an obedient wife—instead of changing my mind at the altar, which seemed rude after all the trouble that he went through to plan a wedding. That was the first marriage.

I originally tried to call it off, but everyone around me had me convinced that he was more of a catch to me than I was to him, because how could someone with my abusive upbringing do any better? I operated from a place of low self-esteem, thinking it was humility, second guessing myself because I figured they knew better.

The first time I married, I did it after talking to the people I thought were my friends—not anyone that I had established a long-time bond with, but I at least honestly believed they loved me, and mostly gave me the green light based on what they would have done. I had so much doubt about his intentions that I kept saying, "Girl, I don't know!" Right up to the wedding day, I mean, you cannot walk away after your great-grand-mother drove 8 hours in a car at 70 years old to see her first great grand-daughter get married.

This is why you need to trust yourself and your gut over the advice of others when making critical decisions. Remember, you always know what is best for you, and the key is to trust yourself.

He only married me after I gave him an ultimatum: I was not going to be the girl who was a lifetime companion. I did not trust myself to believe that I did not even need him at all. That was after I started going to church, and back then, church was the club, you know, that other place where you go to find a spouse. We dated for two years, and I trusted that all of the red flags I saw were just my imagination and upbringing that blinded me. Knowing that we were not compatible, I went against my better judgment and said he was the one. He decided I was the one based solely on my being so submissive, and my predisposition to do as I was told.

The wedding and reception played out like a Hollywood production of *Our Town*. There were over three hundred guests, none of which I knew personally, and seven bridesmaids that were all strangers except one. That was my little sister. It felt like I was a character in a play instead of a bride on the happiest day of her life.

I was just another stupid girl, and did not know it until after we married. He sat me on the shelf to collect dust like a forgotten elf on the shelf! I lived alone most of the marriage—without a relationship or any kind of bond—and I lived that way for the next ten years. I had my children to raise, so eventually I focused on that, as most women would.

At the time, I was sold on the idea he was a good, church-going man. In my mind, there were only two types of men. The first kind were men like my father, who was a pimp, drug dealer, and user, with a nine to five mechanic job to cover his tracks, and the other were the guys that went to church. His kind happened to be the lesser of two evils, and I didn't know of any other kind as of yet. My grandfather was a church going man, and he always took loving care of my grandmother, so I chose from that, and never did know any more of the man except surface traits. Nothing concrete.

Granted, I was still discovering whether there was any merit in marrying a good, church-going man. I just assumed they were better! That's because I only had one example of a church-going man growing up.

My second husband is the one I had to drag to church, but his parents had a strong connection to the church, so I felt there was hope that he had the potential to be a good man—like the apple might not fall far from the tree! The last thing I wanted to do was end up in a second unhealthy marriage, yet here I was because I thought, well, he was more fun than the first. He was not as controlling as my first.

My second, however, did the love bomb thing and had me believing he loved my children. He pretended to be better than the first, and I fell for it because I thought he was the catch, not me. And I desperately wanted to get as far away as I could from the father of my children. I was so afraid of my first husband at the time because even after granting me the divorce, it is as if he was a ghost waiting in the shadows waiting for me to fail and coming running back to him. I believe I married to make sure I was out of his line of fire.

My first husband knew judges and lawyers, all types of people who could make my life a living hell until he got me back in his prison of power and control. I believed he was waiting for me if I wasn't careful. As the old folks say, I moved in or "shacked up" with my second husband even though I managed to stay single for two years after my first marriage, with a decent job and a home for my children awarded to me in the divorce. I never truly felt safe alone. I had the victim mentality that I could not do it alone, as most divorced single mothers think. Let me say, that is a lie!

So, with that victim mentality I let my second husband talk me into moving in with him to share the bills and financial responsibilities, plus he promised to keep me safe from any fear I had of the boy's father. Again, I believed in someone else more than I did myself.

He popped the question with a cheap cubic zirconia ring that came in one of those tiny zip lock bags in a basket next to the cashier's register. I didn't know that because he took it out of the plastic bag and put it in an old jewelry box he had laying around. I saw the red flags, but since I had such a low opinion of myself and two more mouths to feed, it did not matter that there were newspaper articles about an old arrest he had back in college. When I questioned him about it, he told me that he was young and that he was not that man anymore. The arrest was for a peeping tom charge that he told me was a misunderstanding, that he was on campus looking into a window for someone he knew, and it was taken off his record. Seemed believable enough, college can get crazy for most, so I tried to be non-judgmental.

It wasn't until after I married him in a shotgun courthouse wedding that I came to the harsh reality that I had married a habitual liar who had no intention of keeping the "m" in marriage monogamous.

What did I do? I figured if you can't beat them, join them, literally! I was very transparent. No, I was not cheating, and I didn't do anything illegal—I just thought I would become the fun, open, super cool wife, and we could do the open marriage thing, women only, no men. I was not looking for another man. I was looking to keep my husband from being with other women away from home, so I allowed him to bring women home. And I became the "hostess with the mostess" out of the fear of looking like a two-time divorced loser. I could not admit how ashamed I was that I allowed him to fool me, and I did not want to move my children again.

Don't judge—you would be surprised at what you might do to avoid looking like a fool. It wasn't hard because I have never been the type of woman who was jealous of other women. Some men love the idea of having sex with two women, and unbelievably, some women will go to their graves with the same secret that I put it in a book, that's for sure. I will not lie and say it was my first time with a woman. It had been a coping mechanism growing up as a teenager, but it was my first time knowingly and willingly agreeing to share my husband.

Sex and marriage can get complicated, and most people will opt to get creative to save it to their own demise. Something I will never do again because I learned a hard lesson. The lesson is that three is absolutely a crowd, and turning to such unnatural measures will in no way save a marriage, but it definitely will prolong the divorce.

It wasn't until after I had egg on my face that I took the rose-colored glasses off and saw how much I devalued myself to keep a man who had no intention of ever being faithful, or even loving me. Truth is, as a broken hearted single mother, I was an easy target. The straw that broke the camel's back was when I said I was done fooling around bringing other women into our marriage and still being disrespected. After I had decided that the European-style sex life was not my thing, I told him no more. I was going to get back right with God is what I told him, and he agreed.

I thought we both agreed, and it wasn't until one of the women that I had toxic bonded with called and told me she was still having sex with my husband, and that it was a courtesy call because she respected me for going cold turkey on the whole thing.

I gave them both "back to the streets," as the saying goes. I figured if I go where no woman has gone for you, and you are still acting greedy, then you can "free yourself," as my girl Fantasia says!

I returned to the house I thought was home and demanded answers about why this woman gave me details about situations we agreed not to partake in any longer. I told him that the audacity was she called me while I was at work, and I sat through the rest of my workday feeling like an idiot. He just went on to be who he always was without me, and I learned he never intended to change. After that, he even stopped going to church with me. And I had to make the decision alone to repent and ask for God's forgiveness for my stupidity!

The gig was up altogether, and my children were ready to go as well, seeing they were also victims of his mental abuse. He went from a cool stepdad to a daily dictator. They did not deserve that and neither did I. The worst thing a mother can do is allow her children to witness her being taken advantage of and degraded and be able to do nothing about it, but I didn't run away this time. I left with my head up, knowing I was making the right decision, even if in the eyes of others I looked like a fool again!

This time I stood in my authority as a woman with a made-up mind. I gave him sixty days' notice and took the proper steps to leave, and no matter what he pulled out his bag of tricks, I stuck to my guns to show my sons that I was serious about giving them the type of happy home they deserved. Even if it was a single parent home. I also had emotional support from my little sister. She has always been my biggest cheerleader. My boys were ready to go, too. My first born came to me one day and said, "mama you know we can't stay here, right?"

Ultimately, I had a compelling proposition from a woman that was the only friend I thought I had. The Lord used her to seal the deal. She told me she could not be my friend if I didn't leave this man.

At the time, she was someone I considered a godly mentor, so I believed this to be God warning me to turn away and get as far away from this man as possible, before I was overtaken by a fate worse than I was willing to admit. After her admission I started doing the inner work to heal from the hurt of this devastating betrayal. If you think marriage is hard, divorce is harder, so it's better to wait and make sure you're marrying a friend instead of a foe.

You cannot even imagine how many times I hit my head against a wall thinking, *Jiminy Cricket! I'm a two time divorcee!* My baby sister told me that I had better forget what people will think of me, and get out of that house. I took the necessary steps to find an apartment. I moved out before the beginning of the summer of the same year—the last week of May to be exact—and I left without taking one red cent or asking to get anything out of it. He threw in $500.00 to pay my deposit and functioned as if it did not bother him at all. After he saw I was serious he tried to bargain with me and offered me $20,000.00 plus a weekly allowance to stay.

He said, "you can stay in the guest bedroom and I stay in the master, we can do our own thing until we figure this out."

I told him in no uncertain terms that what he was proposing was not a marriage, and refused. I loved my freedom more than the money!

When it was time to move, I took just my children and a few miscellaneous things so that my tiny apartment wouldn't be empty. As I was packing the U-Haul he stood at the stairwell, threatening me with a mean look in his eyes as if to intimidate me, but I had learned my lesson.

I was more afraid to stay than I was to leave, so I told him "Not today! I am leaving, and you should have taken me seriously when I asked you to, instead of playing me for a fool after I already told you how much life left me damaged!"

And we walked right out of that front door, handing him the key on the way out, and making it clear that I was not going to change my mind.

Once again I found myself starting again from scratch. At least I am grateful I did not have any children from that marriage. I had already decided after my first divorce that I didn't want to bring any more children into the world to have to endure what my sons had. During that first marriage, though, I also took in my baby cousin — a beautiful little girl of five, and raised her until she was twelve. Sadly, I could not manage the weight of 3 children as a single mother, and I did not want any harm to come to her during my transition to single-parenthood on my own. I left her in the care of other family members for safe keeping. It hurt like hell, but I know it was the right thing to do at the time.

One broken family was enough for me to understand how devastating divorce is for children, and I did not want to take the chance on raising any more children of divorce if I could help it. I made the choice after my first marriage to get a tubal ligation done. I was proud of myself that I was careful not to have children out of wedlock, so I did not want to take the chance for any unplanned pregnancies after that. Leaving this second divorce free from the burden of co-parenting. He was also free to be single again, not that he ever stopped being single in hindsight. Truthfully, we were only married on paper anyway.

After my second divorce, I had to dig deep and figure out where this drive to be married came from, because for the life of me I could not figure it out. Then it hit me like a ton of bricks: my mother and her mother. I come from a line of women who knew what it meant to wait on a man hand and foot. I realized the only examples I had growing up were of women that worked very hard to be good wives by going above and beyond what was healthy in order to "keep their man happy," so I thought I had to do the same. I had no idea that was a toxic characteristic!

The women in my family majorly had toxic relationships with men that demanded to be treated in the old-style traditional roles, where the woman did as she was told and was better seen and not heard. I believed any attempt to speak up for yourself was defiant, now understanding it was a basic human need to be heard and healthy to have a partner that wanted to listen.

Instead, I grew up with women that made themselves door mats for a man, only for those same men to use the same hands and feet that God gave them to enact abuse over the women and children they were supposed to protect when they didn't follow instructions. I was raised by the type of women who were groomed to serve, and that is what I perceived would make a great wife. It's the kind of wife I tried to be too, except it becomes taxing when all you do is give, and all they do is take.

I didn't learn about true love, where the feeling is mutual and there is an unconditional exchange of support and adoration. I learned that what you do to get a man, you did to keep a man, and if you slack and he slips up then it was your own fault. I didn't grow up around women with careers, soccer moms, carpool dads, and the two parent household power couple. So, I did what I knew at the time. I was so fixated in that mindset that it was not until the age of forty after two divorces that I realized, "what's good for the goose isn't always good for the gander!"

The women in my family also didn't have the greatest sixth sense when it came to men, and I felt the same dark generational curse that fell on them had somehow caught up with me. I was terrified to even dream of a happy relationship without seeing a tragic end. All I knew was that I hadn't found my person yet, the way Cinderella found her prince or Snow White found hers. I mean, Ariel was a fish, and she had a good man. All I had was the hope that the fairy tale at the end was going to be a real thing for me, too. Honestly, think about it. As little girls, all we were told is that one day a man is going to come and sweep us off our feet.

All the unrealistic Disney movies of the prince coming to find you and making you a princess and you live happily ever after? I was looking for that. Not the Lifetime Movie Network dramas, which were the only real stories life had given me so far. Even so, that was my upbringing in the seventies, when a girl could only dream of being a homemaker and raising babies.Now in these more modern times girls have so many more opportunities than what our grandmothers did, and I feel awful about the way this present-day society of young girls are being gaslighted into thinking that what's between their legs is more valuable than what is between their ears, because a woman's brain is her most valuable asset!

Truly we have gone from one extreme to another. We have gone from the Barbie doll Disney princess conservative examples that left most women hanging in abusive, one-sided marriages with no identity, to the nuances of the 20th-century toxic example that a man isn't good for anything except what he can contribute financially. Using men for money is just as damaging to men, and it leaves young girls believing their only worth is physical, when in reality a woman's most important asset is her mind.

The truth is, friendship and partnership are the missing elements that create space for both to thrive as a power couple—the bond that cements any lasting union.

After I had moved into my tiny apartment with the boys, I was not much for casual dating, men in my mind were scary enough as it is, and the fear of standing alone in the dark face to face with what looked like the devil with the lights off was complicated. That was the scene that hovered in my mind after I left the boy's father. Him standing in the dark, heavy breathing like the boogie man, it was a terrible scene that I would not wish on my worst enemy. I hadn't seen anything like that since my last encounter with my father in my adolescent years. Truth is, you never really know a person until you see them upset. How someone manages their anger reveals who they are at their lowest. I did not want to take that chance and date a total stranger!

I stayed strong through two toxic marriages, holding on longer than I should have. But if those were the lesser evils compared to the cruelty I saw in my father, I had to search my soul and wonder—could this really be all that relationships offered? I needed to be careful not to let my vulnerability show. After you leave a toxic relationship, you must discipline yourself to suppress the need for outside comfort and learn to hug yourself through the hurt. I grew up watching my mother date men after my father moved out and hated being introduced to different men wondering if any of them would be a repeat of my dad. There was no way I was going to make my boys suffer that emotional stress!

I was not mature enough to know what support looked like. I only knew how to serve, not how to be served, so I supported their dreams, and they let me. Whenever I started to take the time to pursue my own dreams, it was as if I was being selfish or I was lead to believe I couldn't handle too much pressure of being a wife, mother and a successful business woman, every time it looked like my life was going to take off, there was always a reason. The bottom fell out, and both times in both marriages, they figured out how to distract me from the things that made me successful and concentrate on the things that made them successful.

That is my opinion and my belief! All I could do was trust we would co-parent more effectively than we did cohabitating after the first marriage. He was the best at making me feel incompetent and unqualified to achieve anything without him telling me how to milk the cow and drink the milk.

Anything other than that I was not doing it right in his eyes, and it wasn't until I started working as Prevention Program Director at the Domestic Violence shelter that I realized he was a liar. I worked that job 8 years as a supervisor with employees underneath me with a whole crew of people that thought I was the absolute best person in the world, there I was succeeding without him telling me what to do, and it hit me hard how he made me feel incompetent all those years just for his own personal insecurities. He liked me better stuck in victim mentality mode, but you do not know until you know.

In my second failed attempt at love, I was simply grateful I did not have any children with him. He certainly pushed the envelope when it came to living in the shadows. I cannot tell you how many pairs of binoculars I had to take from him, with the promise he would never do it again. I learned the hard way, the little incident he had in college was a fixed character trait as a man and it was one of his many unhealthy addictions!

I was just grateful that I could completely sever ties and never look back, not even to coordinate scheduled pick-ups and drop-offs. He called me absent-minded to a fault. An insecure man will try to break a strong woman every time she starts doing well because in his eyes, she will know her own capabilities to succeed without his help, therefore taking away the only tool they can use to assert power and control over her. Helplessness or hopelessness makes a woman feel she needs a provider or protector like a little girl without the power to make her own decisions.

Having success means that no one has power and control over you, something that does not intimidate a confident grown man that appreciates having an intellectually strong woman at their side. He obviously did not want me to identify my strengths, something I was taking a good look at after all of this, I needed to dig deep and do this on my own if I had too. I needed to put my sons first, even if I could do the same for myself. My sons were all I could think about. *Do this for them,* I kept telling myself. In my mind I had nothing else going for me, save for being a mom, and if I failed at everything else, I would not fail at this mom thing. I couldn't!

Looking back, all I'd known as a little girl were two kinds of men: good and bad. The good kind went to church, like my grandfather, and the bad kind were womanizers and abusers, like my father. I did not know a man could be both good and bad by the condition of his heart, not the façades they put on. Contrary to popular belief, any man can and will change for the person who is right for him. I had to rethink my whole life. I felt like I was never enough, no matter how much I tried to be. That can be a very depressing thought!

I had learned how to degrade myself to appease others. I kept putting myself down to put others ahead of me. I learned that behavior as a child growing up in a home plagued with domestic violence. My mother took the abuse quietly, not realizing she didn't have to. She always says, "I didn't have to, so now I don't." Now, at the age of 65, she has learned her own lessons as well.

That's the mentality it takes to forgive yourself and press the reset button. Negatively reinforced, learned behavior will produce toxic confidence in some, and destructive self-sabotage in others. I unknowingly took the path of destructive self-sabotage. It didn't look like sabotage to me when I thought I was serving others, by putting forth extra effort and going above and beyond to ensure those around me were happy. I thought I was just being nice!

The toxic part was that I didn't understand those qualities of mine should be earned and not handed out. People do not see you as priceless if you just hand yourself over on a silver platter, a bad habit developed from neglect. No one showed me that it's self-taught. Growing up in a toxic household, I had no choice but to learn my abusers' patterns to keep situations from becoming explosive. That instinct was ingrained in me as early as five or six. That, coupled with some false religious teachings later in my 20s, made me the perfect candidate for mind control and psychological abuse. As you continue to read, you will see what I mean by "being the ideal candidate for psychological abuse," which I will discuss with you in the forthcoming chapters.

I am so proud of myself that this time, I did not fall into the same toxic pattern as before. This time, I succeeded at focusing on myself, and it feels great. It took me so long to pray for real, like, Lord, I am done doing what I think is right. I prayed a prayer of surrender:

Lord, I desire what you have for me because I'm missing something all these years, trying so hard to do better and be better yet continuing to hit brick walls only to have the audacity to get back up and try to climb it again. I never gave up! I am proud of myself because I never gave up on myself and believing I was born on purpose for a purpose. Amen!

It seemed important for me to tell my story. I finally saw the big picture when I started to put it on paper. I had to work on not being overwhelmed, just sitting down to write it all out, but I thought what if the same story that others in my past were tired of hearing was liberating to someone who had never heard it before? What if someone needed my story to heal? Are you letting your story defeat you, or are you using it to propel you towards purpose? We all have a story. The key is not to be ashamed of your past. Own it! Taking accountability is part of the healing process. You were born with a purpose, with breath in your lungs for a reason. It is up to you to figure out for the reason for yourself. Even though I looked at my life like another #Metoo story, for someone new—it could have been just what the doctor ordered.

Over the years, whenever I took the opportunity to put myself first, I would sit down and write about myself until some convincing distraction came along, to cause me to put myself on the back burner. I folded myself up like an old patch quilt in a box on the closet shelf for later. Each time, I had to press through so much pain just reading it back to myself, since I have been through so much more than I believe one person should, it was bittersweet sharing it. I wish I had someone to consort with that had a similar story at some point that understood me enough to help me write the darn thing! I learned the hard way I had to do this on my own, no excuses if I was going to finally break through the invisible glass ceiling.

I did not want to be the person to write the book with so much blood on the pages,—blood, sweat, and tears. I did not want anyone to read my pages and feel sorry for me, or try to rewrite my story with negative opinions and false narratives. I was simply happy to be alive and have peace when I did, but I felt that I could not be selfish with my story, isn't that what testimonies are for? As a disciple of Christ, the whole foundation of faith is to share a mixture of your accomplishments and failures to the Glory of God when all things work together for your good (Romans 8:28).

I have had to move around a lot in my life to find a place where I could even think straight, without having to go through some mental valley of the shadow of death experience, constantly looking over my shoulder.

Now, I can help someone else escape the psychological victim mentality prison of the mind, or what I call, The Great Get Out!

Especially as an adult, when you still haven't figured it out, yet carry such a powerful story that—if you pulled yourself together—you could help someone else still searching for inner peace. You realize how badly you needed guidance from someone who would keep it 100 with you, whatever that looks like, since the journey is genuinely personal.

I had to question whether I could offer the same transparency to another person who needed it in a mentor or friend. Yes, because I survived. I was not dead. As the saying goes, what doesn't kill you makes you stronger, but after you become stronger what you do with that next is what makes it a testimony!

> *He replied, "Because you have so little faith. Truly I tell you,*
> *if you have faith as small as a mustard seed, you can say to this*
> *mountain, 'Move from here to there,' and it will move.*
> *Nothing will be impossible for you."*
> **Matthew 17:20**

That was a testimony, for sure! After reading this book, you might consider me someone you can learn from. I had mixed feelings. I wanted to write the book and see it become a best-seller, but doing so meant risking vulnerability—putting my shortcomings on paper for the world to see. Even so, that's what the world needs: more transparency!

Still, I was a complete homebody, and thrived better personally as an introvert. I just had to throw my comfort zone to the wind and walk out my dreams by faith. The only thing stopping me now is me. My children are not babies anymore. I now have a husband, who is my best friend, and my children are my biggest supporters. So why not me?

We all have a story. I am just finally strong enough to heal through the triggers of this process. I'm 49 and finishing a book I started writing 20 years ago. I began it by telling the story about my childhood, how I was molested and abused, ran away from home as a teenager, living pillar to post, so to speak, until I graduated from high school, and yes, how can I forget those years. It was a miracle that I graduated from high school. Man, how many students were there that didn't graduate because they didn't have a healthy home environment to thrive in?

My entire high school years, and even in elementary school, I loved school. I loved learning the most, because learning gave me something new to feed myself as a distraction to keep me from drowning my own troubles throughout my childhood. School is the only thing some kids have to help them find their own identity, to teach them how to have healthy interactions socially, without parental influence, which simply teaches them how to grow up, and handle success and life as a responsible person.

I was in the dance and arts program under the most skilled and no-nonsense director. She reminded me so much of Debbie Allen of *Fame*, and all I wanted to be when I grew up was a ballet dancer.

I told my Gangster Granny once when I was a little girl that I would go to heaven with a boombox on my shoulder. I loved running around the house singing and dancing as a little girl when I could. I felt free when I danced, and from elementary through graduation I followed the path of the best Magnet and Fine Arts schools, where I grew to love life's eclectic offerings.

We did not have a lot of money growing up, none to be exact, and it was a blessing to go to the type of schools that offered more than just numbers and letters. I learned about music and arts, biology labs, baked cookies, acted in plays and talent shows, had dance class and the coolest gym teachers—but dance was my favorite.

I became the *Eat, Pray, Love* girl early on in life, which left me learning how to fight the fight of trying to transmute the negative realities of a very dark childhood into a bright future of opportunities through music and movement, reading and writing. Inside the music was the only place that made me believe that I had not lost my connection to The Man upstairs, so that became my happy place, and wherever the music was, I wanted to be.

Well, this story of mine is the greatest leap of faith I could make when I got tired of being who I had become. At some point, I realized that the problem was me; All me! I could only blame others for so long until I ran out of people to blame. I pushed everyone away after each painful encounter. Not to say that I didn't have a good reason, because I did. I really kept going with no doubt that I was doing the right thing, so why stick around? I learned the hard way that you cannot take folks at face value many times, and even family relations mean nothing without the same essential character traits to make sure they are not a threat, just as anyone else.

I suffered so much abuse—mentally, emotionally, physically, and most definitely sexually. I moved right on! That is why you better do your homework before letting anyone into your personal space, home, car, or any closed-off alone space. Life can be heaven or hell, depending on your mindset. I developed a bad habit of becoming a skeptic about everything. I didn't realize it was a crippling viewpoint because I missed several opportunities to help myself become better in the past.

I was walking on eggshells, thinking the sky was falling, and I was usually right, but only because I was looking at life from a hopeless mindset! Not because the sky was actually falling, but because it seemed that no matter how great a picture God painted for me, it usually turned out to be a nightmare in the end, because I wasn't really seeking God for what was best for me. Without a vision, the people perish—and the only person that could change that for me was myself.

I knew I could not go on being afraid. I had lost the strong little girl who survived the worst, only to become a weak woman with a victim mentality. I got angry with myself when I looked over my life and had hardly any happy memories. That's when I understood why I was such a skeptic. I had good reason, but did I want to die like that? I wanted to live and see what a good life was.

I was attempting to gain footing as a divorced, single mother of two beautiful, very wonderful sons. They held my heart, and I had to figure out how to keep hope alive for them and keep the lights on without asking for handouts or favors. I just started doing what I do best, I went to work! I worked two jobs, I have worked two jobs as long as I can remember, up until now. So, I worked at the medical center in the business department and as a public speaker with the aspirations of becoming a full-time motivational speaker and children's book writer.

I was ready to start my life for myself and my children alone. My tiny box apartment in the corner by the woods was so peaceful. The medical facility where I worked was a steady job, and I could even take days off for my speaking engagements. It looked like things would be okay!

Tragically I had one more lesson to learn, I call it a lesson because looking at life from a healthy mindset you have to find the silver lining in every sad story, or you will sink with the ship when you should be sailing with the tides. My last lesson was about being too trusting. I went in over my head, and wasn't watching my back anymore. I had relaxed my boundaries—that whole face value thing again. I accepted a lunch invitation from another newly divorced mom I knew, and guess what? She also had two kids! Two newly single ladies out for a night of venting and figuring out in what direction we wanted our lives to go.

I was a certified homebody then, so I was being unfair to myself by not going out and treating myself. I was going on a mom date, trying to move on and be social. The sun was shining, and the boys were safe and content. Mom was going to treat herself, out to eat with a friend and told them who and where. I kissed them and told them I was coming right back.

I will not go into details, because I owe that much privacy to myself. I will say I did not make it home that night and barely lived to see it the next day. I cannot figure out why anyone would have wanted to put me through that horror, but they did. Yes, I said they did. I was a good person to anybody I met. I worked in my church as an usher and, occasionally, as a children's teacher; I tried to be the kindest person you could meet, and just when I was getting back on my feet one wrong invite almost cost me my life.

My children were almost left without a mother. I will never forget the hell that was unleashed on me that day just by agreeing to go out to a restaurant with a woman I believed to be a woman of principle, a fellow mother, what mother does that to another mother? She put something in my drink and allowed the most horrible things to happen to me, she was not any friend at all, she purposely wanted to see me fail, she took my life for a joke. I never knew such horrible women existed till that day! Some people will go to extreme lengths to watch other people fail.

I survived again. The next six months I spent fighting for my freedom and my sanity, and everyone, I mean everyone, treated me as if I had just imagined it! And I know they knew, but I could do nothing about it. Not even the police helped me. I was on my own. A zombie for months, I stopped going anywhere, and for all my personal and professional progress, I had to fight to regain credibility. My children were so confused, and no one offered them any explanation. It was a mess, but we got through it again, my boys are real champions. They have grown up now and are still just as wonderful as they have always been. Thank God, we prayed together every step of the way. I am growing, and I am healing. I will not pretend anymore that I'm strong enough not to at least acknowledge that it hurts like hell, but I survived. It is true what they say: what doesn't kill you makes you stronger. If people understood how deep that goes, they would not mess with a person who has looked death in the face and survived. Fear is the least of their concerns. It was not until recently that I took a good long look in the mirror and thought, I need a whole brain transplant. My old mind could not do anything new for me; I had no choice but to change!

I put others before myself so much that it almost killed me. As I sat in my new reality that had just crashed down around me, deep calls unto deep and said, "Girl, you got this." I got up and prayed, "Lord, you kept me here for a reason. Let's do it again!" Who in their right mind would say that? Right mind, yeah, right! Because you must get out of your old mind and into your new mind, since old ways don't open new doors.

I recently went to 6 Flags with my husband and son, and I don't understand how they got me on a roller coaster after all these years, but they did. And I immediately thought, *girl bye.* I'm not just being extra. I mean for real, for real! I had my eyes closed, the little fastener bar they say is "so secure" was flapping up and down with every turn, and I thought my skinny behind would fall flat out! I kept screaming, "keep it closed, Jesus!" True story! My husband recorded me, just laughing so hard!

After I got off, I said never again! My point is I will not ride another roller coaster, but God; I will obey God. I'll write a book exposing all my weaknesses and errors if it means someone will be less afraid to give life a second or third chance, and if possible, give their life to Christ because they see me living my best life for the same Christ that rose from the dead for them as well. It is not an exclusive invite; salvation is free to "whosoever will!"

Dumb it down, Jerri Lynn, okay? Well, it's not us humans who work everything out for our good, not us who raise the sun in the morning, or set it down during the nighttime. I don't understand why we can't acknowledge the presence of an unseen God who wants to help us walk in the newness of everything we prayed for. If you don't pray because you say there is no God, then okay, let's say you imagined a life different from the one you have now, and you have said to yourself at least once, "I wish!"

Like Dorothy in *The Wizard of Oz*. She went through all that, and when Glenda, the Good Witch, told her at the end that she could have clicked her heels three times and just went home, I could have just thrown the remote at the TV. She fought off lions, tigers, and bears, flying monkeys, and almost lost her dog, Toto. You can't tell me you weren't at least a little angry watching it, realizing Glenda hadn't told her all that from the start. You must keep moving and watching to learn part of development. You just have to walk through some lessons just to show someone else the way. Dorothy helps three others along her journey, one to have heart, the other courage; the scarecrow didn't even have a brain. Her faith in the wizard kept her going, only to discover that the wizard was not real. But we do have a Creator in Heaven that is real and does show us the way.

If your steps are ordered, it's not for you. It's for others who otherwise wouldn't have the heart, courage, or brain to find the way. Some days, the lesson and blessings are not just for you; Jesus was never selfish! When the perishable puts on the imperishable, and the mortal puts on immortality, the written saying shall come to pass: "Death is swallowed up in victory." Your victory is that you are not ashamed of your experiences because you're alive to read this!

That is how it worked out for me. That's my story. Your story does not have to be mine, but you *do* have one. And you owe it to yourself to heal—to see the outcome for yourself. Anyone can do it if they believe. If you can take the bull by the horns, if you have a supportive team that you can equally love and receive love from, then okay! You can do this. The point is to get somewhere and get yourself together. Love yourself first. You can't help anybody wounded and lost. Self-care is a ministry, too. Either way, here we go!

Chapter 1

Betrayal and Rebirth

———■———

*"Now, the serpent was more subtle than any beast of the field which the
Lord God had made. And he said unto the woman, Yea, hath God said,
Ye shall not eat of every tree of the garden? And the woman said unto
the serpent, we may eat of the fruit of the trees of the garden. But of the
fruit of the tree, which is in the midst of the garden, God hath said, Ye
neither shall ye touch it, lest ye die.*

And the serpent said unto the woman, Ye shall not surely die."
Genesis 3:3

Of course, this is a bible story, and most people take it for granted
without realizing it happened. That is how humanity was stolen
from mankind. Not understanding or knowing how to interpret
what is said is the reason most people fall victim to psychological sabotage.

Eve was one of many people in the Bible who fell victim to the smooth
words of the soothsayer Lucifer. A logical excuse for Eve's ignorance was
that she just happened to be the newest member of the garden. Some
translations say the serpent beguiled Eve, which means charm or enchant,
to cast a spell. Her husband, Adam, was not written in the scene at the

time. Both were created with free will. We will never know what actually happened in that story since most of the bible was not properly translated from the original scrolls.

This passage is so important, because who *is* the devil? When you can identify "the devil," that thing that has held you back from successfully living in a place of ultimate bliss and abundance. It's the temptation to etch God out of our lives! The devil's advocate in our head is when we reason God out of our decision process. He does not have any new tricks. He plays the same trick on everyone by pretending to be something he is not. In order to provoke submission by fear or self-sabotage, when you forfeit your life, the devil needs another soul. He swindled Adam and Eve out of the Garden of Eden and inherited the world by default. Satan does not care how he wins because he doesn't play fair. And he always comes back to collect. Jesus paid the debt!

It happens to the best of us. Judas, for instance, was a disciple and was with Jesus from the very beginning, watching Jesus perform miracles right in front of his eyes, and still fell victim to allowing himself to be the one to betray an innocent man who offered him a family of salvation, from sin and teach him the ways of the Kingdom of Heaven. He was hand-picked by Jesus to stand beside God and usher in a new era as a disciple. Then before it was all over, he was deceived by the idea of having Judas as a treasurer over God's money, and the devil convinced him to sell Jesus out for 30 pieces of silver! Which back then would have been about $300.00. He was tricked out of his position as a disciple at the right hand of God to usher in a new era and a steward as the group treasurer. He probably had more than that in his pouch. What a tragedy!

Not only did Judas sell out his future as a great leader to Christ, but the money also he negotiated for himself cost him his life! The devil came back to collect, so he hung himself because his soul was needed.

We can all see ourselves falling victim to the spirit of self-sabotage if we look closely at the value of what we have beyond the dollar amount. We don't even know what we are worth as human beings, and that is why we don't understand the cost of the blood on the cross or why the devil fights so hard to trick us out of our salvation. On Earth, as it is in Heaven, you are not required to die to enjoy the benefits of salvation! We must search ourselves for the answers. Life is not fair. There is nothing fair. That is why we have rules to make sure evil doesn't win.

The day my husband read it to me, I cried like a baby, the story of Eve and how she had no clue what was really taking place at that moment. I had read it so many times before; most of us know that story even if we have never read the bible; we know that the story is ironic because that's the beginning! The most prominent impression made on women still to this day. Is that in the bible, the woman was portrayed as disobedient to God, ate the apple, and gave some to her husband.

It sounds evil and intentional but at the end of the day, she didn't mean it. This is why we can't make decisions from an emotional place. As most women do! Usually, for most women, every decision made is made from an emotional place. She is either operating from an area of hurt or operating in the office of a nurturer, trying to make sure everyone is okay! Most women are not intentionally evil. There are a few in the army of Cruella de Vil floating free, but women were created with a good-hearted nature.

My husband and I had a discussion the day before in which I shared with him how the stories of the bible were used against me in a ruse to manipulate me as a new convert in the church some 22 years ago. This particular morning on his way to work, he listened to the bible via his bible app. It was the story in Genesis about how Eve was deceived.

We were having a conversation about me taking responsibility for my part in allowing the victimization to continue by not putting an end to it after the first incident. I was explaining to him I was a young adult barely over twenty and made an idol of a preacher whose words were, "Follow me as I follow Christ." When that happens, especially as a new convert, you live off every word that comes out of the preacher's mouth because, as far as you know, the preacher is the closest thing to God. We did not have a Me-Too movement back then. I did not even realize I was beguiled by the serpent. I called the whole experience service to God. Not only was I a new convert, but I was in a new city all alone, with no one to depend on except my new fellow Christians from church. I arrived by Greyhound with two cardboard boxes, which is all I had to my name.

I left my hometown in '99 after having a final run-in with my biological father. I discovered after being separated for 12 years from my father that even though I was an adult, he still had a sick mind and wanted to see me back under his spell. I went to visit a church in my hometown one day, and my biological father was there. They said he was a deacon. I had to see for myself because the father I left behind was a pedophile, and it wasn't safe to leave a child alone in his company. He didn't know anything about my unannounced visit, and when he noticed me walking as he was up sweeping the porch, he froze and ran off. After composing himself and returning to the front stoop, he stared at me like I was a ghost. Gathering his words, saying how happy he was to see me like we were long-lost friends, I smiled and nodded, also in shock.

The church minister escorted my father and I to dinner to try to see if reconciliation was possible. It wasn't, of course. After dinner, on the way back to the church, he threw a narcissistic temper tantrum, demanding they allow me to live with him in the church. He was the custodian and in-house resident. They said absolutely. Later that evening a kind motherly elder in the church offered me a spot at the women's shelter that she just happened to be the administrator of. She just so happened to be employed by the same church my father was a member of, but he was forbidden to come anywhere near me. That was an interesting setup, but I continued to attend church, and my father was told to keep his distance.

The downfall of religion is mixing restoration with reconciliation, and by doing so, we suggest it is an unspoken rule that forgiveness is a buy-one-get-one combo. You are encouraged to function as if nothing happened. People shove forgiveness down the throats of abuse victims like surviving wasn't enough. We inevitably forgive those who have harmed us in this thing called "life." After that, there should be no contingencies on restoration. You can forgive someone and move on. Forgiveness, you would think, should motivate your assailant towards change, but no! It does not work that way. You must forgive them, for they know not what they are doing, and they have their own free will to choose. Hopefully, they no longer desire to be the person who gets a dopamine rush from harming others. You just need to set up boundaries so that in case of regression, it will not be you playing the part of the victim. Change is a product of understanding, not circumstance.

I told the house mother about my childhood and how I had escaped my family by running away. The streets were no place for me. It was more than I could bear. I told her I needed a place to get my life together, a place free from abuse. That's all I had known my whole life. I needed peace to think!

I went to that church for a little over two years. I was safe if I stayed in the confines of the house, and I grew tremendously in that year. I spent much of my time reading the Bible, a book I grew to love because of all the fascinating stories. Mother Helen said I wasn't any trouble and didn't take up much space. She was exceedingly kind and allowed me a safe space to discover God.

Meanwhile, the whole time I was there going to church, trying to find clarity, my father was waiting in the shadows on a mission. He kept trying to come over and visit the house, but the house rules were no men allowed. He was like a predator waiting to seize the moment. It became increasingly uncomfortable to even think with him around. He was just waiting outside my door like a wolf.

Mother Helen thought it would be safer if I stayed with her after a while when she noticed him behaving like a snake. So, I did. We sat around drinking tea and discussing the stories of the bible. She planned to go out of town for the holidays, and she took me for a visit to Alabama in the second year of my stay to their sister church, which was a branch of the original church. Her son and his family happened to be the pastor. They seemed like a wonderful family. Everyone was so warm and welcoming, very charismatic, and driven for Christ!

"Behold, I send you out as sheep in the midst of wolves,"
Matthew 10:16

I longed to be in a place where the atmosphere was all about Jesus, and I was free from my father. After our trip, I prayed for several months about Alabama, and when I received my answer, I believed that was my call to ministry. I waited almost two years to be called by God. As the saying goes, be careful what you pray for, because even in ministry you can think you are being used by God, and you can just be getting used by opportunists. Some of the people over the ministry were for it, and some were against it. I felt I had to follow my own mind and once again get out of this dead-end cycle of fellowship with a father that had not changed at all. He was hiding behind a religious mask. Little did I realize that was The Lord showing me what a wolf in sheep's clothing resembled, giving me a glimpse of the upcoming struggle.

I moved down South, and for the first few months, everything was great. I proudly started what was my call to ministry as an armor bearer. I did not know what that was—an armor bearer—but I did know how to serve. My people pleaser kicked in, and I jumped right out of the boat like Peter wanting to follow Jesus.

In the scriptures, zeal without knowledge is used as a very powerful parable. In Proverbs 19:2-3, it tells us that it is not good to have zeal without knowledge, and a man's own folly ruins his life, yet his heart rages against the Lord. The zeal of believing that I fulfilled a request of God towards following Him, leaving what I knew from my broken childhood. That is what we do. We believe there is something better out there for us, and it is the reason people wish upon stars and blow out birthday candles. They are hoping, believing, praying, and wishing for better.

Then, true to the word, I found myself a sheep among wolves. My new pastor was nothing like his beloved mother. I learned that he had an addiction to crack cocaine, and struggled also with the abuse of women. Abusing his wife and allegedly accused of molesting his stepdaughter. I had no idea such evil existed in the church. I was too familiar with the notorious character of my father, and I never imagined preachers being that way. I watched the Jim Jones story on television when the phrase "Don't drink the Kool-Aid" became popular. I never thought I would live it. I thought the years I spent under my father's spell was the last of the abuse, especially after closing that chapter by moving on. This was my first personal experience of being thrown out of the frying pan into the fire.

> *"He that receiveth a prophet in the name of a prophet*
> *shall receive a prophet's reward."*
> **Matthew 10:41**

\Zeal without knowledge is having desire without an understanding of healthy boundaries and expectations. A man's own folly ruins his life, yet his heart rages against the Lord. My new shepherd used scripture to justify the abuse of women in the church coming from Genesis 16, where Sarah, who is Abraham's wife, gives him permission to be with Hagar, his handmaiden. I, too, fell victim to the guise of being a handmaiden. When you read it in the bible, you believe it's true because the bible is supposed to be true, right? So, you find yourself gullible enough to do whatever they say because that's God using you, or so you think. You have to be careful in every setting that you are alert to BS on every occasion, even in the most seemingly holy places.

Now before you know it, you're carrying bibles, pouring water for one that calls themselves a prophet, doing laundry, cooking meals, you're a maid and free babysitter for the children, and one day he says to you that God sent you as a protective mechanism for the Kingdom of God to help him make it in his weak moments, so he doesn't have to go outside the church and risk being exposed for his weakness of perversion and adultery.

It's the same lies Jeffery Epstein told and the same lies R. Kelly told, except they had a god complex offering record deals and a better life. This man offered you a prophet's reward for covering the prophet. It is written in red letters.

Just like any predator, they seek out the people that have a history of child abuse and the ones that have a history of trauma. Those victims usually give in without much of a fight because they have already been groomed for abuse. Long story short, they know the drill. That's how many victims of abuse end up in abusive relationships, and it is a trigger. In the end, I became disgusted with myself and left the church, calling out the pastor and telling others what had happened, hoping to be supported by other members of the congregation.

Instead, they wanted to stone me, blaming me for tempting the man of God, calling me terrible things. I left alone once again in my journey, running away from abuse, but this time a place I never expected, the church. A couple of years later, when that same pastor was arrested for sexual molestation of a minor, then they wanted to believe me. I pushed this story far back into the black hole of my mind where the other abuses and trauma were stored; that was how I survived. Twenty years later, it popped up in conversation with my husband, and that is the day God dealt with it, coming back full circle to Eve and the serpent deceiving her.

That was not the last time I found myself in a vulnerable situation that led to rape and abuse within that 20-year span of time. It's something about being a survivor of child sexual abuse that makes you a magnet for abusers even in your adulthood. And that was the point my husband was getting to. Even though for the past six years I have lived my life free from abuse, he was trying to show me how every time I gave an ear to the enemy and for me to stop pointing the finger at others. You cannot heal from the wounds if you keep giving people the knife! Now, I do want to say this acceptance does not mean taking responsibility. It's like blaming someone for being too nice! However, you can acknowledge the red flags given off by your intuition and say no when a situation makes you feel uncomfortable.

Most victims of abuse are afraid to say no due to the severe consequences of angering their abuser. This is why most of us question adult victims of abuse; we don't understand how someone can be an adult and act like a helpless child stuck in a bad situation. Lately, there have been several stories in the news of adult victims coming forward, the Me-Too movement, the Surviving R. Kelly series, Jeffery Epstein, and his partner in crime, Ghislaine Maxwell story, on Netflix. The Jerry Sandusky scandal is another example of such crimes. A retired football coach who had the

Second Mile youth camp for underprivileged children used his status in the community to lure young boys into gaining his trust only to sexually assault them. It's never the victim's fault. The only thing we can do is to get the word out and tell victims that they do have a voice and to use it and scream to the top of their lungs, if need be, to fight back if they have to and show the bullies that enough is enough.

Today, I found myself in a time and place where my life was finally coming together, and I'm happy for the first time. The disclaimer is I am constantly working on my trigger response to natural, unrelated life occurrences. Writing this book has helped me tremendously, simply by "writing the vision down and making it plain upon the tables, that he/ she may run that readeth it," as it says in Habakkuk 2:2. What is the vision, you ask? Healing! The vision is to heal from the trauma and triggers that broke me in the first place and become more than a conqueror, losing the victim mentality!

What is a wilderness journey, you ask? It's symbolic of the time it takes to get from captivity to freedom, the Great Get Out! The children of Israel wandered through the wilderness for five chapters of the bible in the Old Testament, you may ask yourself, what was it all for? To bring them out of captivity, which is not only a tangible place of enslavement like the African American experienced but also the victim mentality that hangs around in the back of your mind long after your release. If you're thinking right now, what does that have to do with me or this book? Hold your horses, and I'll explain.

Technically, we were all born into a dysfunctional family and governmental world system. We like to put the blame on somebody when we operate in the victim mentality state, but if any one of us really wanted to make the world a better place, we would do it by starting with ourselves! We call that breaking generational curses. It is just a fancy term that says I won't repeat the same mistakes made by my dysfunctional family members who came before me breaking free from the victim mentality.

For me, that cycle started with my great-grandparents on my mother's side, particularly with the women. There had to be some type of pattern of repeated behavior in which they always wound up with abusive men. I know very little of my great-great-grandmother Corrine, who was 4 generations before me, but I do know her story describes her going from one abusive marriage to the other, and the only child she ever gave birth to is my great-grandfather, who himself turned out to be an abuser, he is deceased. JC grew up to marry a 14-year-old girl by the name of Mae Lois. He was 19 and, in the military, back then, they married young, so it was common to see a young woman get married off to an older man. Those two I knew a little better because they moved from Alabama to Ohio, where I was later born. They were alive most of my childhood before I moved away.

The cycle of abuse continued with them as my grandfather was allegedly physically abusive and had pedophilic tendencies. As horrible as it sounds to say it, that was a common trait for the men in our family. They gave birth to 3 children, two sons and one daughter. I have heard rumors that one of my grandmother's children was a direct result of being raped by her biological father.

As it relates to myself, I, too, could have been a victim of pregnancy due to my biological father raping me as a youth. I can remember one day after I started having my cycles thinking oh wow, I hope I do not get pregnant. I thought about the story of Ms. Cealy in the Color Purple. We do know most child pedophiles initially start with a grooming stage to gaslight the child into believing the molestation is an act of love and not violence. At that early time in a young child's life when they would reluctantly agree to sexual acts believing the person was someone they could trust, like taking candy from a baby, most pedophiles would confess, which means very easy to accomplish, saying the task is so easy it's almost unfair to the child that they don't actually know what they are consenting too since children really have no clue what sex is.

My mother and I recently had a conversation about her childhood and how this very same thing happened to her. Up until about three years ago, my mother and I never had a mother-daughter relationship because the hurt she endured and the hurt I endured kept us separated from one another instead of loving one another. I recently forgave my mother for her actions against me growing up with the help of the Holy Spirit. I kept my mother at bay for years. During my childhood, instead of being a loving, nurturing mother, she was physically abusive to me.

It was only after I heard the Holy Spirit whisper to me to give her another chance that I did, and she finally told me her story. The scenario where a child had a child at the age of fifteen, was robbed of her youth, and it took her childhood. She had to drop out of school and get a job to raise me while my father went into the military, abandoning his responsibilities. My grandmother forced my mother to marry my father at the age of 15, a common thing back in the day you got pregnant, you got married. I asked my mother what happened because I don't remember my father being around much for the first few years of my life, not like the memories you would have if your parents actually were living under the same roof. They were off and on due to my father's infidelity. My father was not in love with my mother. I doubt he even loved her at all the way he treated her. My parents were just two people who had a child. While he was away, my mother and I lived with my grandparents, so they lived separately for a long time.

My grandmother took over as my mother, raising me as a seventh child to her already six children. My grandmother and I were close due to my mother being so young it felt like she was another sibling. She had three sisters and two brothers. We were all raised together, and I saw my grandmother as my parent because she was the one who enforced the rules when anything went down. My mother dropped out of school to work, and my father went off doing only God knows what. All I had was my grandmother, who at the time was a stay-at-home mother.

My father was several years older than my mother and really had no business touching her. I guess as a young man in his late teens, he had an affection for children early on, and that's how my mother got pregnant. Her story of sexual abuse started initially with my great-grandfather and his affection for children. My mother was one of the many family members who endured sexual abuse at the hands of my great-grandfather. By the time I came along, my mother had a lot of built-up anger from having been passed around by men before the age of 18, and motherhood is no place to unload your baggage.

I knew that I obeyed God when she said to me, "Because you forgave me for my sins against you, I can forgive my mother for her sins." Because I was able to face my demons and understand my mother, too, was a victim at the same time, I was a victim. It was only fair that I let go of her past in the form of forgiveness in order to let go of my own past. Forgiveness is a hard pill to swallow when it comes to childhood incest.

My great-grandfather was several years older than his wife. She was 13 years old when he married her. The fact that she was just a child herself at the time, taking on the role of a wife in the 30s, already gave him seniority over her, therefore quickly establishing himself as the Alpha in the marriage. My great-grandmother was one of the sweetest women I'd ever met. My great-grandfather, however, not so much, he was a very grumpy old man with a less-than-tasteful sense of humor as I remember it. Nonetheless, they were the head of the family on my mother's side. I was blessed to have known them being that I was born later in the fourth generation of women on that side of the family. I just knew he was a grumpy old man with one leg, and she was a saint.

However, like most families, we went along with dysfunctional family traditions because that was the "norm." We met up every family holiday at Big Momma's house like clockwork. She was always in the kitchen cooking, and he was always sitting in the chair liquored up, watching the baseball game as usual. Like most families, we started the festivities by breaking open a fresh deck of cards, unlocking the liquor cabinets, and blasting down-home blues until you couldn't hear yourself think.

What looked like tradition was the mask we used to hide our family's dysfunction. Behind the food, liquor, and loud music is where the demons of incest and dysfunction hid themselves at every family gathering. It was the place where you make the best out of a bad situation and even worse, it's the place where the groomer secretly found their next victim in the younger generation. The gathering place for the hunter and the prey. The main villain was sitting at the head of the table all the time, calling all the shots.

It was the place where we opened a fresh deck of cards and played a game of spades to cover up for the lack of communication in our family, to the things that could have made us better and healed us from the hurt that we just kept sweeping under the rug year after year.

Little did I know at the time that my great-grandfather had established his dominance through incest and abusiveness. Not respect. He was the abuser in the family. He molested his daughter, who, for lack of a better phrase, turned the other cheek when it was done to her daughter, my mother, and inadvertently taught my mother to turn the other cheek when it was done to me, by my biological father. My mother knew because her mother knew, and I guess everybody felt helpless in the end. Therefore, one unresolved abusive marriage being swept under the rug opened the door to every generation after that to struggle through abusive marriages and divorces, for that matter, until eventually, our family consisted of a bunch of strong single women with unhealthy baby daddies.

Unfortunately, somewhere along the way, it gave birth to a lifestyle of homosexuality for those of us running from the dysfunctional, one-sided sexual encounters that we thought were love between a man and a woman. I felt that somewhere along the way if this is what God intended when he created relationships between a man and woman, he had obviously made a mistake, and I wanted no part of it.

Even to that end, my father was abused when he was a boy. I didn't know that until later after he had passed on. Sadly, boys are subject to being molested as much as little girls, it's just a topic not to be spoken much of because most men are ashamed to speak up, and abuse makes them look helpless. Women are supposed to be the damsel in distress. Men are supposed to be the hero, but it's just as painful for me to learn my father was a boy raped and beaten by other broken men.

By the time I was born, my mother was a 15-year-old little girl broken, battered, and overlooked in a family of six other siblings, who had lost her identity to a cycle of generational abuse, finding herself pregnant by a man carrying the weight of his own cycle of generational abuse, at the hands of men that were supposed to be his protectors and father figures.

He carried with him not just the embarrassment of physical abuse, but the shame of sexual abuse as well, being that boys are supposed to be able to fight off their attackers. Also, the shame of sodomy because his abuser was also a man. Leaving him emasculated before he even had a chance to grow into his adulthood. His abuse stripped him of his manhood early on, and my father had something to prove.

This was the motivation that allowed me to find the courage to try to make the world a better place, but first, I had to heal. And it's hard to heal without a teacher! I understand now that my parents were just broken adults with a kid living out the cycle of generational curses, as were their parents. Unhealthiness was the norm in our dysfunctional family.

Fast forward to me being the age of 7, my mother was accepted into the program for Section 8 Housing, and instead of moving into government housing projects, we were able to use the grant to move into our own three-bedroom, two-bath house in a decent neighborhood. It was honestly an incredibly beautiful home. It had a long sidewalk leading up to a large front porch with white wood banisters. The front door was glass with a wood frame. When you walked into the front door, the main living room had three large bay windows, deep, rich cherry hardwood floors, a fireplace, and a wide cherry wood archway leading into the dining room.

Because it was a tri-level home the front living room had a grand staircase with about 15 to 20 stairs leading up to the second floor that turned the corner up at the top, with three large bedrooms and a large bathroom. The whole house had an antique look to it. I loved the deep red wood everywhere you looked. Back downstairs the large living room thru the archway led into the dining room that was big enough for a table set and a couch set. Then we had the kitchen and attached bathroom with a back door that took you outside to a fenced-in backyard. And we had a full concrete basement with a door to outside.

It was a dream for someone who grew up poor like I did. That was just the outer shell, though. Inside that dream home turned into a nightmare.

This was my first official home with my parents as a real family. Before then, my mother and I lived with my grandfather and grandmother in the home she shared with her siblings. So, this new home was our first real chance to be a family. And instead of my father and mother laying new roots of their own, they repeated the cycle of abuse. My mother spent most of her younger years taking care of her siblings cause that's just where the lot fell for the oldest female born into a large family, then she had a child at 15, and now at 23 in her own home, you would think she would have the mindset to want better. It just didn't work out that way. Being naïve plays a role when you don't believe in yourself. It is what it is, and who am I to change it? My mother repeated the cycle of negative, abusive behavior she grew up with. She and I were never on the same page. So, I just kept quiet and stayed out of the way. My mother had given birth to my baby sister, and I love babies, she was like a little doll to me. I took very good care of her. I made her my own.

My father was in and out of my life the first few years, part of those years he spent in the military, and the other half just dodging responsibility. When he finally settled into the home with us, things took a turn for the worse, my father set his affections on me, and it pushed my mother and I further apart. He'd come home after work and find me, and he would demand I take a bath, to which he would also make sure he was the one to bathe me. I won't tell you exactly what happened in that bathroom, but I can assure you I never came out feeling clean. Our home became the house of shadows, everyone walking around not saying anything. Don't ask, don't tell! He often told my mother whenever he left the house to make sure I was clean and ready to go with him. My mother did as he asked without question.

I hated leaving my baby sister behind, she was my only friend, but my daddy said she couldn't go. He'd take me to different places, to other women's homes. It wasn't until later in life I realized that they worked for my father, like street women only not standing on the corner. Most of the time, we were alone, and it was then I understood that he took me with him, so he didn't have to sneak to have sex with me. It was rape, but I didn't know it because I was naïve too. I didn't understand it then. I was just being a good girl, and I definitely didn't want to make my father angry because he had a horrible temper.

The few times I mustered up the courage to say no, I paid for it. He never laid a hand on me to beat me, but he would abandon me, leaving me stranded alone in strange places for hours at a time, then coming back later to ask me if I had learned my lesson. My father had molested me so many times growing up I stopped counting and stopped waiting for someone to come and save me. I just learned to do what he said to get it all over with sooner. When he took me to strange places, homes I had never been in before, I would just lay on the bed and focus on the clock, he'd always say just five or ten more minutes until he was done. So, I would watch the clock and wait in a numb, dead haze when the minutes had gone by, waiting for the right moment to ask if he was done. Then I'd go lock myself in the bathroom and cry. He would often get high in front of me. He had several different drugs of choice, I often think it was like growing up with the devil himself for a father.

It wasn't until I got older and the little girls in the neighborhood started inviting me to sleepovers that I noticed the other fathers didn't have the same relationship with their daughters as mine did. The other fathers didn't give baths, and the girls had such good friendships with their mothers. It all started to look strange to me and I began to question my mother as to why my father was different from the other fathers, and her response was silence. The more I asked, the angrier she got, but she never stopped it. After a while, she'd beat me in her anger, and I spent a lot of time in my room when my father wasn't home like she didn't want to look at me or deal with me. My father started coming into my room in the middle of the night. It was like I wasn't safe anywhere. My father and mother argued a lot, so there was no peace at home at all. I would go to a neighbor's house for normalcy whenever I got a chance.

One day, a friend of mine asked me why I was so different, so worried and self-conscious all the time. I confided in her about my home life, and she immediately told her parents. Her parents marched over to talk to my parents, and they denied everything. My father moved out a few months after that since the Department of Human Services was called in, and they told my mother he had to leave. I didn't know exactly what happened, but I did know that they helped me enough that the molestation stopped after that. My mother and I were still the same, though. Both of us were angry, and the love and affection most daughters receive from the nurturing of a mother. I didn't get it. I was almost a teenager then, so I was responsible for my siblings just like my mother's mother made her do.

I lived like that until I couldn't take the silence anymore, and I asked my mother why she allowed my father to molest me. We got into a huge argument, and in her blind rage over being confronted by the truth, she pushed me down a flight of stairs and started to strangle me. She was told to be quiet and, in true tradition, forced me to do the same. I ran away from home that day, leaving behind my sister, best friend, and a very adorable baby brother, who happened to be the newest addition to my dysfunctional family.

I felt so bad leaving them behind, but at least the molester was gone. I just couldn't protect them from Mama anymore. I lived from house to house back then, and I worked odd jobs, so I didn't have to rely on anyone to provide for me. I didn't want to owe anyone anything for taking care of me. I became a ward of the state and lived with different relatives to stay focused enough to graduate from High School. People were kind enough to help along the way, but I never had a real home after that.

I went back to visit that house recently with my husband, Kenn, and it was gone. There was not even a trace of evidence that the home ever existed. It's like the Lord was giving me permission to start over because the past was gone. My nightmare no longer had an address.

For a very long time, I struggled with identity issues. I never had an opportunity to be my own person. I found it necessary to put others' happiness before my own, even though the sexual and physical abuse was over. No one told me it was not my responsibility to make sure everyone was happy. All I knew was to do what other people told me to do to keep down the commotion. I would do as I was told, and as quickly as it was over, I'd find a peaceful corner to retreat to.

I'd watch my grandmother sit in a chair and read romance novels for hours on end whenever I stayed over at her house. It was so peaceful that one of my coping mechanisms became the love for reading books. So, when I wasn't catering to others around me, I would go off to read books and daydream of what a normal life might have been, but then who was I to wish for normalcy? I finally earned enough money working odd jobs to afford my own apartment at 18. I stopped living with everyone else and finally had a place for myself. I liked it because I was alone, with no one to bother me. I'd go to work, take a few college classes, and back home.

Whenever I tried to make friends, it was frustrating because I thought people liked me because I was nice, only to find out they liked me because they thought I was gullible, and they'd laugh at me behind my back. That's when I learned ghosting people was easier than facing the truth about myself, and I allowed people to take advantage of me due to my lack of confidence to say no to things that made me uncomfortable.

I'd suffer through awkward situations because I had no one. My family was dysfunctional, and most of my friends were only friends with me because they felt sorry for me that I was so alone at 18. Even then, I felt alone in a room full of people; I could never take my guard down. And I don't know how to act with people that didn't go through what I went through. I didn't know how to carry on a normal conversation without sharing the story of my childhood. I mean, that is what you say when someone asks where you came from and why you don't have any family. I could have tried to visit my family and blend in. It's just the atmosphere was so toxic that I couldn't even fake it. I wanted nothing at all to do with my mother, and I refused to stand in any room and share the same oxygen with my father.

I grew up thinking I was the problem, and something was wrong with me. I labeled myself weird, so I didn't have to answer for my inadequacies. Life was different on my own around total strangers, so l learned several different types of coping mechanisms in order to survive alone. As I set off into the world to find a place that felt like home. I didn't know much about anything but my love for books and learning is what kept me up and going. I read a lot of self-help books and grew very fond of poetry. Maya Angelou is my favorite writer.

It took a long time to learn how to love myself because I always put everyone else first. My life stopped and started so many times I can't count. I lived somewhere for a while, giving everyone the benefit of the doubt before I even really considered if they were good for me. I just knew I had so much love to give. I wanted to make the world a better place and to be nice, so I tried not to make anyone feel like I had felt growing up.

Growing up, I felt like a burden, so I learned early how to do everything myself so at least I could be independent enough to stay out of everyone's way, and being people-pleasing was my survival mode. That way, I made myself useful to my abuser, and gaining favor with your abuser makes you indispensable in some cases.

I realized that was an unreasonable demand to place on myself, and I suffered until I learned most nice people get used. In the long run, I looked up and had not made one true friend from being a people pleaser. All I had done was wasted a lot of time, prolonging my state of mental imprisonment. I had told myself to appease the beast in every person with power and control tendencies. It was learned behavior and how I survived living with a sexual predator.

I had to turn the mirror and face my own stupidity. God took me out of the abuse, but no one ever taught me what "normal" was, and I thought putting myself first was mean and selfish. I became more of an introvert to protect myself from the dangers of life. I found a little of my father in the first two men I married earlier on in life. That dominating familiar spirit I wrestled with as a child haunted me years later as I tried to marry and have a normal life, but I was still the naïve girl just looking for love but didn't know what to look for. Studies say most little girls grow up looking for traits of their father in the men they choose, even if he is toxic because unconsciously, we gravitate towards what is familiar due to the fact we have learned how to navigate.

I was divorced praying for answers when I became more acquainted with Kenn and he helped me to see that a husband should be a friend, not just a man that had rule over you. He is the second reason I learned to love and put me first. Together we have three sons, 2 from my first marriage and 1 from his first. I can't begin to tell you how peaceful and amazing our home life is. It's what I felt was possible, but I never found it until now. I can only imagine him being a healthier, nontoxic example of what a man is. Woxic was all I knew until now. He understands that even though I was broken, I'm working on my healing, and he is a great support system for me to develop and become the woman that has escaped me my whole life. It is important as a woman that once overcame abuse to see yourself as more than just an accessory to a man, but to see yourself as a whole human being!

See, the enemy that lived within my father stole a lot from me: my virginity, my childhood, and my right to say no without fearing repercussions. Even with my ability to defend myself physically, because at times I had to learn to fight off my attackers, I also grew up very submissive because it was my survival mechanism when I could not fight back. I still grew up to be the kind of wife who was labeled a good wife because I did what I was told without question, believing that was the definition of a good wife and when the stress of having no identity and the weight of feeling like a slave got too much for me, I ran and left.

Just like I did as a little girl running from my father and then I ran from the same narcissism as a woman that I ran from as a little girl. It made me stop looking at others and start looking at myself. I had to ask myself the question: when was I going to stop running and just stand in my power as an adult, not just a girl subject to the improprieties of men, but a woman with the power to stand in my truth and be unashamed of my testimony! The truth of how the power of God set me free.

At some point I had to get serious about life and I became responsible for setting the example for my sons because I knew I needed to grow up and stop running, in order to show them how to stand. My boys were my first true blessing in life. I only ever wanted to be a good mother, a better mother than my mother and her mother before that. It worked with the help of the Holy Spirit, they are amazing. Focusing on my role as a mother became my inspiration. Now our boys are doing great, I say our, because I am not alone, now with a great man in my life, Kenn is also such an amazing step dad to the boys a God sent for me and them. They have such a laid back relationship that they call him KO, it's a bond that they have never had before with any one in my life! He is definitely not an abuser, and they have no fear of watching me live out any of the same cycles repeated in my life.

I wanted to give them a better life than mine because I needed to break the cycle, so they wouldn't have too. A child is so innocent that they will develop a bond with a groomer out of sheer desire to be nearer to someone they admire because that person presents themselves as a friend. A groomer is a term used by someone that has not yet abused but is setting the atmosphere of falsehood for a child to have a false sense of safety with them, so the child will let their guard down and not become suspicious of inappropriate behavior.

The groomer, however, in his or her attempt to manipulate the innocence of a child who trusts and loves them, tries to deceive that child so the child will let down any natural discerning defenses, and the groomer then becomes the molester pretending that the inappropriate touching is a normal part of touching. It is the worst kind of emotional manipulation, even before any molestation takes place, this is a type of psychological abuse that children are absolutely oblivious to and don't even understand is happening, which is why parents have to be vigilant in protecting their children from the exposure to such individuals.

My ignorance was my father's weapon, and he used this same type of psychological tactic on me, just like he used me. When I spoke up about something that didn't feel right or basically that I did not want to participate in, my father ignored me and pretended that what I was feeling was wrong and that he was right, that it was okay, that it was acceptable for a father to touch his daughter this way. That my perception was the problem, not his behavior. Not knowing any better, I obeyed, suppressing the hurt and repulsive feeling inside my gut because I wanted to make my father happy.

We did everything together. We had what I thought was a father-daughter bond, just keeping me with him at all times so no one else could get to me. Every time he touched me, I died a little on the inside. Your abuser will tell you everything is okay when it's not. You can see it and feel it and know on the inside that it's wrong but if you don't have the right help, the abuser will do everything possible to make you believe that you are just imagining it! It will feel like you're on the inside screaming no while on the outside, you are being held captive, all the while wishing it will stop, feeling powerless to even lift a hand against it. You have to take your power back! You have every right to say no to anything that makes you feel unsafe.

Back to the conversation I was having with my husband about Eve's naive nature, when the serpent said to Eve, "You shall not surely die" on that particular day some 47 years later, when my husband read it to me, that repulsive feeling came back up in my spirit like regurgitated words, and it broke me. When I understood she did die that day, not in person but her innocent nature was taken, and she was left with the stain of knowing what the shame of sin felt like after being manipulated by the devil. In theory death can be delivered in more than one way, my death was the death of my innocence as a little girl that never had the chance to be pure, to know what it was like to be a virgin. My reality is that it didn't kill me, but it did take something from me that I could never get back, I only have the chance now to be pure at heart and forgive my father so I can turn the page and be free of the shame that tried to hold me back!

I figured out all this time the word "shame" held me captive to a lifestyle of letting people get away with doing things to me under the guise that my belief was the problem, not their behavior. The beginnings of the wakeup call for a people pleaser. Except this time, I have someone in my life who wasn't in it to take advantage of me, my husband Kenn wanted to see me free. That is an example of true friendship. The tears escaped my soul like a flood setting free the little girl that was forced to sit on daddy's lap. Now, as a grown woman, I understand for the first time the meaning of following your gut and how I had never followed mine. The deception takes place when no one tells you that you are slowly dying from the inside out every time you accept the challenge to do something you don't agree with for the sake of making others happy. That is a major reason why most people commit suicide without any warning because their heart has already stopped beating in their chest due to the pressure of not speaking out against fear. You can become crushed from the weight of the grief, and the belief that you have let yourself down again in an attempt to make others happy, the lies you tell yourself when the pain starts to make your stomach curl to the point where you vomit or come down with a serious case of diarrhea because of the nervousness of not listening to your gut.

That's what is called being strong, when you go against the fear of what may happen when you stand up for yourself and just stand up for yourself. It's a terrible weight for children to bear. No child should ever be asked to betray themselves in this way.

The post traumatic effects of believing that the definition being strong means you must sacrifice yourself and your beliefs to make others happy, is the hardest to break free from because it's been programmed into you like the broken record, that plays over and over in your head as if you're being selfish for saying no. Therefore, if you are not careful to break free from the post traumatic stress syndrome effects, "no" can become a word you take out of your vocabulary in an attempt to be a "nice" person. In such cases when someone wants you to do something for them but it doesn't sit well with your soul, you hesitate to oblige and feel as if saying no makes you the villain, but I am here to tell you, that it does not at all make you the villain.

It's only when you don't use your power to say "no" but go along with the deed that you find yourself holding your stomach balled in a corner somewhere, wishing you hadn't. It's the look on the devil's face after they've gotten what they wanted that leaves you feeling one step shy of giving yourself over to what you thought was love. This cycle of child abuse is usually passed down from generation to generation. Until some-one, says no, like I had too.

Children grow up believing that touch is love especially when it's withheld from you, except in instances where you are rewarded with affection after you do as you're told. The trade, however, is self-betrayal, and it cuts like a knife long after the blade has left the body. This very same cycle of self-betrayal continues with you on your journey to adult-hood. That's how you become naïve as an adult when you don't deal with your childhood trauma.

Being naive carries with it certain insecurities and trust issues that make forgiveness hard to achieve when your reality is that someone know-ingly pulled the wool over your eyes using your own innocence to violate you. But you must forgive in order to heal! Healing means letting go of the shame but it does not mean that you have to allow the abuse to con-tinue, not at all forgive and close the door to the person that abused you, giving them over to God to deal with in his own time in his own way.

In hindsight, you think forgiveness makes you feel stupid, as if you allowed yourself to be used, like you could have done something about it. While blaming yourself by playing different scenarios in your head, trying to envision how you could have stopped it, beating yourself up for not being your own hero.

The truth is most of us did not even know it was abuse. We thought it was love from family members or friends that we looked up to as the per-sons in charge of protecting us. So, there was nothing I could have done because I didn't know it was abuse, even though something on the inside of me felt unclean. Over time and with trial and error I learned to stand on my no when it went against everything in me. I had to learn myself in order to know when someone was taking me out of my original state of peaceful being. That uneasy feeling is always a red flag to alert you when something is not right.

To understand groomers, we must understand certain qualities make children easy bait for groomers. One is that groomers look for children that are free in their bodies, ones that don't think anything of nudity. As parents we must know that touch is a primary love language for children. The affection they receive from being held and cuddled is what they thrive off. When an abuser grooms a child, they will use the very thing that is a necessity for a child to thrive to woo the child into the web of sexual perversion. We as parents must teach children the difference between a good touch and a bad touch, that when a touch is uncomfortable it's okay to say no! And to understand that a boundary is being crossed when their no is not respected. To not keep a child in the same environment as the person that disrespected their boundaries.

This means when it's time to forgive, you understand you are forgiving the person who intentionally used your innocence to manipulate your love language for their own benefit and perverse dark nature. Knowing it's okay to close the door to manipulation, ending the cycle. Forgiveness is not easy because you must realize this type of abuse is no accident, and to forgive means forgiving someone who was perfectly aware they were snatching your innocence away from you. All because you believed it was love and the necessary building block of growth and development. Knowing better means doing better for yourself and understanding what love is and what it is not.

Forgiveness can feel like letting someone off the hook scot-free without any repercussion or punishment for the crime they committed against you. Instead, I will tell you the truth is you are letting yourself off the hook from believing the lies and freeing yourself from blame that was not yours to carry. Letting go of the thought that you could have done something to prevent it and just being happy that you survived.

This brings me to the point when my mother said to me, "Because you forgave me, now I can forgive my mother," and my mother sat at my grandmother's bedside when she died with a pure heart, because she forgave as well an act that only her abuser was responsible for because, her and my grandmother had the same abuser. Wow! The majesty of it all at that point was that there were simultaneously two generational curses broken at one time, because I had the courage to see past my pain in order to look at my mother's pain and then her mother's. Rest in peace to my grandmother, a beautiful soul.

I come from a long line of strong women who were strong because they never had a childhood as so many women from that era. It was stolen by incest. They grew up having to play the role of a woman early on in life, not really knowing what happens when a young girl is introduced to sex before they have the mental capacity to understand what having sex truly means. And that the role they played that mimicked that of a sexual partner that was nonconsensual or forced. Bless the heart of all those that survived childhood abuse.

Most young adolescent girls lose their innocence to the game of hide and seek with some neighborhood boy behind the bushes, curious about the birds and the bees or in a relationship with a high school sweetheart, whom you think you are madly in love with. Either way, sex is supposed to be a conscious choice you make, thinking you are giving yourself away in the name of love, like in a romance novel or an after-school special. If you are spiritual you wait until marriage because you want to wait for someone that is agreeing to be monogamous and singular with you for a lifetime commitment the way love and sex was created by God, our creator.

Incest, no matter how you try to twist the truth, is not right and I pray no child from this point on goes through what I and many of us have previously endured. Deception is the foundation of incest. It's a phycological game played by the groomer that uses the naïve nature of the child to trick false consent from the child, so it doesn't emotionally feel like rape or doesn't trigger the threat of danger in the mind of a child.

Like in the garden when the serpent said, "You shall not surely die". He wanted to make Eve comfortable to spark a false sense of security with something that was forbidden. Children were not created or designed to have sexual experiences. The child is less likely to act out of fear towards the abuser if the act is presented as love or nurturing from a supportive caregiver, which is consent under falsehood. Falsehood is misleading the child with lies to make them feel as if they are agreeing to the act by taking part in it without understanding the end from the beginning.

It also doesn't always have to be an adult, it could be a sibling or cousin, sometimes of the opposite or even same gender. It's not until the child grows up and realizes it was wrong and nothing that was presented to them was nurturing at all, that the blinders come off and the healing begins.

By the time the blinders come off it's too late to change the truth, and you can't change what happened, but you can heal and move on with the understanding you survived and your trauma did not get the best of you. The tragedy of incest is that the shame falls on the victim and not the abuser, leaving the impression that the child did something to provoke the abuser. Placing the blame on the child and not the adult is the reason incest is visited generation after generation in many families and never resolved, because when we sweep it under the rug and victim blame, the primary person responsible for the abuse is not held accountable for their actions. No one wants to admit that auntie, uncle, daddy, mama, grandpa, grandma, cousin so and so is a child molester, we'd rather be quiet and do nothing before we get involved and be labelled the black sheep of the family it happens generation after generation because we are not acknowledging the infestation of incest within our families.

This type of behavior is the reason we have so many generations of family dysfunction as we continue to mimic the covering up of trauma as the siblings branch off into having families of their own, and they carry that baggage into another household when we grow up and have families of our own.

If Dad can get away with it, then the son can when he has his own family and so on, so on generations later until someone speaks out. If Mama can get away with it, then the daughter can when she becomes a mother, and then the granddaughter when she becomes a mother, you get the point. The fear of "messing up the family" through the acknowledgment of the dysfunction allows the abuse to stay hidden.

Being naïve comes into play because when a problem is not dealt with justly, it appears that abuse is masked as "that's just how family is": a very dysfunctional perspective to hold onto and pass down to future generations, and there is nothing we can do about it since no one ever has. This is the distorted mentality we pass along. The naive part is due to the fact that it becomes believable in the wrong spaces where people have not been exposed to truth. When dysfunction is programmed into society as normal, that dysfunction can bleed over into other relationships like friendships or outside associations, like our churches or our jobs.

We as a society turn what is supposed to be normal plutonic interactions, average everyday encounters with people, into sexual encounters because sex becomes part of the requirement for survival when we have been victimized, we were taught to use our bodies as a form of exchange to get what we think we need or to pacify the narcissist in our lives. There is no progression of relationship, romance, or intimacy which is the healthy approach when we operate out of healthy behavior, unhealthy behavior will have us doing as we are told to gain approval or acceptance, whether we agree with it or not, because unhealthy behavior has no boundaries and it teaches that a person has no rights to speak up for themselves.

It creates a 'do as you are told' mentality in someone who has suffered from sexual abuse. Allowing yourself to be used for the benefit of other people is part of the norm in unhealthy social circles. Except for those that take on the role of the Alpha, the Alpha male or female in the equation of any dysfunctional environment are usually the only ones that are allowed to call the shots.

That is why most people who suffer from child abuse end up in one abusive situation after the other because they permanently take on the role of the weaker vessel to anyone who proves dominance over them. We all need to heal, but we are mistaken if we think we can do it alone. I have had the help of the healthy men in my life like my grandfather, adopted father and my husband Kenn. Until Kenn I never had a man ask to be my friend, and I never really knew what a male friend was supposed to be.

I had such a struggle identifying what a good man was, I had almost given up on being married again at all and decided that all I wanted was to be an amazing mother. All I ever wanted was a happy home, but I kept living out my mother's generational curse which lead me to having to file for divorce twice. It was not until now, that I am living my best life through the good and the bad, when I kept starting over and over just trying to provide a happy home for my sons and a place of peace and normalcy for myself.

Now, I am a serial entrepreneur, an author. I'm healing, and I am writing this book, things I've waited decades to do after decades of allowing others to push me to the back of the line with fear! I hope to be a light and a matriarch for those who understand what it means to be broken but not beyond repair.

I was blessed to meet Kenn when I did because he helped me see my own potential and invested in me as a woman to know what was already inside of me. After all that I had been through, I wasn't going to let anyone else into my broken soul to crush it more.

Besides my sons I had no one that I truly believed loved me, and I honestly learned through raising my boys, how innocent men have the potential to be, when loved correctly as boys. That is why I did my best to raise my sons in a loving home. It is for this reason the pages of my story come together so eloquently because no matter the storms of betrayal I build my foundations on love. I was naïve to believe my only purpose in life was to serve others, even at the expense of possibly defaulting on my own purpose, I looked around to see that I had no joy. I was naïve to believe I didn't matter in the full scheme of things. Naïve to believe my feelings weren't important and that happiness was a gift I could only give but was too crippled to receive. I never looked in the mirror to even love myself because I wasn't allowed such privileges of vanity growing up as a little girl. I didn't even think I was pretty. I felt guilty for even thinking it because I thought flaunting your beauty invited rape. I covered my beauty with the disguise of being a tomboy, so no one would find me attractive and start talking to me. I didn't want them to be interested in me. My husband came along and, in the name of friendship, took the veil off my eyes and told me it's okay to be beautiful. Helped me dress in clothes that were even my size because I dressed in oversized clothes, now I dress in modest clothes that at the same time were my size and yet helped me feel grown and sexy.

Love changes things, especially self-love. Yes, we can do it alone, a strong woman on the verge of showing the world her iron-clad heart after being hurt so many times. Yes, we can, but I didn't want to. I wanted to dream of a happy home of a family that loved one another. Maybe that was the source of my blind ignorance, but I kept praying and kept believing that one day I could say I knew what pure love was and that the curse was broken.

I'm happy to say that day has come for me, and I couldn't be more overjoyed to be walking in my purpose of living and breathing what I thought was unattainable as a little girl, now here I am manifesting dreams come true.

I won't say I'll never be naïve again. I still live in a world where we have knowledge of good and evil, but now I am able to see the good in myself. To be a role model for other women that need help out of the valley of despair. Yes, there are plenty of people on the sidelines, eager to make an even bigger fool out of me but, oh well you can't control people, I have learned that I was destined for greatness and so be it! I will say I have learned that putting myself first is not rude or mean and that wanting a good home filled with love and laughter is not out of reach for me. I will say I've learned to be careful of who and what I let into my life, and I take claim to the desires of my heart. I won't stop dreaming. I won't stop praying and expecting better days ahead. The past is behind me, and it no longer defines me.

I do not have to live out the generational curses of my father and mother. I will always strive to become more aware so that my family and I will live a healthy life as well. That I can write my own story and if you are reading this so can you! I will be the friend you need to light the path for your journey out of darkness until the Lord sends you a mate or a loving support system to walk hand and hand with you through your healing. Healing is coming, just keep believing and don't ever give up. You would think the years of abuse and lack of identity would have broken me.

However, somewhere along the way, I realized God favored me, in that no matter how many times life knocked me down and even though most of the time I was an emotional wreck, I learned how to be strong for my boys and then myself, because I wanted them to have a good mama. So, God gave me the grace to be what I never had back then, a good mother, and that kept the door of my heart open for what I never knew as love to flow out of me for their sake. And from there I learned how to start loving myself, even the broken parts.

Chapter 2

Identity

———————————

"To be or not to be, that is the question,"
Shakespeare

The words "Identity Crisis" are enough to raise alarm. It's a personal red flag. You're just out here in a worst-case scenario, hoping every day for a miracle, faking it till you make it. Identity Crisis is defined as a period of confusion or uncertainty about one's sense of self. It can happen at any time but is often triggered by a significant life change.

For me, this was most of my life, the times in my life when I realized I was nothing like my family. I could not be like them, no matter how much pressure the abuse put on me to perform acts I didn't feel at one with. I grew up in a family that was always partying drunk or high, and the room was always filled with negative sexual energy. No one was safe from being groped or pulled into a corner. My parents were wild. I felt trapped and always on guard. So, I didn't ever feel like one of them. I always looked for somewhere else to be, over a friend's house, over my grandparents' home, great grandparents, anywhere but home. I never felt like I belonged. This was my first identity crisis.

When you don't know who you are in the midst of what's happening, you do your best to blend in well. The lack of self-control in times of intense danger and an identity crisis will thrust you into survival mode. Identity crisis and survival mode are a deadly mix. You wind up acting out of the need to please people, believing they are your key to survival. You take on the role of who you're told to be, and of course, you feel like you can't live on to the next moment. Your brain functions come to a halt because you never use your brain, never learn to logically solve problems, just rushing to decide based on life and death circumstances. At first, there is no way to know if what you're feeling even has a name, that adrenaline rush just feels like part of your identity. You are considered hyper and technical names like anxiety or panic attacks won't come to mind, but it's just fear from having to survive one moment to the next.

All you will know is you feel sick in your stomach like a tiny fist balling up and twisting your intestines. It can be hard to breathe, and it is like an extra 10 lbs. on your shoulders. This is how I felt as a child, just using the terminology child since I never had a childhood. The only time I truly felt free as a little girl is when I lived with my maternal grandparents early on before my mother and little sister and I moved into the house with my dad when I was around 7. It was then when the worst part of my abuse began to take place, thrusting me into an adult mindset.

I can remember the panic overwhelming me at times, so much so that even when I would take a bath with the bathroom door locked, I still felt very nervous because I knew my father was coming up the stairs, and I knew I would have no choice but to let him in. He had a temper so enraged that telling him no was not even a possible answer. I had no privacy whatsoever growing up. I suffered tremendously from panic attacks that I didn't even know I was having. The feeling of an overwhelming rush of emotions passing through me living in the shadow of the fear of the unknown, every minute I lived at home was a war zone, me against them.

Everyday my father came home from work he would tell me to go take a bath before dinner, and every day for so many years there I was sitting in the tub staring at the door, listening for his footsteps, waiting for the knock. Laying under the water, covered by the same towel I was supposed to use to dry off with, but who cared about drying off with the devil at the door ready to do his dirty work, always against my will with no help of rescue from my mother or anyone else. It was just him, her and my new born baby sister at home.

That was the worst anxiety, no one can imagine unless you've experienced it firsthand. What it feels like to be a child enduring the confusion of feeling this is wrong, the act itself and the person just pretending it's all okay. Even as a child your body functions like that as an adult with the same senses and reflexes as if you are having sex like an adult. It's the most horrible and confusing reality having to grow up before your time, body and mind. No child should ever have to endure that agony.

You can't think at all. The only thought in your brain is that there is no one to rescue you, and the only way out is to just wait until it's done, waiting just to get it over with. No wonder they call it trauma. Trauma defined means emotional shock following a stressful event or a physical injury, which may be associated with physical shock and sometimes leads to long-term neurosis.

The emotional shock causes you to lack the ability to believe it yourself, here you are in a waking nightmare. Your only hope is to wake up from it and you can't because you are not dreaming. Your brain try's tells you it's just a dream but the pain says its real. I grew up having such a high tolerance for pain due to the fact that I learned how to bear down and endure the unimaginable until it was over. Holding in the tears going somewhere else in your mind so you won't show your pain to your abuser, not allow not one extra second of gratification that what is happening is even bothering you. A twisted way to overcome mentally but truly the only way, when you know that no one is coming to save you, because I lived the reality over and over day after day with the same outcome. Wondering when the day would come that it would be over.

"A mind is a terrible thing to waste" was a drug commercial that came on TV when I was little, but it also in my opinion applies to where I was mentally. It is also a waste when you can't take the driver's seat in charge of your own life! The reason being survival is a mind over matter technique that you learn how to apply daily in order to not allow your reality to win and conquer you.

Survival mode is a life-and-death brain simulation that immediately triggers your fight-or-flight responses. This means you never sit still long enough to gain your bearings and daydream peacefully about who you are and what you believe in. To even imagine like a child because the carefree innocence that comes with your youth is snatched away from you in the dark terrors of an abusive reality.

It keeps you from standing your ground long enough to leave an imprint in the universe—to dream that something better exists. Imagination is the key to manifesting your dreams, and when you are comfortable with yourself, you will be less likely to do something that goes against how you feel about yourself. The only thing left is for you to walk out an exit strategy in your mind of how to get out, coming up with excuses as to make yourself unavailable. Pretending to be sick or any excuse I could come up with to see if my father and mother would have any mercy for me, but it never worked. I grew strong because it was that or commit suicide, but my mind kept telling my heart not to give up!

When you can't think straight, your imagination grows more anxious about escaping the personal prison called life growing around you. You spend all your time daydreaming of how to get away because you're such a nervous wreck walking on eggshells every moment. You have no space left to imagine that your life even has purpose. You feel like one person on the inside and on the outside struggling to survive, that is the recipe for identity crisis.

When you are suffering from an identity crisis, you don't even have a belief system; you do whatever you believe is best at the time to wake up the next day because you're dying on the inside, and you don't want to die in the dark place. So, you decide to walk through hell hoping that someone left the light on at the end of the tunnel.

Survival mode is death on the path to purpose. I was dying and didn't even know it. When you are constantly troubleshooting life, there is no room to think ahead or plan for the future. Your brain is like a car with the check light engine on. There is always this nagging thought that you could be without transportation at any moment. Although you're driving right now, there is an underlying concern for your safety whenever you are in the vehicle on the road to where you come from to where you are to where you are going, hoping that the car doesn't give out at any moment.

You know something is wrong, but you don't know what, and you hope you can fix it before it becomes one more problem you have to fix and still find a way to get around without losing time and momentum to get where you are going. It is difficult to find peace or think positively about where you are in life and the great things that will happen for you in the future.

That's how our brain works during moments of trauma. Your body is driving right along. Life is doing its thing and amid all you have to do, your mind manages trauma and uncertainty while smiling and ensuring everyone else's day goes well. Because your assigned identity is to be the person that bends over backwards for everyone else without breaking under the pressure, the whole time wishing you just disappeared into thin air if you could. You are missing out on yourself and focusing on the needs of others 24/7 even in your sleep. I never got a moment's rest even in my sleep.

Identity crisis trauma causes you to constantly second-guess all your decisions, stuck in the moment, managing trauma with a smile, and forgetting all about the future. It's like the movie *Groundhog Day* except the Halloween version because instead of cute fuzzy animals, you're stuck with monsters. Until by some act of fate the chains are broken, and you wake up one day free. Now remember Jeremiah 29:11, that God birthed you into the Earth with hope and a future. You have a future!

Gaslighting and or Power and Control are two methods narcissistic abusers use against their victims to strip them of their identity psychologically, this is the underlying cause of identity crisis. Gaslighting is a form of psychological abuse or manipulation in which the abuser tries to sow doubt and confusion in the person they are targeting, to distort their mind.

Typically, gas lighters seek power and control over the other person by distorting reality and forcing them to question their judgment and intuition. Giving up your willpower and ability to reason for them to live out their will through you, like a puppet. They are psychologically cloning themselves into you through mental manipulation hoping you will have a nervous breakdown and become so catatonic that they can take over your person, like a body snatcher. You just become a face with no name, becoming an empty void less object. Your mind is not yours and leaving you lifeless and clueless to question them, giving them a chance to fulfill whatever sick twisted game plan they have in mind.

The behavior of a gas lighter is to deny what the other person knows is true, swapping the truth for the lie by disregarding that the truth is absolute and actual, so your brain flickers back and forth between what you see and feel to be true and the lies that you are being told, creating a smoke screen of lies. Their primary goal is to break your spirit and make you their prisoner for life.

The psychological impact of being gaslighted is a powerless feeling over one's own life and circumstances, keeping you confused over small details or unsure over your next move about the simple things like whether or not you should make a right hand or left hand turn while driving in a circle, that type of confusion. Having you isolated from others, whether self-isolation or because you have been boxed into believing you are unable to function properly around others, leaving you mentally exhausted to make any choices at all. Therefore, you give up on thinking for yourself and allow someone else to make the choices for you, doubting yourself. This creates low self-esteem and debasement in the targeted person. Making you doubt your own competence altogether and life in general, just a bag of useless purposeless flesh. That is the goal of a gas lighter and folks this is not a game at all.

Gaslighting in relationships is not limited to sexual or intimate partners. This could be family or friends, colleagues, peers, members of your church. Anyone who likes to keep you around because you are useful only if you are willing to do everything their way, this is all conditional. The end game of Gaslighting is to have Total Power and Control over the targeted person's mental clarity and decision-making progress in as many, if not all, aspects of their life as possible.

> *Then God said, "Let us make mankind in our image, in our likeness,*
> *so that they may rule over the fish in the sea and the birds in the*
> *sky, over the livestock and all the wild animals, and over all the*
> *creatures that move along the ground."*
>
> *So, God created mankind in his own image, in the image of God*
> *he created them; male and female he created them.*
>
> *God blessed them and said to them, "Be fruitful and increase in*
> *number; fill the earth and subdue it. Rule over the fish in the sea*
> *and the birds in the sky and over every living creature that moves*
> *on the ground."*
> **Genesis 1:26-28**

Let's go back to the story in the beginning to look into the true format for humanity when God created mankind, Genesis 1:26-28 tells us that God created an Equality Bond in the Garden of Eden; "Let us make man in our image, after our likeness: and let them have dominion". The balance of authority and power is oneness in the phrase let "them" have dominion, not over one another but over the responsibilities to live and thrive together in the image of God, which is love. "Over the fish of the sea, and over the birds of the heavens, and over the cattle, and over all the earth, and over every creeping thing that creepeth upon the earth", the clear picture that we were never to have power and control over one another but over the earth as a means of a manager over what God entrusted to us as stewards and ambassadors. Never over each other. Wow, sip on that tea!

It was not until after the fall of man, the balance of authority became unbalanced and unhealthy. Without God—which is love—as the center of any great relationship, it turns into a Power and Control struggle of who is right and wrong. This dynamic is considered a "fallen state", which further solidifies the argument that narcissistic abuse is the further from God we as humans can be.

In the garden, they both sinned, so the accountability should have been mutual and equal as well. Instead, we blame Eve for her involvement. Only God did not ask for Eve; he said, "Adam, where are you?" Adam blamed Eve for the fall, not taking any accountability for his behavior. Eve didn't even argue when Adam blamed her. She stayed quiet and was still a perfect partner by honoring God in her part of the disobedience to God. And not tit for tat in the pointing of fingers, like so many women today!

However, the story never even shows that Adam took any responsibility for his disobedience. Jesus had to come and take his place as atonement for sins. Jesus took accountability for the fall and offered protection for the New Bride of Christ, which is the old Eve washed clean. Where would we be now as a society if Adam, in theory, had taken accountability when God asked him where he was and had taken responsibility for the part he played in disobedience to God? Things could have gone completely different since God resists the proud but gives grace to the humble.

The first example of an unhealthy imbalance of power struggle is Genesis. Christ restored us on the cross, to the original blueprint in Genesis 1:26-28, which is how we are redeemed and resurrected from the unhealthy narcissistic, gaslighting, abusive power and control hold of the devil's hold over humanity because love should be the foundation of every one of our relationships. Only pure sexual love for that of your partner, not the masses, chronic sexual promiscuity reveals a lack of self-esteem because love loses its value. Having a spiritual bond with those you are related to and in your community and reserving the Eros love connection for your unconditional forever partner. This saves us from having to deal with sexual assaults, abuse of children, lust and lascivious lifestyles, and gender confusion when we put love before sex. Some people do it because they are lonely, and the need to be held and comforted is sought out in less healthy ways.

It was later in life that I understood what this meant. I watched and experienced it growing up. My father was my first exposure to gaslighting. Not just me he was a serial narcissist and would do little things to my mother to make her doubt her mental processes and recall. As I reflect on the events of my childhood I can see now that I grew up thinking that being gaslight was a normal way of life, no wonder it took me so long to wake up to the truth!

I remember him going into the basement to turn on the washing machine in the middle of the night and then returning to bed with my mother. He woke her to say, "You left the washing machine on!" She tried to recall the events that evening that led up to her going to bed to remember when she could have left the washer on. And when she didn't remember, he would guilt trip her into thinking she was too absent-minded even to remember turning the washer on just moments before going to bed. In hindsight, I believe he did it to make her defenseless not to second guess him at all when the question of molesting me came up or anything at all for that matter, he was so horrible there was no telling what all he did in one day. So, he had to behave in such a way that would cause her to question her sanity that way, when she tried to reason within herself whether anything she saw or heard was real, he could strip her of reasoning to make her points invalid.

He also did the same to me to interfere with my logical reasoning processes when I questioned our dysfunctional father-daughter relationship. He was a skilled narcissist and had many people afraid of him, had a terrible temper, there were other women that he introduced me to, I can only imagine those were the women he pimped because they did whatever he said, as well and they always treated me with well and with a lot of respect, but I can remember seeing the fear they had of him in when I looked in their eyes. He had the personality of a monster, and I know very little of him other than this he was a victim that became a victimizer, he obviously never healed before he died or at least I hope he did.

Gaslighting gives people the ability to do dirt right in front of your face, and you don't even question it because you believe you are only imagining things. It's like a form of being under a conscious hypnosis, or if you've ever been roofied I compare the two because I have been gaslighted and roofied and the two feelings are similar except you don't eventually crash out from the gaslighting, it keeps you stuck in a loop repeating the same certain set of behaviors that is focused on pleasing the person that has the power over you. You can only break free from it by changing your behavior by doing something different, unexpected for the betterment of yourself, to the good of all and the harm to none.

It paves the way for an identity crisis by making you question your sanity when discerning the intent of others around you. It disarms your senses, leaving you open prey to manipulators. And left unhealed, you go from one abusive encounter to another. Your abusers change faces, this is worth repeating "your abusers will have different faces but the same spirit of tyranny attached to them", like the phrase "same BS different day", yeah that part! Sadly, the abuse continues because your lack of ability to track back to the source of the abuse remains unresolved.

I always knew growing up that my childhood had a detrimental effect on how I saw myself and how I related to others. I just had to break the cycle concerning my identity. I had to stop being what others wanted me to be and become what I needed for my own advancement. I seldom bonded with people who were good for my growth and development because of such deeply rooted, legitimate trust issues because I was constantly giving the wrong ones the benefit of the doubt. So much so that when good people came along, I was so ashamed of myself, that I didn't let anyone worthy help me heal. I was too embarrassed from the choices I made in the name of being a "rider", not anymore. I will take several seats now, will sit down on somebody really quick if it isn't on the up and up.

Most of the people I met over the years have re-victimized me due to my own naive tendencies, you have to be careful who you share your story with before you heal. I was living in a repeated cycle of abuse due to my own big mouth. Figure that! I had to learn the hard way that everything is on a need to know basis, here I thought that it was my duty to share my life history with others as a means of being transparent and honest. Not fully understanding that was the thing that the narcissist used to guilt me into thinking I was not worthy of love as if I was to blame for my own trauma.

They twisted my truth and created false scenarios to make me believe I brought the trauma on myself. Like when someone tells a child they are bad for not doing what they are told, when in truth the child's natural instincts kick in and they perceive the information being told to them is wrong, but feels guilty when they don't obey the person asking them to perform the act, so they override their natural instincts and do it anyway feeling horrible after and are rewarded for the improper behavior because that's how the abuser twist the child perception of right and wrong. The same tactic works on adults too. I am here to tell you that you don't owe anyone anything, your pain and your story is private, especially before they have earned your trust and confidence.

I thought I was the problem in every scenario, and I just turned up my people-pleasing skills, hoping I would make the people I was with happy enough for them to approve of me. In doing so, I was losing pieces of myself to the identity of others, becoming a blank canvas for others to create whatever was beneficial for them. My life somehow slipped out of control, and I just became a zombie. I was constantly questioning my self-worth and sanity outside of whoever had power over me at the time.

That's why I started running from everyone and everything, which made me feel like I was going crazy. It's impossible to win an argument or make a valid point when you're up against someone skilled in manipulation because they are never wrong. They will twist your words and make it seem like you're not making any valid points and have you questioning your recall of events until you feel stupid for even speaking up in the first place. That place, for me, feels like what the Twilight Zone would be if it was a real tangible place.

It wasn't until after I gave birth to my second child at the age of 34 that I was able to see that my imagination was not playing tricks on me, but my life has shifted from living out the pains of an abusive childhood to religious power and control in the church, to force me into a place of submission to man by using the guilt trip that I would be disappointing

God if I did not do as I was told. It was an issue of authority every time. First through my father and mother's parental authority, to the ungodly authority of the church I was a member of, to the authority of a previous husband, who says the man is the head of the household, and a good wife was a submissive wife and not to question the authority over you was something I was taught not to do. So, everyone in my life was winning around me except me! Money is not the only reason people come into your life to take advantage of you. Sometimes, people will settle for locking you into a type of psychological slavery where you become a servant to them forever. And they will have you believing being a servant to them is the Will of God for your life, and if you do not do as you are told, you will grieve the Holy Spirit. That's the basis of Religious Abuse, which is the cruelest trick of all, using God as the foundation to justify abuse.

Apart from the brave face that you wear every day is a piece of you screaming out to be set free; you don't know how to set yourself free because you second-guess your ability to make sound, reasonable choices. Since you've been taught through gaslighting and manipulation that you're not good at making sound choices, you end up making no choice at all, which is actually a choice to do nothing, believe it or not. This is a partially correct observation because the person telling you this knows you wouldn't be wasting time with them if you knew any better.

Being too afraid to ask questions plays a huge role in you not knowing. You have not because you ask not, asking questions helps you to make decisions based on truths instead of misleading assumptions. It's not until you get to the point where you are willing to take a risk on yourself that your life takes a turn of fate or shall I say from doubting yourself to having faith that God gave you a brain all of your own to think with, cognitive skills to reason with, the scripture says in 2 Timothy 1:7 "For God has not given us the spirit of fear; but of power, and of love, and of a sound mind," so when we began to use scriptures for a book of wisdom and instruction instead of a tool for condemnation and judgment we can see why it was written a handbook for life to those that love God and desire to understand why you were created.

It doesn't matter how the dysfunctional patterns of identity crisis crept into your life. What matters most is when you recognize that you do not belong to anyone as if you were property to be bought and sold, but a creation meant to be appreciated like fine art. It is not until we are willing to make the proper changes within yourself to break free from the mental bondage, that keeps you in a cycle of thinking you are not enough and that you are undeserving to be treated with unconditional love and respect, when we break free from that mentality by making sound choices, then and only then can we receive the gift of Salvation that sets us free.

I wanted to be loved and not controlled. I was tired of pouring myself into people who picked me apart by keeping what was beneficial for them and shutting down the parts of me that made me the master of my life and choices. Some people are so good they will have you believing it was your choice to be the lesser, weaker vessel in the relationship/ friendship or the dummy in the group. When you decide to change or take charge of your life, that's when you win, until then possibly everyone you meet, will make you feel you are doing them a personal injustice by taking the bull by the horns, for lack of a better phrase and drawing boundaries for self-respect.

There are some really sick individuals that benefit from our ignorance and lack of self-esteem, and they won't be taught a lesson until they see their behavior is absolutely unacceptable. It honestly wasn't until after my second divorce that I had some serious soul-searching to do. I felt utterly lost. I had spent most of my life getting my heart broken over and over. I found myself constantly falling into a pattern of abuse with family and "the church", and then two failed marriages.

That's when I just stopped and took a pause on going hard for everyone else and started to look at myself in the mirror and ask, "girl, what is wrong with you!" I only attracted friends that were with me because I would give the shirt off my back while standing in the rain. Which for me meant I was usually alone when the going got tough, because the truth is no person has true respect for someone they can walk all over. Accountability to self is realizing sometimes that the problem is you, especially when you keep repeating the same cycles. Even if it's just that your perspective is off and you need to reevaluate how you think, your heart could be in the right place but like Tina Turner said, baby "what's love got to do with it", and I will add if it's killing you? To the end of that question. I had to dig myself out of the pit that my lack of self-care put me in, that's called accountability.

One example as I reflect on the gaslighting I experienced was when I became a certified aerobics instructor. I was super excited. I taught several classes at least twice a week, and they were so successful that the class was always packed. I printed business cards with my name to pass out, and my first husband, told me to put his number on my business cards so he could filter out the type of people that called. For my protection, he said, however, I didn't feel as if I was in any danger. Plus, I was a capable woman with a full schedule, working full-time at the local hospital during the day and teaching nightly aerobics classes at a nearby gym in the evening. I was more than capable of answering the phone for myself and setting up any personal training sessions. He, however, convinced me that because I was molested as a child, the negative effects of my abuse were something too profound for me to understand, and it was his job to protect me. Like a dummy, I put his number on my cards, and guess what? That was the beginning and end of my business. According to him, no one ever called!

Another example was one day, he said he had a surprise coming in the mail for me and wanted to check the mail himself so I wouldn't spoil it! Well, so much time passed that I don't think I ever checked the mail again. I forgot about it, trusting him that a surprise was coming. The surprise was that there was no surprise. I am still trying to understand why he asked me to stop checking the mail.

The last straw happened several years later when we agreed to raise my youngest baby cousin. She lived with us for a while about 6 years, and due to several stressors in the marriage, we had driven her back to my hometown so I could focus on raising my two sons, whom I had given birth to over the time she lived with us. She was born addicted to drugs at birth, and several of us in the family took turns taking her in as we could.

Nevertheless, when we got back from our trip, which was an awful emotional strain on me because I loved her dearly, and I only took her back home because I started to notice he shifted his mind games from me to her and told me, he told me it was for her good that he became the primary caregiver for her to help me focus on the boys. He said he knew better how to deal with her because he was a professional counselor dealing with cases like hers every day. Well, when I finally decided it was in her best interest to return home, he and I were pillow-talking after we returned home from the trip, and he explained to me how he lied about submitting the adoption paperwork on her because he knew I didn't know any better. He was doing me a favor by holding off on everything, that raising her was just an emotional decision I was making without thinking. At that moment, I realized I had given ten years of my life and my youth to a man who lied to me with a smile the whole marriage. That was an "ah ha" moment for me for sure. I wondered who I was really married to.

I thought of myself as a failure. Not only did I not fulfill my word to a vulnerable young girl who trusted us to provide a safe home for her, but my sons thought of her as an older sister and didn't understand why their sister had to leave. There was so much pain in my heart and tears in my eyes. All the while, he was smiling. I knew that day that something was wrong with him and not me. I knew then I had to leave, and now the pain of breaking up the only home my sons knew, in order to leave a man that would eventually drive me mad for his amusement, was at the front of my mind like a dagger in my brain. I didn't know who would raise my sons if he succeeded. It was that moment that the mask came off and I saw him for who he truly was, a joker.

I couldn't even find freedom in the one place most people claimed was the ultimate answer: the church. It blew my mind that not even in the "House of God" could you find refuge from being taken advantage of. When I sought help, everyone made me feel as if he was a good man and that my upbringing was the problem. I had no idea why people felt the need to use my childhood trauma to justify his behavior, he had people so fooled that it was me and not him that had the problem because of his many years of experience as a counselor, well sometimes the counselor needs counseling. Because the truth is he hid behind his credentials and political connections, I can't begin to accurately convey to you the truth on how he was able to gaslight others concerning me. Now looking in hindsight it's as if he told the story of a woman that was incapable of making sound choices for himself, as if he was a self-appointed savior over my life. As if with him in my life I was better and without him in my life I was a threat to myself and others.

The reason I say this is because I felt when I left him there was a social manhunt to get me back in his clutches, I had a story to tell about a man that I felt kept me bound under oppression of his superior identity and when I tried to explain my dilemma of the marriage dynamics, it was as if when I spoke about the details of my oppression under him, the stories were flipped on to me as if my childhood trauma blinded me to his greatness and that was the reason the marriage was not working. As if he was not at fault for his treatment of me because he allegedly gave others the impression that his many years of social work experience canceled out the truth of my testimony of his behavior.

He painted the picture that I was insane or delusional because he had inside knowledge of my father's undiagnosed mental issues, because obviously my father having been such a beast of a man there was something wrong with him. I told my ex-husband when we were married of how my father would shoot up with heroin and go through a physical psychosis right in front of me and crash out acting under the direction of the drug to behave insanely and how he would cut up hundred dollar bills into tiny pieces and throw them in the fire. Afterwards he would molest me while under his drug induced state, it was the most horrible memories I have of my biological father, his drug induced tantrums in my presence. The demonic energy he operated in was terrifying and the protection of God and his angels is the only way that I survived. Well, with stories like that in his mental archives and years of social work training he was able to paint a picture of me to others that made them feel I was best under his care, but the truth was actually that he was a liar and I was scared of him and no one would listen to me because he had more friends than I did. I was an introvert with a troubled past and he was an extrovert that had the ear of judges and magistrates and a tightly knit social work network professionals that had already decided that I didn't have a leg to stand on against him.

He won that battle judicially, and all I could do was make sure I was never alone in a room with him again and be cordial enough to go along to get along because he had shared custody of my children and there was nothing at the time I could do to change that fact. That is the sad truth concerning most women that were childhood victims of abuse that are married to professionals in the fields of psychology and social work, and law enforcement. All the narcissist has to do is paint her as crazy and his colleagues and social circle will follow, like the blind leading the blind.

My ex-husband knew too much about me because he had been collecting his scientific data on me since he met me in 1999. When I sat under the sadistic pastor that I had escape from, during my first unhealthy church abuse under the pastor that went to jail for sexual abuse of a minor. I don't know if it was really scientific data, but I call it that because of the way a narcissistic brain works. They collect information and process it in such a way they can weaponize it against you later to trigger your post-traumatic stress disorder responses to gaslight you. Looking back for a second, I can see now that because I met him as I was transitioning out from underneath that church leadership, I shared a lot of my horror stories about my church experiences with him and I innocently thought it would be okay. I later learned over time everything is not for everyone, you have to discern who you can and cannot vent to because not everyone you meet has your best interest at hand.

My cult-like church experience started when I left my hometown in 1998 to move to the preverbal bible belt to do what I believed was to follow Christ. I make the difference between occult-like churches and actually "households of faith churches" because not all churches are the same.

Moving to Alabama from the Ohio "sister church" pipeline, was my way of trying to escape my childhood and the drifter life of a runaway, and as I mentioned earlier, this time I wasn't exactly running, in my heart this time I was actually answering the call of Christ for my life. I was so excited I felt as if I was on a quest to redefine myself, to be better. I was leaving the old for the new. I spent so much time in the women's transitional home sponsored by the church, that I felt for the first time that I was ready to get out into the world and live a life that was going to be different than anything else I had done. I got on that greyhound bus with two taped up cardboard boxes and a dream. I had decided to follow Jesus because the love I felt just reading the Word of God in a peaceful environment under the guidance of the kind house mother that took me under her wing.

It's an indescribable feeling when you read that Jesus died for you to have a better life, how noble and romantic like a love note from heaven only pure, there is nothing sexual about God's love, it is love in its purest form. So, we don't get it twisted and sell ourselves short comparing God's unconditional love to human conditional transactional love.

After surviving so much childhood trauma, running away from home and living a few years going from place to place not really able to find myself with no stability and then after the two years getting cleaned up living in the women's group home, trying to understand my life, praying and studying the bible. I felt like I was ready to make the biggest turn around ever, I was off to be a servant of the Lord and preach the gospel of Jesus Christ. So, I took the leap of faith to move somewhere I thought I could continue the work.

I stepped off the bus to smell the same fresh southern air that captivated me a year earlier and from 1999 to 2001, I only later realized that the same dark souls hiding in the corners of the Earth from Monday through Saturday that I was running from also lived in the pews of the church on Sunday Morning. Some were even preaching behind the altar on Sunday morning, go figure. The reality blew my mind, but I thought maybe it was just this church over time things became clearer.

The first pastor I sat under had a bad problem with adultery, drugs, and a few other things. He was a wolf in sheep's clothing. Now of course I did not know this right off the bat. It took some time to realize, once the zeal for my decision faded and I started to see the truth. He hid it and was not honest about his struggles, it's not that anyone is perfect, but transparency keeps us accountable to God and one another. And what is hidden cannot be healed.

Nevertheless, having lived a life of abandonment and sexual abuse, I had severe daddy issues, which is the worst place for an abuse victim to be, under the leadership of a person who has problems with perversion, especially a church where you associate the personality of the leadership with that of God himself, a common mistake of new members. It's like they can smell your vulnerabilities on you. I was looking for a father figure I could trust, let me also say that it's okay to have a history of childhood trauma and NOT grow up looking for surrogate parents to replace the ones that abandoned you as a child, that is a mistake many of us make when we have mommy/daddy issues, instead it's better to self-parent and find that love by good self-care. Anyway, I moved far away from home down South to what seemed like a quieter, less congested place to heal, than the fast-paced hustle of city life.

When I joined this church, they told me I was an armor bearer, which means personal assistant to the pastor and his family. This is an Old Testament tradition that is taught in the church that should no longer be practiced in my opinion, because it causes codependency to man and not dependency on Christ. It teaches servanthood instead of adoption to the family of God as children of God. We are children of God not servants, we serve one another in love yes, but we are not servants. That part of the scripture commonly gets twisted in its interpretation due to selfishness of false leaders.

I had never heard of such a thing, but at the time I would have been whatever I needed if I believed God said it. Having lived with two abusive parents, I was all too familiar with doing what I was told. So, I agreed to be this armor bearer because I thought it was a noble thing to be, and I went from a life of abandonment and runaway to being the pastor's family personal assistant.

I slowly began to realize the pastor had a habit of using his influence to manipulate the women in the church. This is only important because if you are already suffering from an identity crisis, not knowing who you are other than a victim, you will keep being a victim, and not even church will save you, because there are bad people in the church as well. You must be careful wherever you go, whoever you are around. I went from living in their home, cooking, cleaning, washing, and babysitting, to being the full-time church secretary, slowly falling under his control, believing I was doing something good, bettering myself. I was a single woman with no children, wasting my time and my skills for a narcissist wolf in sheep's clothing. This man was abusing his wife, and she just went along because she just wanted to be a good wife to the man of God or maybe she wasn't strong enough emotionally to fight for herself and protect the women in the church. My blinded desire to be good led me into the home of someone just as bad as my father. The man I had traveled all this way to get away from. The response from most people when they hear something like this is well, "you were an adult and should have known better and just said no!" This is logically if you have not been indoctrinated to idolize leadership as if disobeying the pastor is comparable to disobeying God, that part!

He told me this story in the Bible of a handmaiden named Hagar (Genesis 16:2) and how her life was of service to the people of God. How completely devoted Hagar was, and just like Hagar, it was my duty to make sure I was just as devoted and could not refute scripture.

Most people will tell you that the Bible is the irrefutable Word of God and not to question it. They won't tell you, however, that people will use the Word of God to lie to you and manipulate you, which for them is a delayed punishment in waiting because the Lord's representatives take a vow to do good. However, until that time since you are without a credible reputation are just another victim to the system of false doctrine, as I was. And to cover their tracks the church will paint a false narrative against you like you are a jezebel that tempted the pastor, not that he preys on vulnerable women which is the real truth.

So, years after the religious abuse that conditioned me to be this docile, submissive person, coupled with childhood trauma. I went from the frying pan to the fire when I met my first husband. He was raised with the idea that a woman was the lesser, weaker vessel to be seen and not heard, and I fell right into the trap. Because as I was fleeing the church with this cult, I met him at church one evening at a revival and he asked me for my number. He was a member of a community choir that sang gospel music, so I was under the impression that because he was in church that he was a good person. In the meantime, I openly told him what was going on and that I was leaving the church, but I didn't know anybody in town, and I definitely could not go back home to my family. He presented his best persona, giving a sense of false security to me and a couple months later we started dating. We started out slow. He wanted me to feel safe to think that he was a gentleman and to show me his best god-like character. It was not all bad love bombing never is at first, his polite behavior was convincing that maybe he wasn't like everyone else. However, on the inside by the end of the marriage he was just like every other church going man of God and I was the fool.

I want to take a moment here to suggest to every person that has been a victim of sexual abuse, to please take a break to heal and learn about yourself before moving on into the arms of someone you feel will be a hero to you in your circumstances. There is no hero you have to do the healing.

He took my trauma and vulnerabilities and used my weakness to fuel his lust for power and control. In the end I truly believe that the only reason he married me was to exercise his right of control over a woman that he knew was already easily controlled. From that period, the best thing that has happened to me is that I gave birth to two beautiful boys who have been the soft center of my heart ever since. I left the marriage after I realized I kept living the same repeated pattern over and over. He thought nothing was wrong with him and blamed my childhood for any issues we had in the marriage. That pill was a hard pill to swallow because how could I ever escape my past and the abuse I grew up in constantly being reminded of it?

My advice to anyone is never to stay with someone that constantly throws up your past trauma as if you are that same person. Even the stories I tell you in this book are old stories, and I cannot guarantee that maybe the people I speak of have not changed and become better, I can only tell you what I experienced back then 20 years ago, who knows now maybe they have changed. I don't know because I made it a point in life not to let the same person hurt me twice.

It is okay to help people, but never to your own detriment and in certain circles where the takers outweigh the givers you can get beat down with overexertion. It becomes draining because what others are taking from you cannot be replenished with something as quickly as drinking a bottle of water to rehydrate. The type of exertion I am talking about is a mental draining, financial draining, physically if you have someone around you that like to start physical fights or worse sexual abuse. These type of abuses take days or even weeks to heal from and repeated attacks of any time keeps you in fight or flight and you never relax. That type of draining takes miles off your life so please, if at all possible, stay away from such people.

I would never be able to grow and become stronger in a place where I had to live in the shadow of religious power and control, which enforces gender roles to keep you bound mentally to certain behaviors. That is no place for a person who has grown up in an abusive household, no matter how strong your belief in God, when you have no voice and are constantly silenced into submission, especially women and children.

A person needs to be in an atmosphere where they can take off the weight of an abusive childhood and unlearn unhealthy behaviors. They should be able to make mistakes without feeling they are letting God, their family, and the church down by stepping outside the box. Identity Crisis happens when you are chastised for simply being yourself. I'm in no way condoning reckless behavior. I mean just breathing, laughing, crying, and doing things to help you find what makes you happy. Identity Crisis happens when you are put down for simply being yourself.

The people around you need to be aware of your desire to grow and become a better version of yourself. Those people should be okay with and super supportive of your healthy decisions. This means there needs to be a "judgment-free zone" made for you, that allows you to make harmless mistakes on the road to self-discovery. As for me, when I decided to stop smoking, it took a while, and among other things unhealthy habits I picked up along the way, since the only true safe space was with my children. I didn't hide my truth from them, I healed in front of them.

When I told my sons, they were very supportive and held me accountable for my decision. However, some days were more stressful than others, and I fell off the wagon plenty of times until I was able to kick the bad habits one at a time. For a couple of months when I was trying to stop smoking, I drove to the gas station down the street to buy those little cigars and smoke for 5 minutes then flush the rest down the toilet. You may do that 20 times before you realize it's a waste of time and money and energy, because it never solved any problems. But having that space to mess up and be imperfect means everything. Even people who attend Alcoholics Anonymous give you the grace to start over as many times as you need to without judgment and have a support system of sponsors on standby.

Another example that most people need to realize is an area that needs improvement is over apologizing. My oldest son used to say "I'm sorry" a lot, and when I noticed how much he did it, I told him, "You only get two "I'm sorry' s" in a row before you have to move on from whatever you're sorry about. If you're not careful, it turns into a pity party and could give way to a moment of low self-esteem. Be sincere in your apology and turn the page to a more positive note. If serious and significant issues arise from your actions, plan to resolve the issue effectively and then turn the page. This is what I mean by not being reckless. You should have room for the new and improved you through trial and error, with a goal for improvement at the forefront of your mind.

Not all churches are based on the power and control theory. I want to add room for churches that teach the Salvation of Christ and not judgment. Anyone can manipulate words to teach you one thing and show you something different. That's not what Jesus did. He practiced what he taught. He taught us about the goodness of God and forgiveness—about the unadulterated, un-perverted love that God the Father stands for. Remember all of that as you heal it's good self-care to have positive thoughts about yourself.

If you choose to attend traditional church services, find a place to attend that offers you a healthy environment to grow in Christ. The goal is to draw people to a God that loves them, not scare them off by painting God as a narcissist. God is love, not hate. If you have experienced church hurt and choose not to attend a traditional service, it is okay, yet important to put your relationship to source or creator first in daily meditation or worship to center yourself in alignment with the vibration of the living God our Father in Heaven.

Coming out of abuse means you must find your groove because you've lived a life of being told what to do or else! Even to the point that the church will tell you to do and what to say or go to hell. No one can make that call, but God, no human should have the audacity to feel so superior over you that they will force you into a box using hell as a fear tactic to seduce you into submission. It's crazy, and no one deserves that type of torture.

Nevertheless, by the end of my unhealthy journey, I lived through a severely abusive childhood and two emotional and mentally draining marriages, that I entered into believing that I was on my way to bettering myself through a union of partnership where you vow to love, honor, cherish, and obey. Both left me empty and worse off than if I had stayed single. I found myself constantly giving, and others were taking until I wanted to give up on life altogether. God already knew what it would take to keep me fully vested in this race called life. He gave me two beautiful souls called children that He knew I wouldn't and couldn't possibly give up on.

So, I vowed to pull up my big girl panties and start the journey to find myself. I moved into an apartment in early 2018 while I worked through the trauma from my second divorce. It was the year before COVID-19 hit the scene like a storm. COVID was a blessing in hindsight; when seemingly everything on Earth shut down, the church included, that was the first time I was left alone to pray and meditate to God and ask Him what my purpose on Earth was. The only purpose I had at that very moment, at the age of 41 was being a mother, and since my boys were growing up fast, I found myself needing more from life than just being a loving mother.

Even though my boys constantly showered me with love and gratitude for being a great mom, I know projecting your brokenness onto your children is unhealthy for them. Children become increasingly wrapped up in your emotions, and they start to focus more on you, the parent, and your issues instead of their own growth and development, which is a much-needed step for them to have their own functional identity as healthy individuals.

So, during the Covid pandemic, I went into deep prayer. I knew then something had to change at once, or I would keep going through the same cycle of violence, and this time, someone tried to take my life, which was shocking and frightening. I had reverted to self-isolation after moving out into my apartment with the boys. I didn't even visit or spend any time with my then-estranged second ex-husband. He was more of a lesson than a husband, I did not wait on the will of God to take root in my life before I married him, and I paid dearly for not having healed before I made the choice. That's why I call him a lesson learned, I truly understood then why prayer and patience is important before you marry.

He kept calling, asking me to visit our old home or at least communicate with him. I told him no, I needed time and space, and he owed me that. He demanded that I talk to him. He pulled the "husband card" on me as if demanding me to see him because we were not legally divorced yet, and I had a duty as a wife to have sex with him. I refused because after all the stress I endured finding out he was having multiple affairs, I told him I was not having sex with him, and I was taking time for myself. Plus, I did not want my boys to see me compromise myself with someone who didn't love them or us, and there was so much peace in that little apartment without him that I didn't even invite him over.

This was in the later part of May 2018. He wasn't happy about it and eventually quit asking. Another issue was finding a good barber for the boys because he did the haircuts for them, and I would not call him for a haircut. So, I found someone I knew. I was vaguely familiar with his female cousin who owned a salon. I was reluctant because they were related, but I didn't sense any obvious danger then.

I took the boys, and they got there faded and fixed up well. While we were there, she suggested that we hang out and have girl time to chat it up, girl talk. She said she, too, was going through a divorce, and it might be great to get me out of the house. The first time we planned, I canceled as I usually did back then, so we rescheduled because I felt bad for bailing on her. Well, that next time came around, and I hesitated because the boys and I were painting pictures in the living room, but I figured I'd go and come right back. The restaurant was less than 15 minutes away. My oldest son was old enough to watch his little brother, and they knew where I was going and who I was with since she was almost like family. And again, I never went anywhere other than work and home. So, I kissed the boys and walked out the door, telling them I'd be back by 7-7:30 at the latest.

We went to dinner and sat and chatted over a plan of action for the future, throwing out random ideas like a podcast or a business idea in my newfound free time. Suddenly, two guys she knew walked in. One was the barber, whom she introduced to me as her boyfriend, and the other was a stranger I didn't know, whom she introduced as her brother. I wasn't expecting company, but back then, I wasn't the type to do something rude like refusing people from a table.

Not long after they arrived, they went up to the bar to get us some drinks, and next thing you know, I felt completely disoriented, like the feeling you get after waking up from surgery under anesthesia. I'm missing chunks of time from the events after that. I will tell you, I found myself in a room full of strangers and passed out. When I came to, I found myself behind the wheel of my car, not knowing how I got there, driving in the pit black dark hours after I told my children I'd be home. It was horrible. The police were behind me, and I had no idea what to say to them. I was disheveled in appearance and very emotional. I was arrested by 5 officers after being thrown to the ground and tackled and put in jail instead of taken to the emergency room.

Later, when I woke up in the freezing cold box and bright LED lights shining on me, they told me I had to wait 18 hours before my release. I tried to explain that I believed someone put something in my drink and attacked me, and trust me, I looked horrific. I asked for help, some medical attention, a nurse, or someone to help. They bluntly refused me any treatment and slammed the door in my face. It was cold, and I was barefoot, not even wearing shoes. I had no idea where my shoes were, and all I could think about was my children were at home, not even knowing where their mother was or what had happened to me.

I couldn't believe the female officers on duty didn't listen to me at all. They never offered help, and the worst part was they laughed at my distress. One even grinned at me and asked, "What happened to you?" rudely. They were still offering no help. That night I was roofied, raped and left for dead by a close relative of my then-estranged husband's family, the same person that owned the salon and the two men that showed up to our dinner. No one gave a d*mn about any of that almost heartless behavior, towards me, I can't imagine how many sexual assault victims have been mis-handled by the judicial system.

After my 18 hours were up, I was reunited with my children but denied the right to press charges by the police. It may seem like a coincidence that my ex-husband's father was a retired police officer, but I can't assume anything I don't know, however it was the only information I had that made sense to me why there was no investigation.

Not long after, I confronted my estranged husband about the incident and asked if he had anything to do with what happened to me since they were related. He denied any involvement and, next thing you know, filed for divorce. I gladly signed the paperwork and gave him everything in the divorce. I didn't want anything from him or to do with them.

I spent the next five years in court trying to defend myself against a judicial system that victim-blamed me and continued to re-victimize me by not investigating that horrible night for me. I eventually dropped the issue because it wasn't important enough for them to care. I survived by the grace of God. Obviously, it was in God's plan for me to live and do exactly what I'm doing now: write this book. Amen.

I only pray they can never do that again to anyone else, so that the judiciary system learns not to ignore the cry of a woman asking for help or medical attention. Those officers on duty could have taken me to the emergency room instead of locking me up in that cold, awful place. I never had a criminal history or anything on my record before or since then. It was unjust treatment. I was glad my boys were not left without a mother that night by the sheer grace of God.

After this, I buckled down and tightened my circle of friends and those I allowed to influence me. My life seemed to be broken up into stages of abuse. Stage 1 was my abusive childhood. Stage 2 was my introduction to religious abuse. So, in my mind, not even church was safe. Every place I ran to for refuge had a type of dysfunction all of its own that helped me to understand there is nowhere to run. You have to stand still and face life from the inside out!

The only escape for me was no escape at all, just alone with God in my apartment with nothing left to do except heal, like Jesus's painful journey to the cross, which led to the path of ultimate purpose and his resurrection. My resurrection was the revelation that God kept me alive, and I don't have to fall for the same schemes of the devil that I did before that incident.

Even though the church and the religious sector itself left me hopeless and broken, I never blamed God because I lived through every horrifying experience that was meant to destroy me. And I knew that was the power of the Almighty manifesting himself in my life with his favor. I'm a woman who has been hurt so many times like Job, and my ability to not blame God for what others have done to and against me but, look within myself to find answers on how to set boundaries, like if you have been robbed you don't move you put in security cameras and alarms to keep the robbers at bay, this reasoning was the avenue I needed to heal from past trauma and finally take on my true identity and not just be a people pleaser.

I'm 49 and writing this book because it took me that long to learn how to love myself. To resolve an identity crisis, is to learn about how to love yourself. It took me 49 years to learn to love myself because I had to let go of everyone else's idea of who I am. I had to figure out I couldn't be what others needed me to be.

I spent that time with my sons, healing, when God sent me a true friend, someone who would wind up becoming another source of peace and strength for me, a man who would help me break the generational curse off my life, that stretched back to my father/ daddy issues. I poured out to him, and he listened. He never wanted anything more from me than what I was willing to give, and same, I didn't have any ultimatums or conditions for him to be in my life a platonic companion until we both realized, that time and space of isolation were for us to meet and carry out the will of Heaven for our lives. He has been my best friend ever since. We've known each other for 20 years. It was a blessing right under our noses. We lived parallel lives in the same surroundings: cities.

He knew the people I knew, but over the years, we were both married to other people, and we respected that and did not want to make a mess of one another's lives for the sake of what could have just been lust. God honors marriage so if someone is married even if the marriage is on the rocks, leave it alone. In my opinion if someone is miserable, they need to respect the covenant they made and work it out or divorce before it becomes toxic. Misery loves company so don't let a coward drag you along as a side piece.

So, after 20 years of knowing one another, he asked me, "Will you be my friend?" I had never had a man ever want to be my friend. He saw me hurting and tried to protect me from what he knew to be a cruel world. At the time, he was also newly divorced, and we both just needed a friend. That started a vital piece of healing for me because, for a girl who never had a father to protect her like the role of a father was created to be, my friend took me under his wing and was just a phone call away if I needed it. At any time I called, he came through wanting absolutely nothing from me. Every man I'd ever met, including my father, took something from me, and he came to reciprocate in exchange, friendship and support.

That man is my best friend and husband, Kenn. he is a beautiful soul to me, and a vital piece of the puzzle to assist me on this life journey. We have 3 sons together, two from my first marriage and one from his first marriage, and every day since he asked me to be his friend has been a catalyst for the necessary and overdue healing in my life. I have a healthy place to find myself without having to run. You can't heal until you stop running from the pain.

I look and sound different. I can kick down the boundaries that were once closing me in, suffocating me, to find myself. The generational curse of unhealthy relationships does not bind me, and I'm not bound by religious power and control, we both live to fulfill our earthly purposes, and reach toward something greater than anything we've ever known together.

Chapter 3
Habits

———————————

If I speak in the tongues of men or of angels, but do not have love, I am only a resounding gong or a clanging cymbal. If I have the gift of prophecy and can fathom all mysteries and all knowledge, and if I have a faith that can move mountains, but do not have love, I am nothing. If I give all I possess to the poor and give over my body to hardship that I may boast, but do not have love, I gain nothing.

1st Corinthians 13:1-3

Most people are troubled because they walk around unhealed with a massive hole in their heart looking for someone or something to fill it. Love is the only true remedy to the wounds of the soul that make us complete in our being, it should start out with love for yourself, then that cup overflows to others. We have it backwards and try to operate out of what we think is love and we fail when we pour from an empty cup.

There is nothing to gain from pouring out of an empty cup (heart full of holes), and after a while it's all just hot air and empty words. How do we keep from being that type of person, someone that is empty? We must develop healthy habits of self-care to love ourselves back to health and oneness with our creator. Then and only then from a healed version of ourselves can we pour love into others and pour from an everlasting cup of the love of the Father into our community and the world around us.

Learning to make healthy choices for our greater good is the highest form of self-love. That is how to successfully love your neighbor as thyself, by loving them also in the highest form for their greater good and if we can do that one to another it will allow us to pass on the highest form of love.

My son and I were having a conversation one night and we brought up the order of "healthy love". First, we love God by acknowledging God exists by proof of a force greater than us to raise the sun and set the moon in the sky. That same force that allows us to live and breathe, the spirit of the universe flowing through for your greatest good.

Secondly, we must know God, our Father and creator. He created you because He loves you and his love is unconditional, constant and everlasting. Pondering on this love removes low self-esteem and fear from your heart, try speaking good things over yourself and forgiving yourself for the choices you made in your past—that if you knew back then what you know now you would have done better.

Finally, we must transfer that love into others by pouring from your overflowing heart the fruit of the spirit Galatians 5:22-23 says, *"But the fruit of the Spirit is love, joy, peace, forbearance, kindness, goodness, faithfulness, gentleness and self-control. Against such things there is no law."* Learning how to pour from an overflowing heart with the fruit of the spirit, in my studying, is the best way to heal and help heal others from a pure heart.

"Be ye transformed by the renewing of your mind."
Romans 12:2.

It all starts with your choices and habits. Don't copy the behavior and customs of this world, but let God transform you into a new person by changing the way you think. Then you will learn to know God's will for you, which is good and pleasing and perfect.

Habits dictate your patterned behavior, partly because if you can't change your habits, you can't change your life. That also means you can't go where you used to go or do what you used to do. And that's where discipline comes into play—a regular practice. Do what you've always done, get what you always got! That's a true statement, the good thing is that if you are practicing walking in your highest good then you will continuously live out of your highest self. The not so good thing to do is make the same poor choice you always have in the past, never breaking the generational trauma off your life.

Understand regular, which refers to the ordinary or typical, is what keeps us from walking in our higher self. Now, there are typical habits that all people have, like eating the same favorite foods or having a regular daily routine. These are what we call good habits for an enjoyable, productive life.

Some habits in our daily routine are not good for us or anyone else in our immediate circle. Those "bad habits" we refer to as toxic traits, produce unhealthy habits produce unhealthy behaviors. The unhealthy behaviors usually develop from our typical regular everyday habits that go unchecked. We need to do self-checks and evaluate our choices from time to time, especially when we feel held back.

Abuse is unhealthy, and since we know this, we need to make sure we do not bring an abusive mindset with us into the future. Not all of us are the same, so we have to leave room for interpretation, so no one is forced into submission to behave like another. Remember we are transforming and not conforming. To conform means to follow existing rules, standards or laws. To transform is to make a thorough or dramatic change in form, appearance or character.

Whatever causes you to stumble is unhealthy for you. Drinking may be a healthy recreation for some due to their ability to have self-control over how much they drink because they know their limits and if they can keep their composure. Drinking for someone else who doesn't know their limit and getting drunk beyond reasonable limits, would be considered unhealthy for that person.

"Do not get drunk on wine, which leads to debauchery.
Instead, be filled with the Spirit."
Ephesians 5:18

So, how do you create new healthy habits or break old unhealthy habits? First, you must identify what is unhealthy for you, those behaviors that usually come with lessons learned are the ones you start on first. Suppose salt causes you to have a medical condition like high blood pressure. In that case, your first step is to listen to your doctor, practice reducing your salt, and look for alternatives to seasoning that help you gradually cut salt from your diet because, for you, salt is unhealthy.

Your motivation for forming a new habit of keeping salt out of your diet is that you love yourself enough to try to reverse the symptoms of high blood pressure due to salt intake. We can do the right thing with a good enough motive. Now, apply that to anything that you desire to see change in your life to become a healthier version of yourself. A recovering alcoholic will in no way be able to hang out in bars once they've become sober. You can't continue to live in the same old patterns, you must make some new ones, old ways won't open new doors.

When you are unhappy with your life or have endured tragedies, it's time to set new goals. As children, we cry and throw tantrums when we don't get our way. As adults, we develop coping mechanisms to help ease the pain of reality, and it also numbs our perception of truth. The key is to decrease your need for coping *mechanisms* and learn to cope, by understanding it's better to face your fears and overcome them than to allow fear to defeat you mentally.

Coping mechanisms are patterns and behaviors to deal with unusually stressful situations. Humans lean on these strategies to stay calm until they fully adjust to the change. A coping mechanism could be drugs, binge eating, smoking, alcohol, sex, or fighting. Other coping mechanisms can be things like overthinking, committing minor crimes, becoming a hermit using self-isolation, for more than a healthy amount of time to recharge, self-sabotaging behavior that tells you giving up on your goals and purpose is an option, and becoming emotionally detached from life, altogether. When you have been through horrific events in life, any number of coping mechanisms can cause you to become dependent on unhealthy habits or behaviors to separate yourself from the love of life, giving into the thing that sneaks in to destroy your soul and destiny.

I developed coping mechanisms early on in life to deal with the pain of my father molesting me and my mother's physical abuse. When both parents are abusive growing up, you have no escape and no other choice but to rely on your survival skills. I learned it was easier to do as you're told than fight your parents. That submissive trait became the key to my survival and as it went unchecked became a stumbling block to my progress. My parents were drug addicts, among other things, so, technically, they were always out of their minds. On top of that, my father was a drug dealer and a manager of several women at one time, or a pimp for a less classy vocabulary.

My mother was deep off into marijuana. I wish I could remember a time when she wasn't high versus when she was, but she was happier. I understand why she lived that way, it was a similar vibration of the one my father lived on, and you will either beat your oppressor or join them because the mental strength it takes to keep negativity from devouring you, the best way out is through positivity however some environments are so toxic it's hard to see through the gaslight smoke to see the exit. It's a battle children can visually see the struggle of their parents which is how trauma passes' to the next generation. I could see that my parents were under the influence of their coping mechanism, but I had to function in order to stay alert and alive at home. Not all children understand that observation early on and can't beat them, so they join them and become "troubled youth". When adults ask "what is wrong with today's youth?" Well, the answer is poor adult role models, too much do as I say and not as I do mentality in the Gen X Era. We grew up in the do as you are told, not as I do and the what goes on in this house stays' in this house era. That's where we learned to shut up about our trauma and not discuss as a family how to heal.

I can only imagine how miserable my mother was, having lost her whole childhood and married off at 15 to a young man, with abusive coping mechanisms that was not himself ready to be a father or husband. My father was abused growing up, and so was my mother, and that miserable generational curse trickled right down onto me as well. I learned how to smile through pain as a child. That was my coping mechanism. No matter what happens, people keep walking when you keep a smile on your face. And that's precisely what I needed them to do: keep walking because I couldn't explain anything that was going on trapped behind my smile. My mother made it very clear, as most households do. The famous motto is, "What goes on in this house stays in this house." Every kid I know has heard it. To an extent, I understand the persistent nosiness of the outside world that tries to take a peek into your life so they can judge you and make you out to be someone you're not. Trapped by a toxic environment forced to remain silent and deal with the effects of its poison. Painted with a joker's smile to keep the tears from escaping the corners of your eyes.

On the other hand, it's some very dysfunctional households that need outside assistance to save the family from domestic abuse. That's why what goes on in this house stays in this house rhetoric is so toxic. First of all, secrets are usually the by-product of lies constructed together as a psychological prison to keep others bound to false teachings that manipulate and destroy a person's sense of self, the same tactics gas lighters and abusers do to keep the "secret keeper" feeling obliged to perform certain degrading or humiliating acts for self-gratification of their abuser. This is why we must allow children to have a voice and be heard. It is their human right, to speak up against the things that make them feel justifiably uncomfortable as we all should.

For example, when an groomer, tells a toddler that it's okay for the adult to touch them inappropriately on their private parts when helping them to the bathroom because that type of help is expected and needed to assist them going to the bathroom, but keep it a secret because others may not understand how helpful this is. So, the child feels trapped to speak about the incident, even though the help leaves them feeling yucky for lack of a better term afterward, because they are unknowingly being gaslighted to think keeping the secret is good and the reporting of the incident as bad. When the truth is in fact the opposite, which is why truth has become so twisted and hard to unlearn. Our moral compass was compromised early on and now it's time to untwist it.

Children in families where the generational trauma gets passed down, are bound to keep the secret because they were told others may not understand. That child grows up to act out particularly more immoral behaviors and activities because of the negative psychological effects of the abuse, due to the twisted lies they were told.

Let me take a minute to expound on why keeping secrets can be detrimental. The first issue that arises from keeping secrets is that it prolongs the abuse; if you don't speak up, the abuser will not stop. Abusers are borderline personality narcissists without a conscience for self-control. It is delusional for us as a society to think someone who thrives off abuse will one day unexpectedly say, "OK, today I'm done being a rapist, or today is the day I keep my hands to myself!" The truth is without proper intervention or guidance, an abuser will eventually devour anyone in sight, leaving no stone unturned. Speaking up and fighting for your freedom is imperative. How can anyone help you if no one knows? Your abuser is not going just suddenly to confess.

Secondly, the combination of trauma triggers and post-traumatic stressors will pull you into a deep depression that will cause you to become a hermit and a self-isolator. After a while, you will be too afraid even to walk outside and live life for fear of more abuse, so much so that you will begin to project that fear onto others who have no intentions of harming you at all. Moreover, what they do not know will cause you to build up a wall against the wrong people. What I mean by the wrong people is the good people that are sent to you to help you, the ones that can help you if they know because they would exercise the powers of authority over the abuser to make them stop, and your silence will be the catalyst that will open the door for trauma triggers and PTSD. Instead allow your child's voice to be heard and speak up against anyone they believe is harming them and be the person with the power to stop their abusers.

I want to help you understand the symptoms of trauma in an abuse victim. The American Psychological Association (APA) explains that in the days and weeks after experiencing trauma, unpredictable emotional and physical symptoms can result. Trauma symptoms can include feeling nervous, jumpy, or on "high alert", irritability, difficulty sleeping; flash-backs, intrusive memories, nightmares; trouble feeling positive emotions, avoiding people, places memories, or thoughts associated with the trau-matic event.

When you learn how to deal with trauma, you can help yourself resolve these typical reactive symptoms. Post-traumatic stress from abuse or sexual assault events may also be less likely to develop when individuals have and seek out positive sources of support. However, those who may not have the support to deal with traumatic events may develop some-thing called acute stress or post-traumatic stress. This type of stress may snowball and affect your everyday life, perhaps even leading to post-trau-matic stress disorder (PTSD).

This is why it's so important to address the aftershock effect of abuse, we can't keep putting a band aid over the truth of what sexual abuse sur-vivors go through, it's cruel to ask anyone that has been sexually violated to push down or suppress their feeling and pain. If it becomes the habit of those in charge or that have the power to change the course of someone's healing just by speaking out and stopping the abuse, if those people are silent, we as a society keep living out the same trauma. The poor habits of the immoral to keep the secrets of the unjust then we all suffer.

Power to change lives starts with using yours to help change another person's circumstance from bad to good by helping free them from abuser suppression. We have to make it a habit to teach those that suffer from having their voice suppressed that it IS OKAY to speak up and heal. You can only heal once you are freed from those that oppress you, because temporary healing will only bring temporary peace as long as the oppressor is absent. We are working towards permanent healing, not temporary, the most important habit to develop is learning how to use your voice.

Post-traumatic stress disorder (PTSD) may occur in people who have experienced or witnessed a highly traumatic event. A higher risk for PTSD is linked to factors such as: Not having enough social support, being young at the time of the traumatic event. Experiencing additional stress on top of the initial trauma, such as losing a loved one, home, or job, being injured or witnessing others wounded during the event, not having a safe place/ environment to heal. Limited access to counseling and medical treatment, not prosecuting criminals that commit the crimes, fear of being re-traumatized. I understand these traits of PTSD within myself, and I work very hard, every day to tell myself I am no longer the victim but the survivor walking in my victory, keeping the door open to help others.

It's very crucial to make sure we stop sweeping truth under the rug and hold abusers accountable for their crimes, which is what sexual assault is, it's a crime! When criminals go unpunished for their crimes, we send mixed signals to a society we don't care about the abuse or the victims. When victims live with being ignored by the justice system that was instituted to protect them, it triggers feelings of hopelessness. We cannot allow criminals to go with a slap on the wrist or pardon for their crimes, leaving them with the impression that they are above the law. They are not! Speak up and out is the message we need to send to clear up the signal and that you are not alone, and the crime will not go unpunished. Then follow through with doing what is right for the victim, not what is right for the criminal. Criminals give up their rights to be heard when they violate the rights of an innocent victim. We can't change if we continue the cycle of sweeping truth under the rug.

In your mind thinking at some point, you may be at fault because you have been gaslit to believe in some way you were asking for it. All this is a result of suppressing your trauma to appear OK. Pedophiles lead children to think, it is because they are so cute and friendly that they are the cause of their abuse, therefore sexualizing a child because of their need to feel loved and affirmed. The truth is children need love and comfort. Victim blaming is revictimization, it is a form of abandonment to blame a victim for attributing to their own abuse with things they had no control over, one being the lack of another person's self-control.

A child being adorable is not an excuse for abuse, what we must do is offer a safe space for abusers to ask for help as well. Counseling for wayward thoughts and getting treatment to individuals that suffer from thinking they are entitled to abuse others because they have no self-control. We can't keep saying hurt people hurt people like a cliche' without cause and effect. If we know hurt people hurt people, then let us come together to love the hurt people and stop the snowball effect that passes on the toxicity, from one generation to the next.

Some victims are threatened that if they speak up, their abuser will harm the family or that no one will believe them because the abuser will construct a story of lies to lead others down a rabbit hole, painting the victims as liars themselves. We need to help the abuser and the victim, not within the same spaces, but as separate and individual cases.

Lastly, lingering effects of abuse can cause you to seek peace in some very unhealthy places, using coping mechanisms that will possibly lead to further abuse and, even worse, suicide if left untreated.

My childhood home was saturated in abuse. I had to get up every day and get myself together to be what others needed me to be. It helped me to think of myself as a sacrifice rather than a victim. Living in that type of environment is another form of slavery without labeling it as such. I took the abuse like a good girl. In hindsight, I realized that sexual perversion was my father's coping mechanism, which included molestation. His coping mechanism was my punishment, I had no control of his lack of self-control around me. And instead of the other adults around me protecting me by getting him treatment and separating us, in a measure to free me and stop the continuation of his delusion of entitlement to use me as a means to feed his issues. He was not well and that was my biggest problem.

I had to get up every day as a child and strategize how to survive moment to moment only to prolong or to increase the time between the times of abuse. Doing chores or babysitting my little sister gave me another 2 hours to wrap my mind around the fact that I was going to be abused whether I liked it or not. No one was thinking of how all of this affected me because I kept quiet like I was told to do. Instead of releasing the rage inside me from having been treated unjustly by the ones that were assigned to raise me up in love, I was taught to have empathy towards my abuser and try to rationalize why I needed to consider their feelings over my own safety. It's like swallowing a bomb and containing the blast with a polite smile on your face.

I did not know how many victims he had under his belt besides me, but I do know I felt a duty to be as protective of a big sister that I could be to my younger siblings in the home. I always chose to use myself as a human shield growing up, so much so that my sister told me when we were younger, I wrapped her up in layers of clothes at night and hid her behind me under the covers so that when my father came into the room at night, he would not see her. That way, he would not touch her. She was just a baby when the molestation started, and I had to be her protector.

My coping mechanism became the protector. I took the abuse, so my sister didn't have to endure it. Parents fail to realize or choose to ignore the negative effects their poor choices or bad habits have on the lives of the children in the home. We need to bring back the concept of healthy adult role models for our children and stop making excuses for adult poor choices and then ask what is wrong with today's youth. Because today's youth are asking "what's up with the adults and their lack of accountability?"

There were a lot of different dysfunctional behaviors going on at one time, in our household: physical abuse, drugs, alcohol, perversion, and criminal activity. I was too young to use these things as coping mechanisms. Little did I know the devil was sowing seeds of dysfunction while at the same time showing me wrong examples of how to cope with stress that didn't include God. If I had known then that God is love and what that truly means, I would have been able to recognize that what my father was doing to me was not actually love.

When we think of the phrase coping mechanism, most of us cringe and think only of the negative impressions that come to mind. However, when we break it down and define it, there are many positives to embrace. Coping means that thoughts and behaviors are mobilized to manage internal and external stressful situations. Mechanisms are processes, techniques, or systems for achieving a result. Now put it together, thoughts and behaviors that help us process the body's different functions, including but not limited to the brain, nervous system, and other systems in the body, are involved in mental health, which is a person's emotional, psychological, and social well-being.

Therefore, coping mechanisms can be a good way of managing stress, PTSD, or any number of traumatic experiences we humans experience, even things that help us stay consistent in our disciplines of managing our weight and even saving money. Unless, of course, sadly, we grew up without healthy boundaries. Around those individuals that siphon energy and whatever else they can off the others around them, even to their demise, to bring themselves to a state of psychological contentment.

There are people that get an endorphin rush from hurting people as a coping mechanism. A term most refer to as energy vampires! An energy vampire can be someone who drains your emotional energy, leaving you feeling depleted and exhausted after spending time with them. They may be bosses, co-workers, family, different groups of people that don't feel the need to provide you with a safe environment, often targeting sensitive and compassionate people, mostly empaths. Energy vampires may constantly demand your attention, support, or empathy. Interrupt you often, take up too much time, talk about themselves the whole time, use emotional manipulation to make you feel sorry for them, use guilt-tripping, sob stories, or emotional outbursts to gain control. Being around an energy vampire can make you feel anxious, agitated, uneasy, or doubtful of yourself. You may also feel worn out, stressed, or sad after interactions with them.

When you grow up with parents that fit this description, it is a living hell and the breeding grounds for manipulation and mayhem. This is why our Nation's Children Services Departments need to be held more accountable concerning the welfare of abused children, especially the type of psychological abuse that does not leave scars but instead creates a carbon copy version of the adult inside the child, of its environment. Causing so many of our children to be locked up in detention homes and tried in courts unjustly as adults for crimes that they would not have committed if we had a better support system for our youth and families.

My parents were so toxic that I fought most of my childhood to be the exact opposite of who they were. I would say they experienced trauma growing up as well, and for them, they did not understand what it meant to break the cycle of abuse. They simply coped with the same exact mechanisms as their parents before them. The same sexual, physical, and mental abuse I endured, they endured as well. They excused it by thinking: "It happened to me, and I lived through it, so why should you be any different?" They did hard drugs, drank large amounts of alcohol, participated in sexual perversion, and used profanity as a second language. We were out of sight and mind until we were needed for things like cleaning, cooking, turning the TV channel, and going to the store. Back then, children endured a type of treatment similar to that of a slavery mentality for the weary parent. Slavery, I believe, took a horrible toll on our society, which created a false, hierarchal mentality that some were considered lesser than others. That opened the door for some to say it was okay to use the harshest form of punishment, and dominate rule over others. Going so far as to make family members endure rape, beatings so severe that some children were hospitalized or even died. To work children to the point where they had no life or identity outside of what and who they were told to be.

The unhealthiest habit to have as a parent is to raise your children under the same toxic habits your parents raised you. Sadly, we live in a society that needs to break the unhealthy transference of power and control from before the Emancipation Proclamation was enforced. If you ask what I mean by that is whippings came from the mentality of the slave master, and not God. Proverbs 13:24 says that whoever spares the rod hates their children, but the one who loves their children is careful to discipline them. Most people have been indoctrinated to believe the word rod to be interpreted as beatings. However, the shepherd's rod was not for beating the sheep it was for guiding or steering them out of the direction of trouble. When God's word is misused for evil, we create a false narrative for the listeners to follow.

A shepherd's rod and staff are used to tend and protect the flock. The rod is used to fight off wild animals, count the sheep, and direct them. It is also used to prod the sheep during the day in the fields and at night *into the sheepfold.* The staff allows the shepherd to guide an animal without breaching a sheep's flight zone or point of balance. Sheep, if we use this biblical word to translate the scriptures that says spare the rod spoil the child, the term child would be translated to sheep in the text. Meaning our children are totally dependent on the shepherd (parents) for food, water, leadership, and guidance as they move from place to place, just as we are dependent upon God for all that we need.

Sheep (our children) depend on the shepherd (parents) for protection from a wide range of predators and dangers, just as we look to God as our Protector and Defender. That scripture is not meant to build a foundation for abuse towards our children. One of the many unjust habitual lies that have been keeping us under the false narrative that says beating a child will save. The lie is that parents should beat their children instead of becoming better role models for their children, which is the proper way to guide them. The habit of a liar is to twist words to deceive you into believing they are correct because they used the right phrasing but misinterpreted their point by using contradicting vocabulary. Why else would it be considered OK to look the other way at such tragedies if it was not a method handed down from generation to generation? That is not how our children were meant to be raised, and we will never go back to that type of brutal societal doctrine or false doctrine.

Because I lacked peace, isolation became one of my coping mechanisms. It kept me out of the way, and I became the protector of my little brother and sister to keep them safe. I became the defender of those who could not defend themselves. I believe I am still that person. Only now can I find appropriate ways to advocate for those who have no advocate or better yet to teach those who cannot advocate for themselves to self-advocate, the same as my savior Jesus who is an advocate for me.

*"My dear children, I write this to you so that you will not sin.
But if anybody does sin, we have an advocate with the Father,
Jesus Christ, the Righteous One."*

1st John 2:1

Even Jesus is our advocate, when we don't know which way is the right way we focus on Jesus and his character. That is what I have to do to be able to even write this book from an advocate's heart, which is my desire, to bring understanding to the broken-hearted and try to restore peace and love. Something I did not have growing up.

I have, from time to time, used cannabis as a means of coping throughout my adult years. My mother used it, and it seemed less harmful than I saw everyone else around me doing. It was passed down to me as a coping mechanism because I experienced how it quickly reduced the symptoms of the panic attacks that I endured due to having PTSD. I didn't start doing it until I was 18, I did not use drugs as a child at my own free will. I believe there were times my father drugged me before raping me because most of the time I was in a haze for the sexual assaults.

It was one of the things that helped me with the mental images in my mind I could not get rid of early on. What most people that have not been assaulted needs to understand is that after the abuse is over, the mental images stay with you cataloged in your mind as something you cannot forget. That is a primary reason most people use holistic herbal remedies to reduce anxiety brought on by the mental images and flashbacks that happen when you are triggered. The triggers are igniting the memories of the event, both physical and emotional. That can bring on the anxiety attacks that manifest in different forms. Which is why some pharmaceutical methods of treatment are too extreme because some forms of pharmaceutical medicines make people lethargic and unable to continue on with their day, so they stop progressing with trying to manage triggers by living and learning as they go. Depression is a major issue for unhealed trauma victims due to never knowing when and where they may be triggered.

Triggers manifest as fear of loss of control, fear of impending doom, flashing visions, hyperventilation, palpitations, shortness of breath, chest pains that mimic a heart attack, dizziness, abdominal cramps, nausea, and worst cases temporary suicidal tendencies, to escape the trauma triggers. Which is why abuse is much more toxic to children that have no clue what is happening. It has the ability to stunt their mental development.

The truth is even after you heal physically from abuse, the mind needs help recovering from what the eyes saw, and the physical memory that activates the triggers without warning. There is not one way to heal, so the point is to find a healthy way for you to heal and be free and that is a continuous process. Again, there are natural herbal remedies for some who do not want to go the pharmaceutical route of anti-anxiety meds. Most people who have not experienced severe trauma, do not understand PTSD, or why someone would be having any of the other symptoms listed describing the panic attack symptoms. So, on the outside it appears to the onlooker that the person is "freaking out" for lack of a better term, but their body and mind are in the middle of experiencing a real activation of body memory trauma. Which is why we have to practice having healthy habits after abuse that keep us at peace and away from the people that traumatized us in the first place. Forgiveness with distance is good.

Sometimes, you can't get the images out of your mind, and it's necessary to have a healthy way to process trauma. The best help is through a great community support system, such as counseling, group therapy, prayer, AA for those that use alcohol to cope, meditation of music, exercise in the fresh air, and self-help books such as this one.

All these systems should be set up to specialize in your recovery to wholeness of mental health and not a continuance of dependence. You must fight for your sobriety. Most of us stop and start several times before we get the hang of sobriety. I cannot tell you how many times I went into a store to purchase a vape to use it for one or two days to throw it away before I finished it, or how many times I've bought a bottle of wine and poured it out, after one or two glasses because of something or someone that I crossed paths with caused me to be triggered, into a place that sparked a traumatic memory for me that I desperately needed to escape from. The truth is the journey to a better you will never end. We must forgive ourselves many times before we succeed at getting a handle on life; that's the key.

"For a just man falleth seven times and riseth up again." This verse indicates that righteous people are not immune to suffering and that God will help them recover when they fall."
Proverbs 24:16

"We often suffer, but we are never crushed. Even when we don't know what to do, we never give up. In times of trouble, God is with us, and when we are knocked down, we get up again."
2 Corinthians 4:8-9

My hope is that my footsteps are ordered for greatness and not defeat, so I do not condemn myself for the setbacks because I will one day get it right! Even now, as I write this book, I fall short of my expectations of myself, but I know this: in John 3:16-17 *"For God so loved the world that he gave his one and only Son, that whoever believes in him shall not perish but have eternal life. For God did not send his Son into the world to condemn the world, but to save the world through him."*

The Lord has made provisions for me and all of us that through him, we have as many chances as we need to get ourselves together because we are already made whole in him, and he loves us unconditionally. There is no need to try to be something, only to release what was and be made new. The reward of Heaven is already ours once we profess the resurrection of Christ, but when we practice on our sobriety and self-control to not follow in the footsteps of our abusers the blessing of life becomes clearer. As to the fact that when God created us, he said, "it was good" and that we are not defined by our abuse or our mistakes, we just need to practice learning healthy habits so we can stay positive about what life still ahead for us. Positive about the future and enjoy the company of those around us, not living in fear and not living being constantly triggered.

I smiled my way through the pain and became the person who cheered everyone else up. The only joy I had growing up was giving it to someone else, so I became the people pleaser, a dangerous compromise called self-sacrifice. That was the only way to keep the environment as peaceful as possible. I went ahead and did what I was programmed to do without being asked to keep the abusers around me happy. If my abusers were happy the abuse was less severe than if they were angry, the intensity of the abuse was more violent when they were angry.

I was a punching bag for my mother when she was angry, and my father had a habit of isolating me before the sexual assault putting fear of abandonment in my spirit so I could do what he said for fear of worse coming. It was their habit to torment me, and I took it because it was all I could do to survive. Most narcissists and bullies only abuse those that don't fight back, children are not allowed to even talk back to adults because it seems disrespectful which is another reason why children make easy targets. Please start the habit of listening to your children and allowing them the right to speak up when they feel uncomfortable or uneasy. It is not impolite for a child to speak up on their own behalf against anyone that tries to objectify them or passively aggressively bully them into submission.

Fighting off my father and mother never ended well for me because, of course, it was more mental to me, and at the end of the day, I had to obey, even though they were wrong. That is what tears a child apart inside. Being told always to do right while asked to take part is something so wrong. Hypocrisy in adults is the worst. I usually just took a deep breath and did what they said—the abuse was over faster that way. It doesn't matter what it was. My escape was school. When I went to school every day, I had two places I could hide in. They were both in the staircase hidden in a part of the building, and most students or staff didn't go in. I cried in silence when I got there because that was the only time I could cry. I had to be strong. Being strong is a coping mechanism for people who weren't allowed to show weakness during childhood. I had to learn early how to smile through the worst of pain. That's why I believe I have such a high tolerance for BS.

For many years in my life, before I ever got married, my coping mechanism was lesbianism in the early stages of puberty and teen years. Whenever I tried to be intimate with a man, I had horrible body triggers to the point that I would break down in tears just from being touched. Sex used to be almost like torture for me to deal with without being triggered by the idea of having sex with a man after my father. I've also been raped without any justice more than once in my life, so it just was something I did to feel loved without having to be involved with a man that would possibly turn on me in the end. The truth is for a woman that has been sexually assaulted, men—to the touch—are usually not gentle, and are not conscious of what a woman needs beyond just sex. Sex for most women is more mental and emotional than physical. Sex for a man is usually physical and visual, far less emotional or mental. So it was never intentional for me to resort to lesbianism growing up—it just happened one day when I was with a good friend that allowed me to lean on her for the comfort I needed when I was crying because of all the abuse I had to endure and it was so comforting, that later I sought the comfort of a woman because it was not a trigger for me.

I never truly wanted to be gay. I simply struggled my whole life with affection and intimacy. The guilt of knowing being with a woman was not my deepest desire, but opening my vulnerabilities to a man was scary. Most of the men in my life turned out to be abusers. I can't tell you that I was born that way because I was not. I simply resorted to the comfort of a woman because I was never able to find any comfort in men. Not even after being married.

Like I mentioned earlier, until you get to a point that you are in a monogamous heterosexual relationship where you can be vulnerable and the other person gets to know your body, help you through sexual triggers, and allow time for the mental and emotional scars to heal, you will have a hard time healing. Which is a good reason to be celibate for a while after sexual assault so you can find your center and wait for that person who just wants to be with you and you alone.

If not, it's hard to have a mental and emotional attachment with someone that has other options to find comfort in someone other than you. When sex becomes a means of bonding and not just for physical pleasure or something you do because you feel afraid to say no, you will never find the emotional support you need to heal from your sexual wounds. Sexual promiscuity in no matter what form it comes in is not healthy. Maybe you never struggled with codependency in the form of homosexuality, but you were instead someone that was heterosexually so promiscuous that you forgot how many partners you have been with. Either is unhealthy. We have been taught that homosexuality is the world's worst sin, as if God doesn't care about heterosexual sins like adultery, fornication or worse just giving yourself to anyone to try and put a temporary band aid on the hole in your heart. God looks at all promiscuity and lasciviousness the same, unhealed.

To be unhealed is like being sick. If you cut yourself and the cut get infected now it's red and swollen, tender to the touch, with a green pus oozing from the wound, would you not go to the emergency room and get it treated? Well, that's what the hole in our heart looks like when we have been abused and worse if the wound goes untreated. If left untreated, unhealed and then hurt people hurt people that's how the infection spreads in humans.

> *"On hearing this, Jesus said to them, 'It is not the healthy who need a doctor, but the sick. I have not come to call the righteous, but sinners.'"*
> **Mark 2:17**

My father was sexually abusive. My first marriage was religious abuse and physiological power and control. My second marriage was a nightmare, and that is because I was just stupid. I was trying too hard to get someone to love me that just didn't, I genuinely believe, for me it was a rush to judgment rebound to escape constant harassment from the people around me to force me to reunite with the father of my children. Nevertheless, in the end I almost lost my life because of him, I believe he was offended that I left him. He had such a superstar mentality in my opinion that leaving him was bad for his reputation and to "show me" I wasn't just going to leave me and get away with it but God did it. These are all forms of sickness.

I ran from my second husband, someone that wanted to own me instead of love me, just like my first husband. I ran from him and never returned, because it was not a situation that would allow me to thrive. I had already been through so much trauma when I met the boy's father. I was young and weak, and I couldn't defend myself from the church community that thought I was overreacting to minor marital issues, due to past childhood trauma.

Because the church believed what someone else told them I was, they believed the words of someone they thought was more credible in a professional sense, than they did with me showing them who I was right in front of their faces. For that reason, he was more traumatizing to me because he kept trying to psychoanalyze me like I was a patient of his instead of just loving me as his wife. There were plenty of people that came in and out of my life I think for convenience sake.

I was talking to my little sister on the phone as to how some people in the church try to be Jesus without having his character. Jesus went about the Earth having conversations with others humbling himself for the purpose of relationship. We cannot be the judge and jury of someone else's story or circumstances, it is our position as believers to walk in love winning souls for Christ by showing the character of a loving God.

The difference between Jesus and the scribes and Pharisees is that the church was condemning the very people Jesus came to die for. Jesus died for me, and I was surrounded by those that tried to condemn me for a childhood that I had no control over. I was doing my absolute best back then to really transform into the fearfully and wonderfully made person the Lord created me to be, but I couldn't because it was more profitable for me to be kept ignorant of the promise of conversion from old to new. An abuser, including religious abusers, doesn't want you to know you are free because you can choose to think for yourself, make better choices, which in a healed person leaves no room for a narcissist to manipulate you. So, I was never running from the people I loved or my responsibilities, I was by the grace of God allowed to be set free from the spirit of narcissism that plagued my mother and her mother and so on. I constantly kept making emotional decisions out of an unhealed heart. And the Lord allowed me to reset to re-align with him.

I find the need to insert here that we need to unlearn bad theology, it's a type of systematic theology that in my opinion generated from the fall in the garden of Eden. If we go back to the first chapter and focus on when Satan said to Eve "you shall not surely die". The word of God has been twisted by the devil and it has that mentality of entitlement that has been taught and passed down throughout the generations. We have been taught by sleight of hand to discount God's Word for the Laws of Man. Jesus said that the husband is to love his wife Adam said "bone of my bone and flesh of my flesh", Ephesians came back and said "after all, no one ever hated their own body, but they feed and care for their body, just as Christ does the church—", when we put the two together that means a man that loves his wife should love her as if she was his own body and flesh, feeding and caring for her as Christ does the church.

This is presented with a contradictory twist in the 1700's when in 1782 Francis Buller, an English judge who allegedly said that men could beat their wives as long as their rod or stick was no bigger than the width of his thumb. Which should have been unlawful because it is not love! If you do an in depth study you will find that somewhere we strayed from the instruction of God and mankind was taught instead of being a loving husband, that men were allowed to beat their wives as long as the stick was no bigger than the width of the man's thumb. This contradicts God!

God never would give any man permission to beat his wife, Jesus would never beat his bride. So somewhere we strayed from the truth of God's word. I believe it was in the habitual improper teaching of the gospel of Jesus Christ, that narcissistic preachers took God's word out of context to gain power and control of the minds of their listening audience and their families. Why else would there be such an issue with domestic violence in a country that has the brand tagline "In God We Trust"? I say this because if we truly trusted in God, we would not allow the truth of his word to be twisted. And women all over the world would not be subjected to the abuse that has been allowed and gone unresolved. God is Love so if you love someone you do not look to have power and control over them. Male or female, son or daughter, we must unlearn the twisted interpretations of the Word of a loving God by liars that misrepresent God for their own gain. The preacher lied to me by misrepresenting the Word of God for his own pleasure preaching from the Old Testament leading me to believe that handmaidens were still a thing of the present.

God never created handmaidens for Adam in the garden of Eden, so how did we get so far from the truth of God's Word? The Fall! The pastors that preach from the viewpoint of the fall of man when God said to Eve in Genesis 3:16 *"Your desire will be for your husband, and he will rule over you."* We preach that from a viewpoint of power and control and not from a perspective of protection from harm, because mankind at the time was in a fallen state due to the serpent deceiving Eve, however we are no longer in a fallen state. Right, that's what I said, the resurrection absolved us from the fallen state, if we believe!

The untwisting of the Word of God happens when we receive as truth that when Jesus died on the cross and resurrected on the 3rd day, that he restored us from a fallen state. Which means we are no longer under the curse that was once connected to the sins of Adam and Eve. We have been restored to the original blueprint.

"He made Him who knew no sin to be sin on our behalf, so that we might become the righteousness of God in Him."
2nd Corinthians 5:21

"Then God said, 'Let us make mankind in our image, in our likeness, so that they may rule over the fish in the sea and the birds in the sky, over the livestock and all the wild animals, and over all the creatures that move along the ground.' So God created mankind in his own image, in the image of God he created them; male and female he created them. God blessed them and said to them, 'Be fruitful and increase in number; fill the earth and subdue it. Rule over the fish in the sea and the birds in the sky and over every living creature that moves on the ground.'"

Genesis 1:26-28

It is not stated anywhere in the original blueprint of God's word that we as mankind are to have rule over one another but only over the things of the Earth as stated in verse 26. Rule over the fish in the sea and the birds in the sky, over livestock and wild animals and all the creatures along the ground. Why is this not preached or taught? My assumption is because there is no room for narcissism if we teach from this context.

The twisting of God's word only benefits narcissists that want to keep people ignorant for the sake of power and control. Why else would any-one of the men I was married to previously, that knew the word of God that were raised on the word of God, not make me feel as if I was an equal rib and not beneath them? If not to perpetuate the lies of a society ruled by mankind, with an inflated sense of self, instead of by a loving God as it should be!

I currently live in Alabama which is considered to be a part of the Bible Belt. The term "Bible Belt" is typically used for the southeast region of the United States, including these 10 states: Mississippi, Alabama, Lou-isiana, Arkansas, South Carolina, Tennessee, North Carolina, Georgia, and Oklahoma. This region contains most of the Southern United States, including most of Texas and Oklahoma, and parts of the states south of the Ohio River, extending east to include central West Virginia and Vir-ginia, from the Shenandoah Valley southward into Southside Virginia and

North Carolina. In addition, the Bible Belt covers most of Missouri and Kentucky and southern parts of Illinois, Indiana, and Ohio.

Now you ask me how this is related to this chapter of my book entitled habits? Well while I am currently writing this book, we as a people, are in one of the biggest historical election debates of all time, these very same issues discussed in my book are unfolding. The rights of women and human beings in general are under political scrutiny, under the guise as what is best for America according to what was spoken by the Word of God through the interpretation of Evangelical Christians. One side represents law and the other spirit! You can see the rift as if Jesus rented the veil again, once in the spirit and once in the physical realm now.

Evangelicals that of course reside in the bible belt, the very same place that the twisted interpretations of the bible have been preached to me, the very same churches I had to flee from that lied to me and told me I was a handmaiden when I never should have been told that, are the ones vibing to go back to the imprisonment of the law and the rest of us well to infinity and beyond we look to the future where loves heals.

Only after Colonialism did these terms and twisting of God's word even appear to become a thing, which is the exploitation of people and of resources by a foreign group. Colonizers monopolize political power and hold conquered societies and their people to be inferior to their conquerors in legal, administrative, social, cultural, or biological terms.

Colonial settlers invade and occupy territory to permanently replace an existing society with that of the colonizers, possibly towards a genocide of native populations. This place we now call America and in this current electoral administration have been divided by those that want to keep the this old colonial idealism in play, while the other side want to be freed from the unjust and ungodly rule of the colonizers that we abolished by the emancipation proclamation on January 1, 1863. The bible belt past tense was the place that European settlers set up camp for what was to be the worst treatment of humankind ever recorded and that was slavery. Slavery which no longer exists and will never exist again because we are free and were never meant to be enslaved to begin with. The lies that incited slavery were based on the twisting of the word of God by the leaders of colonial rule. Lies that we are being freed from at this very moment, the blinders are coming off from mankind as we seek the truth of God's word and demand we no longer submit to the lies of religion that have been twisted in its interpretation, just like when Satan deceived Eve.

In the original blueprint of God in Genesis 1:26-28 it states nowhere that we are to have rule over one another, not over man or man over woman, instead to live under the freedom in Christ Jesus that he died on the cross for us to be free from all injustice and lies of Satan, and be restored unto God "pre-fall" condition before Satan deceived Eve. Through the resurrection of Jesus. It is only in my opinion that we struggle currently with breaking free from the lie, that we are not free.

> *"If the Son therefore shall make you free, ye shall be free indeed."*
> **John 8:36**

We are only bound to the generational curses of those that were bound by the lie, which is if we allow the same lies to keep us bound in our minds. I was raised to submit to unjust and ungodly treatment by my parents during my abusive childhood and that was a lie. I was preached to as a member of a congregation in which lies spewed from the pulpit, by wolves in sheep's clothing called "false preachers and prophets" and they were liars. And all I ever wanted was freedom from all the dos and don'ts I lived through under the rule of the narcissistic spirit that tried to dominate me all my life.

It was everywhere I turned, and I was too dumb to see it. So, in my second marriage I thought wow I'm free from the religious rule of someone that saw me as a lesser vessel per the lies he was taught. However, I wasn't ready for that type of lifestyle that my second husband was accustomed to, he spent many years living in Europe, a society that has a history of practicing sexual immorality. And I found myself far away from God, living a debauched lifestyle. I quickly felt like I was losing my salvation.

It was like the story of the frog in water. You place a frog in a pot of water and heat it slowly, and as the frog relaxes, his legs become numb, and by the time the water starts to burn, it's too late for the frog to jump out. I learned a very valuable lesson after that. I learned I was too close to God to live lasciviously, and the turn-up lifestyle was not for me. God had to deliver me from the hell I wandered into living with him. There was a balance between enjoying yourself and not taking it too far, while still standing on your principles to do the right things to live a clean life. Living in moderation- avoiding extremes of behavior or expression: observing reasonable limits.

I realized I had no idea what love was, even though I kept trying. Not knowing that one sided love is not love at all, always until now living in the furthest of the extremes. Never knowing that finding balance is about love being reciprocated not how hard you try to be loved.

My mother's generational curse had followed me into the realm of marriage, and she had two very abusive marriages. The only difference is I absolutely could not tolerate physical abuse. I worked for a domestic violence shelter, and I knew blatant hands-on contact was a deal breaker. I never noticed the signs of gaslighting until I saw the classic 1944 movie Gaslighting. It truly opened my eyes to the mind games that were a strategic tactic for sophisticated abusers. I struggled since I married based on the idea of what I thought marriage was, but I never really knew what it meant to me personally. All because I never healed from my childhood. I didn't even know what love was, with one exception: the motherly instinct deep down on the inside that gave me the guidance and strength to be the mother to them I never had. I gained the strength to pray and ask for the perfect will of God to be a good mother.

Throughout my lifetime, I've realized in hindsight that I've had several coping mechanisms that I wasn't aware of. Running away, leaning towards the emotional dependency on others, body dysmorphism, people pleasing, self- isolation, fear of the unknown, a poverty mentality, the list goes on and on of imperfect habits that blind sighted me to my own greatness.

The truth is that coping mechanisms are only an excuse to delay the inevitable. You have to deal with yourself!

> *"Now faith is the substance of things hoped for,*
> *the evidence of things not seen."*
> **Hebrews 11:1**

I can only tell you what worked for me. Number one is faith! There was nothing in my surroundings that I could grasp onto for support or light. My family only knew to do what was done to them. As a child, I had a visitation from what I believe to this day was a bonafide angel. One night, I lay in my bed staring at the door, watching for any sign to see if my father was awake and on his way, because I never knew when he would come into my room at night and sexually assault me. And because of that I would lay awake at night and try to keep up with his footsteps.

All I remember from that one night is suddenly what looked to be a glittering white light in the form of an ageless female, an angel no doubt with long hair and a white gown covering her feet and arms, just dangling in mid-air.

I remember asking, "God, what is this?" I heard nothing. I turned on the lamp by my bed, and she disappeared. I turned the light off, and she was there again. This happened 2 or 3 times, and every time I turned the light off, she was there like she never moved a muscle. When I turned the light on it was like light met light and she disappeared into the light. I was puzzled and a little nervous. Eventually, the figure disappeared into the light, because I slept with the light on for the rest of the night. Looking back, I can only imagine she protected me from my father and whatever he had planned for me that night because he never came in. That was for me one of those moments to be grateful for, sometimes we wonder where God is when bad things happen to us and now I can see that night he was in the light protecting me from the evil that lived in my father. I had at least one peaceful night that I can remember. After that, I believe somewhere in Heaven, God loved me and looked out for me.

As Psalm 27:10 says, *"When my father and my mother forsake me, then the Lord will take me up."* It was true that night, and I believed it even though no one else believed it. I know what I saw, and I know that night my father didn't come in. A seed of fearlessness was sown in my heart that night, and I knew that God was on my side. Prayer became my primary coping mechanism after that, it became my shield!

Please don't blame yourself because someone hurt you, their propensity to give into evil is not your fault! The physical abuse from my mother and the sexual assault from my father was not my fault. I stopped feeling sorry for myself and learned how to survive. I stopped looking for anyone to rescue me, and I started learning how to survive every second of the day in a house full of abusers. That means looking within and learning how to use intuition and watch for cues in your environment to learn how to avoid the abuse as much as possible until you can get free.

Speaking up and not keeping the secret helps, if the people around you are not in on it either. I spoke up, but my family already knew and turned the other cheek. I managed to tell a friend in my neighborhood who was outside of my immediate family circle, and that next day, my father was forced to move out by Children's Services. The sexual assault stopped that day, but he was still lurking around. I managed to avoid him whenever he tried to request to spend time with me.

So, pray for help from God, tell someone by reporting it, and focus on other things to help you heal. I needed dance to help me heal, that has always been my go to, I don't know all the latest moves but I still got it at 50. I've always loved music, so I started dancing as an extracurricular activity in high school. Then, I started dancing with local dance groups and became busy doing what made me happy at the time. I was still being physically abused by my mother but at least my father was out of the picture.

Pray, let go of the secret, and find a hobby to help fill your heart's empty, broken spaces with goodness. As an adult, go to counseling, attend AA, get into an excellent faith-based church that preaches salvation, embrace your wholeness as God your creator, get a hobby, and educate yourself on the particular topic of abuse that you deal or have dealt with to learn how to overcome, fear, anxiety, PTSD, depression, and self-blame. Know you are a survivor and not a victim. Learn how to see yourself as more than enough.

Chapter 4
Gaslighting

———————

The goal of the gas-lighter is a form of power and control
used by manipulators through a thought implanted into your head
to make you believe something that is not true, to distract or
divert you from what is true.

According to Psychology Today, (www.psychologytoday.com) Gaslighting is insidious proceeding in a gradual, subtle way, but with harmful effects a potent form of manipulation and psychological control. Victims of gaslighting are deliberately and systematically fed information that leads them to question what they know to be true, often about themselves. They may end up doubting their memory, perception, and even sanity. Over time, a gaslighter's manipulations can grow more complex like a spider's web, making it increasingly difficult for the victim to see the truth through the lies.

When I first read that definition, I looked over my life and realized it had been happening to me the whole time. I've been gaslighted since childhood. It's a hard truth to swallow, because it's not until you actually see it that you can recognize all the red flags you missed. Just like a spider's web the lies surround you and when you get caught in the web it gets all over you. Once you get yourself clean, you go back and get rid of the web, so you won't get caught in it again. The cleaning up part is you healing and the going back to get rid of it part is to heal your ancestry by breaking the generational curse. That's what it means to be chosen! The one that cleans up and removes the web completely and goes around periodically checking the corners to maintain your healing. My point is once you're able to see it, you learn how to watch out for it!

The 1940s film *Gaslight* delves deeply into the psychological manipulation of gaslighting and how easy it is to fall into traps when you're not thinking rationally. The story revolves around a husband who conspires to make his wife seem legally incompetent so he can claim her inheritance. To achieve this, he enlists the help of the household staff to manipulate her surroundings. For instance, family photos on the wall are subtly rearranged to make her doubt her own memory. Flickering lights on the chandelier create an eerie atmosphere, leading her to believe the house is haunted, when in reality, the flickering is caused by deliberately neglected faulty wiring in the attic.

The manipulation intensifies when she loses her favorite watch, and her husband cruelly suggests she's always misplacing things and that her memory is failing. Devastated, she begins to question her sanity as the web of lies tightens around her.

Eventually, she ventures into the attic and uncovers the truth: the missing photos, her cherished watch hidden in an old dresser, and the source of the faulty wiring. Relief washes over her as she realizes she's not losing her mind. But then the critical question arises: "How did all of this end up here?" The realization dawns that someone is deliberately deceiving her. Determined, she pieces together the puzzle, uncovers the culprit and their motive, and reclaims her life.

"Beloved, I wish above all things that thou mayest prosper
and be in health, even as thy soul prospereth."
3rd John 1:2

Rightfully so, the goal in this chapter is to seek truth and take our lives back. A healthy mind is the will of God for our lives, a gift from The Most High our Heavenly Father. I rely heavily on my relationship with my creator because God was all I had to keep me company to keep me sane, to talk things out with. Sitting alone in my room as a little girl, like Ingrid Bergman in the attic "Gaslight", trying to figure out where I had lost my watch!

I would sit alone in my room on punishment, for just existing, listening to footsteps outside my door pass me by. Trying to figure out what I had done wrong coming up with nothing. I grew up in isolation, mostly alone in a room watching the door knob, bracing myself for the hell I had to endure once I saw the knob begin to turn. With either my mother or my father on the other side of it.

My mother had a habit of punishing me for no reason almost as if she used me as a punching bag to physically vent out her frustrations, because my father used her as a punching bag. Although I spent an unfair amount of time in my room when I stayed with my mother, it was also peaceful behind the door to that small room. Sometimes I thought she forgot about me there, she would walk by the room several times during the day going in and out of her room, our rooms were right next to one another less than a foot apart door frame to door frame. I heard everything that happened in her room and what I could see through the shared antique wall vent whenever I got bored.

I also took solace on the roof outside my bedroom window. Whenever I was left alone, I would climb out on the window and sit on the roof just to be closer to the sky and talk to God. God has been my best friend since I was a little girl, sitting alone trying to figure out what in the hell was wrong with me and why I didn't have normal parents like my other friends in the neighborhood. I'd climb out the window some nights just to look at the stars, the navy blue sky looked like an ocean, the stars like night lights. That's when I began to use self -isolation as a coping mechanism, because no one was molesting, and I wasn't fighting for my life when I was alone.

Abuse was a normal thing growing up in our home, almost as if my parents had settled for the dysfunction, what I call the functionally dysfunction.

My biological father was sick in the mind and toxic, I don't know exactly what happened to him but somewhere along the path he stopped fighting to heal and settled in his dysfunction. I never really knew him outside of the molestation, I don't have many fun father-daughter stories that don't end with me being abused. I have a faded memory of him buying me a big huffy bike and teaching me to ride it. I think I remember it being a soft blue color. We didn't talk much. I don't know his favorite color or his birthday. When we were alone his voice faded to the background of my mind because I was watching his body cues, his words were gibberish to me when we were alone, his conversation was always just to keep my guard down. All I knew was his full name and I have his middle name. I don't understand how my parents were married but I didn't have my fathers last name. I never asked either, even as an adult I thought if he didn't even love me enough to give me his last name why bother asking now that he is dead?

Looking back over my life, I see it's always been there, the gaslighting. My father was my first abuser. I didn't know it, but it takes a skillful gaslighter to groom a victim for abuse. I've learned that in my studies working at a non-profit domestic violence shelter. I was the Prevention Program Manager for 8 years and in that time, I had to read a lot of different books and articles about abuse. Studies on the statistics of child abuse and other forms of domestic violence.

At the time it was the perfect job for me. I went around to different schools facilitating assemblies teaching about "good touch/bad touch", bullying and teen dating violence. They hired me without the fancy credentials because I was good with kids, and I talked a lot. Having the same relatable story as my audience I was able to heal a little in every person I helped. Helping to rescue other children from child abuse from the painful memory of no one coming to save me. And everytime I spoke at an assembly and sang songs and taught the "It's My Body Dance," I healed a little bit more. Reflecting on my own childhood abuse everyday for 8 years, this time on the outside looking in. A different perspective from when I was the one that grew up trapped on the inside looking out for someone to save me.

This moment of reflection reminds me of the poem entitled *Footprints in the Sand:*

"Why, when I have needed you, most would you leave me?"

The Lord replied, "My precious child,
I love you and would never leave you.
The times when you have seen only one set of footprints,
it was then that I carried you."

My father made me believe he loved me for all the wrong reasons. It's as if I can look at the face of my father and see through his smile beyond the facade and see the sly grin of the fox in the hen house. We started by going out on father-daughter hangouts, dates sort of. The truth is the level of toxicity I was raised in was through the roof, I'm grateful I didn't lose my mind as a child. My father treated me more like his girlfriend than a daughter, I honestly did not know for a long time that what my father was doing was even wrong. Even though it was wrong on every level I look back at his character during those times and he seemed so nice, always very careful not to let anyone else harm me, he wanted me in good condition.

I never got a lot of whoopings especially in my younger years after I turned 12 is when he wasn't around much and that's when the beating my mother gave me became severe. Before the age of 12 they used isolation and abandonment to condition me to fear being left alone, in comparison to being in their company but under extreme duress and repeated abuse. It worked for a while.

I thought it was cool to hang out with Dad, even though I didn't understand why he touched me. I remember him taking me to Godfather's Pizza, my favorite place at the time, and they had arcade games that

I loved to play. Every time we went, he would run out of quarters and say well, that's it! No more quarters, I knew that was his cue, and I dreaded it.

He took me out for pizza and spent money on games, and later he used that to make me feel guilty as if I owed him something in return. It was one of the most confusing emotions at the time I had ever experienced. I didn't want what was coming next even though I knew not to throw a fit. I got into the car with him after we left the pizza place, and we drove. It seemed every time a different place, little apartments all over town, it confused me as to how he had keys to all these different places. I was quiet driving from the pizza place, I felt like I was holding my breath. Feelings of ambivalence in my chest, silently looking into his eyes with no regret he stared at me like what he was about to do was okay.

The saying "eyes are the windows to the soul" is true if you pay attention to the expression of joy, sadness, hate, love and how it shows up in the facial expressions around the eyes. And it looked like he loved me with a smile, but when his cheeks rose and the edges of his mouth met the tight creases around his eyes, it looked more like a grin so big he couldn't close his lips. Staring at me while he drove and looking back at his face, I somehow knew what that expression meant, and I told myself it was easier to not fight him and hope this evening it went by quickly.

This is the part that is hard to share, because it may be a little unsettling to the mind. When I decided to not fight him, I decided I wouldn't cry and complain like a baby either. In my fathers mind he did not know why I was fighting him off or to the other extreme crying, I could tell by how he treated me that in his mind he was entitled to be with me because I was his daughter and belonged to him. Like I own this pair of shoes, and you can't tell me that I can't put my feet in them and walk around. He had moments of psychosis, and moments of clarity and some moments when he was a monster. I had to learn how to behave around the monster and how to behave around the man.

This is something no daughter should ever have to go through. He was one man with two completely different sides. When he hurt over his life and childhood, he hurt me thinking he was loving me. Because he didn't know love either, he was molested as a child, so hurt people hurt people. You would think he being a grown man knew it was wrong, I believe in his mind his entitlement was more superior to my rights to not be violated. That was when I saw the monster.

The man was when he was working, driving, and spending time with family. Hanging with his siblings, around his working buddies and boss. Laughing at the dinner table in the pizza place, standing beside me playing arcade games. Driving the car while he let me sit on the roof of the station wagon going down the street, wind in my hair. Yet knowing full well he would be right there 3 hours later at bath time, bathing me, fondling me in the tub and nobody to come rescue me.

I learned as a little girl how to appease the monster and live with the man. That was my childhood, daily. Never mind that he was my father, and it's immoral and illegal to have sex with your daughter. The goal was to make me feel obligated to return the favor of kindness with sex whether I wanted to or not. That's a lot of pressure for anyone, especially a child, but I did it every time because I wanted to prove to my father that I loved him. It was important to him that I didn't make him feel as if he was doing something wrong, if I complained and made him feel bad it would upset him more like I was ungrateful to spend this time with him, because in his mind it made him happy so it should have made me happy as well. It was diabolical. To have to pretend to be okay when you're not, in order to make the person who is hurting you happy.

I wish someone told me I didn't have to do that. I pray to God he stops child molesters, I wish it wasn't even a thing, not even a vocabulary word. To not even be conceivable to woman or man. It's a madness only few survive, the very reason you must fight to stop it in your bloodline by being the one chosen to heal. That's why it's a mistake to pass judgment on someone without knowing their side of the story, without knowing the hell they went through and now taking BS off someone else, that doesn't have a dog in the game.

Ironically, my dad made me feel that he always had my best interest in mind when he wasn't molesting me. With the mentality I'm doing this for you and not to you, but I knew better, I just didn't have any person to rescue me, I had to find my own way out the web.

My mother and I had a complicated relationship. We didn't have that mother-daughter bond while growing up. My father was in total control of his family. She was 14 when she got pregnant, and the thought of being a mother at 14 was absurd, I'm sure. I know history refers to earlier times when women had children as soon as their first menstrual cycle. That was just an excuse to call a girl a woman and rape her, marrying off to someone two or three times her age. I don't know if there is any worse feeling for a little girl than to have a monster on top of her, breathing in her face, taking away her right to say no. Child brides should also be illegal all over the world. Give children room to grow up and develop into intellectual beings which is their birthright. Sex is an adult act between two consenting adults married according to the word of Christ.

Man is flawed in nature and on one end a unique creator in God's Kingdom with the abilities to have rule and authority over the earth and subdue the animals under ranking a little lower than the angels. The other, flawed and broken without the presence of God and the gift of redemption as robes that cover our nakedness daily because of sinful nature.

The crazy part of the generational curse that ran in my family is that my mother and I had the same abuser, just like her mother and my great grandmother. Some families historically have kept the flame going to keep each generation under the spell of the devil, knowing it was wrong but bound to a wicked tradition. Some even passed down through secret societies that thrive on hurting others and labeling it religion. Jesus in the New Testament said there is one God and God is love, so the devil deceived us by lying to us what the truth was concerning love.

The devil told us love was painful and to dedicate ourselves to the idea of the commitment to enduring said pain, is to love the pain as an outward sign of loyalty to God. At the time, the god of evil, was whomever was in control of the dishing out the pain. That's the mind of the narcissist that hides behind religion, the false god, false prophet. I've survived both church hurt and childhood abuse and the two are no different. Just took place in different houses. Only one took a vow to be a good husband and the other took a vow to be a good shepherd, but both failed my already broken heart. The key is to forgive and move on, heal and let them be. Resentment is the venom of the serpent. Seek the true and living God. God is not a narcissist so begin studying to show yourself approved from that perspective. God is love and love is not abuse!

Growing up in a narcissistic household is an insane experience for a child. To anyone who experienced it, I pray you heal so you don't feel you deserve to be treated badly or mishandled by anyone. Child Sexual Abuse should be illegal. You say that it is? Then tell me why it's constantly being swept under the rug and why so many abusers are walking around in our society reoffending because the penalty is nowhere near compared to the crime.

My father was the dominant presence in the household and the primary income source. Just like so many women, my mother couldn't stop him for fear of facing her punisher; my father was so brutal I couldn't even imagine what happened to her behind closed doors with him. She was around 20 or 21 when my abuse started, which means she had six years under her belt of dealing with a monster. Around the house, she was a quiet woman who kept all her pain inside and smoked cannabis to dull the pain. I barely remember talking much with her outside of the basic clean your room and get ready for school conversations. She dreamed of going to nursing school and never did. Her mistake was to allow the boogie man to stop her forward movement to live out her purpose, dream, destiny or call in life, my father made her feel unworthy of it. Her mistake was not standing up for herself by speaking up against false love.

My father constantly ran the streets. Most of the time, I was with him. He kept my mother and I apart and at odds with one another. The goal of a pedophile is to drive a wedge between the child and everyone else to make the child feel dependent on them. That way, the child feels hopeless without them and will do anything to preserve the toxic bond per necessity. Everything is based off the word of the abuser saying their victim is not operating in their full mental capacity, everything you speak becomes twisted and not not credible due to the seed of dishonor by the narcissist. Making the abuser judge and jury of all further interpretations regarding the issue and the issue being your fake mental diagnosis by the abuser. Charming right?

One night, I was with my father, and he took me to his workplace, a local car dealership where he was the mechanic. It was a huge glass building with several boardrooms, a large showroom, and a garage area where the used cars were repaired before being put on the lot for sale.

This evening we stopped in, and I began to play the scenario in my head of what I knew was about to happen, my stomach turned, and I tried to tell myself just shut up and get it over with, like so many other times I had to say similar things to myself, and most of the time it worked. Something grew inside my belly and the word "No" came out. That night, I couldn't do it, and I knew he would be irate. I couldn't make myself go along with the program this time.

My father just silently stared me down, bloodshot red eyes bulging out of his head. It was like the universe paused, and I could see on his face, with all the restraint he had, he wanted to strangle me. Suddenly, he grabbed his car keys and left, closed and locked the door behind him. Before I knew it, I was standing in the dark alone, locked inside, as he got in his car and drove away. I was in shock, afraid to run after him and afraid to stay there alone. I chose to stay there in the dark because I froze and watched him drive away. Grateful to see him leave even though I was shaking in the dark, but grateful to see him drive away. I took a step that day. A step towards defending myself.

After a while you get tired of pretending everything is okay for the sake of not hurting the person's feelings. A person that doesn't give a d*mn about your feelings. For me as a child to stand up to my abuser was life changing because God protected me. He could have broken me like a twig in his hands, he could have beat me, instead he stormed out and abandoned me, but he heard my no. For me it was a small victory because for once he heard my no and it worked. That was not the last time something like this would happen. The older I got, the more wrong it felt, the urge to stand up became stronger.

That night after he left, I sat in that alley for hours staring at the stars in the sky. He eventually came back, and I sat there helplessly waiting. He opened the door and told me to get in the car, so I did. He said, "Don't do that again!" No other words were exchanged other than that. I can only imagine he took his anger out on someone else that night.

"Who taught you to live in fear? For not even God
has given us a spirit of fear,"
2nd Timothy 1:7.

When I got over my fear to tell my father no, the fight started then for me to regain control over myself and my body. My father obviously was under the impression that because I was a part of him, that he was entitled to have "rights" over me. Sort of like the current political debate where the men in one part feel that a woman should not have rights over her own body but has to get approval of a man who believes she belongs to him. Like she is property. How inhumane!

I know what it is like for someone to feel entitled to you, that is an invisible crime leaving no fingerprints, the only witness is someone skilled enough to understand the habits or a narcissist. No one should have rights over another person's body and it's absurd to have the rights over a person who was given the birthright to speak on their own behalf. Telling my father no, felt good even though some would say don't talk back, I was born with a mouth and a voice therefore God gave me what I needed to defend myself. It's only a bully that wants to take that away from you.

A hard truth for me to comprehend as a little girl was that my father was a bully, my father had such control over everything that even when I did speak up and tell family members, everyone turned a deaf ear to me as if they couldn't handle the truth. That's precisely how the abuser wants it to go. The last thing an abuser wants is to lose a victim, especially one that they have spent so long grooming and gaslighting. They will do anything to discredit you, to dumb down your witness.

As a result of learning how to appease my abusers, I developed people-pleasing as a coping mechanism because it became easier to feed the beast than to stop him. I grew up believing I didn't have a right to say no, and that behavior followed me into adulthood. I was the person who made sure I did whatever I needed to do to make the people around me happy because it was safer that way. I learned that people are good with you as long as they are getting their way.

A spirit of fear was cast over me at an early age in life, and I played dead through most of my sexual abuse. My mentality was I couldn't stop him from taking my body as his own. I just had to stay alive through the torment.

Anyone that I spoke of the abuse with treated me as if I was wrong for telling, like why are you bringing this up was the response. No one wanted to talk about it because no one wanted to do anything about it! If it wasn't for God giving me the courage to speak up my father would have never allowed me to go free. He would have kept me his prisoner forever. I remember a time when I was living in Alabama married to my first husband and my father was sending me love letters sprayed with men's cologne and I was 29 years old. Once I moved, I never saw him again, thank God, but his mind was just that incredibly warped.

I grew up being a nice person out of learned behavior. Just dead on the inside otherwise, and my own will and desires became irrelevant. I was taught that my value came from doing as I was told, for survival. So many people do that same thing today, do as you are told for survival. It's like you're emotionally numb, cut off from feeling anything good or bad because you can't afford to feel anymore, and you block everything out, I call that autopilot. You coast through life, not making any waves in constant survival mode.

People can't consume you without first deceiving you. It took me so long to figure that out—first my father, then my mother. Next, as a runaway, I trusted that strangers had my best interest more than anyone I knew. Replacing my logic about life, in exchange for the opinion of others with whom my life was nothing. I was looking for a place of peace, which any person with past trauma knows is unrealistic for most abuse victims, who are stuck in a cycle of victim mentality due to PTSD triggers in unhealthy environments. It's an unrealistic goal because a healed person understands healing cannot be found outwardly, it comes from within.

Peace comes when you are okay with your truth. My truth is life happens, and we were not promised perfection. However, the promise if we would humble ourselves and pray then God will heal us. The promise with the trauma comes healing when we pray. We were born with a free will to choose good over evil, some chose the latter and as a result hurt people hurt people and when we are minding our own business not bothering a soul, life happens to us.

Peace is attainable through hard work and the removal or separation of yourself from the situation(s). Space and time away from the toxicity allow you to clear your mind and reset. Do not retaliate, digging a deeper ditch helps no one. Get out! Staying in a place that keeps you in a cycle of victimization is not wise for any person that can see they are in danger or as some say "Woke". Simply meaning no longer sleep, confused, bound by what holds you hostage to constant gaslighting. Jesus was "woke" in the garden of Gethsemane, why else would he have told his disciples to sleep on?

When he (Jesus) went back to the disciples, he found them asleep.
He said to Peter, "Couldn't you stay awake with me for one hour?
Stay awake, and pray that you won't be tempted. You want to do what's
right, but you're weak." Then he went away a second time and prayed,
"Father, if this cup cannot be taken away unless I drink it,
let your will be done."

He found them asleep again because they couldn't keep their eyes open.
After leaving them again, he went away and prayed the same prayer a
third time. Then he came back to the disciples and said to them, "You

might as well sleep now. The time is near for the Son of Man to be handed over to sinners. Get up! Let's go! The one who is betraying me is near.
Matthew 26:40-46

Simply meaning stay alert, same as stay woke because some people choose evil, and if we keep an eye out for evil then we will not fall for the invasion of evil into our hearts. Out of the heart flows the issues of life. We are to combat evil with good and stay good, God will defend his word. He doesn't need our help defending good, he needs our help spreading good. Satan is the spirit of narcissism and is looking for those that are not alert, woke. I know because I grew up with one and I had to be alert.

It was good for my soul to have endured and know what it's like to have survived such an experience, I am stronger now because of it, even though it does not excuse any of my abusers behaviors, it does show a history of God being on my side!

I am no longer a people pleaser, thank God, I will no longer compromise myself to serve a greater purpose for someone else. That is a self-degrading act. Self- degrading can be explained in a few ways. Negative images we project on ourselves where we think we are unworthy of a hopeful tomorrow because of our past. Tending to undervalue ourselves, belittling yourself as not able to celebrate your achievements or appreciate your own abilities, making success seem unimportant when in truth all people desire success even if secretly! Lastly, not loving yourself unconditionally.

It is a condition that develops when victims feel sorry for or defend the abuser not asking that they take accountability for their actions. They also feel that loyalty in protecting the abuser is above their own safety.

I was running in survival mode. When you are a victim of gaslighting, you live in an unhealthy cycle of co-dependent associations with the people you meet because you're like a zombie walking through life doing what you are told to do. These characteristics are also ascribed to Stockholm Syndrome survivors.

An article in Forbes magazine (https://www.forbes.com/health/mind/ stockholm-syndrome/#) tells us that Stockholm syndrome is a term coined in 1973, about the Patty Hearst kidnapping, after a botched bank robbery in Stockholm, Sweden led to hostages bonding with their captors.

The captor, or a person who wields authority or power over others, creating a dynamic where the victim feels trapped and dependent on their abuser for survival. It's a painful reality, much like when I was left waiting in the alley for my father to come back for me. I protected him, afraid that sharing my story would only lead to more punishment. I was gaslit into believing he held control over my safety, even though he was the very source of danger.

Beyond that, Stockholm syndrome is not exclusive to kidnappings, it can also be a coping mechanism or emotional response for those in abusive situations, whether domestic abuse, child abuse, or human trafficking. It can also be related to abusive work situations or even specific coach-athlete dynamics.

I'm going to add religious abuse, systemic abuse (our governments), pressure from peer groups including but not limited to specific businesses using their authority to demand you compromise yourself for a promotion, promising to promote you to a better position as a power play over you, using your financial resources to manipulate you to do ungodly things for advancement. Even gang affiliations, fraternities, and sororities!

Any position you are put in to choose your safety over your freedom is gaslighting. Even on the airplanes the flight attendant will tell you to put your oxygen on first before helping someone else. When you live in survival mode most of the time, you read the room a lot to stay alert for triggers. It's not until you start to walk in your peace that you begin to believe peace is possible. It takes a true awakening to snap out of it because your survival mode is set on self-sabotage and you have to wake up to the truth, that allowing someone to take advantage of you is not being nice but stupid.

When I was 16 years old, I decided to run away from home and escape my abusive parents to save my own life, even though I didn't know what life was. I kept running after the idea of a better life than the one I had, trying to find something that felt like home. It made me vulnerable to getting pulled into the religious sector, and I gave my life to Christ. It wasn't long after that I found myself living wholly sold out for Christ, thinking I knew what that was. I found a safe place to release myself from all the traumas. I mean, who doesn't believe Jesus is the answer? Except no one told me I had to go through people to get to Jesus. When you have dealt with gaslighting as a trauma, and then you find yourself a member of a church that teaches you that obedience to the Pastor is obedience to Christ, you believe it. Even if it doesn't feel or sound right because that is your learned behavior. You can be gaslighted into believing many different things when you are unsure of who you are.

So, for the new believers who have given their lives to Christ, it's easy to be fooled. You must keep going, overcoming every obstacle and you do not give up. How do you do that you ask? You overcome the obstacle of people by not allowing them to play on your vulnerabilities or aka emotions to compromise your healing by returning to your old broken victim mentality. Stay strong! You can tell church people no, just like you can anyone else, when they are trying to persuade you to do something you do not feel comfortable doing.

The truth of the matter is that "Gaslighted" can apply to just about anything! It's crazy how easily you can believe something, even if it doesn't feel right when it's coming from the right person or wrapped in an alluring package. As I look over my life 40 years later, I appreciate how my experiences helped me grow. I've lived a lifetime of being deceived since early childhood.

Here is the difference between grooming and gaslighting. Every manipulator has a modus operandi or MO. A groomer is a person that softens you for gaslighting. A groomer is someone who builds a relationship, trust, and emotional connection with a person so they can manipulate, exploit, and abuse them. Such persons should be treated by a mental health professional. Most abuse goes unreported because we don't want to see someone we love go to jail. This is a twisted logic because the person committing the crimes is setting out to harm someone and should be held accountable. No more letting sexual perversion get swept under the rug, not just for the crime of sexual assault but also for the mental and emotional damage that results from victimization. Allowing something you know is wrong to slide under the radar is like allowing disease to fester in the body untreated until it kills the host.

Family perversion is a disease that goes untreated when we keep saying "what goes on in this house stays in this house" and we allow secrets to fester generation after generation until we kill off the life of the bloodline because now the whole family is sick. Molestation is family incest which is the worst type of hurt other than church hurt because these are the people we expect to know better and do better. Childhood abuse is not the stranger 90% of the time it's family and that's incest, it makes my stomach turn to think of how many people have suffered from hurt at the hands of the people that were supposed to protect them. God gave us a family to have a healthy place to grow, a place filled with unconditional love and nurturing.

When you don't have a healthy family, the tree is poisonous at the root and must be chopped down and pulled up to plant a healthy tree in its place. That is what I am doing with my husband Kenn. We are planting a healthy tree for ourselves to share with those that love us the most that desire to water and nurture our healthy new beginning.

Church is another place you can have a healthy foundation to grow from, when the church is protected by leaders and clergy that promote a love is not abuse, culture and don't take advantage of people like what I experienced. Like the Jim Jones massacre where the pastor led the people to their demise, if ever you are in church and being sexually intimidated by a member of the clergy get out of that church asap. You should report the incident, but you are not responsible for fixing something you did not break. Never give anyone a second chance to reoffend.

Alcoholics Anonymous is another place that has healthy habits set in place for your healing journey. Sexual assault is a hard illness to heal from and you need a clean place to reset your mindand unload your triggers.

Our new normal is speaking up and fighting for our healing, when we speak out it is not only healthy it's preventative as well! Because when you speak out you can stop incest and molestation at the grooming stage.

Web MD's article on sexual grooming gives us a lot of background and insight (https://www.webmd.com/sex/what-is-sexual-grooming). Sexual grooming is when a sexual predator builds a relationship with a child or adult in order to exploit. They manipulate trust, using it as a tool to control, isolate, and abuse their victims—emotionally, physically, and even sexually. Isolation serves a specific purpose: to keep you away from anyone who might recognize the abuse and raise concerns before you're completely blindsided by their lies. They often start with love bombing, an overwhelming display of affection meant to sweep you off your feet early in the relationship. This tactic is designed to make you fall hard and fast, encouraging you to spend all your time with them while slowly distancing yourself from those who care about you. Once they have you isolated, they begin to distort your perception of reality, replacing the truth with their carefully crafted lies.

A group of groomers, or a pedophile ring/cult, employs similar tactics to manipulate and control, but instead of one individual, multiple people work together to draw you in. They create an illusion of belonging by quickly making you feel welcomed and valued, inviting you to every event and guilt-tripping you if you don't attend. They'll constantly remind you how much you were missed whenever you're absent, reinforcing the idea that you're an essential part of their group.

Members of the group take turns building you up, emphasizing how much fun they have together and portraying themselves as one big, happy family. They'll repeatedly tell you how much of a perfect fit you are and how you're an incredible addition to their circle. Meanwhile, they work to isolate you by keeping you busy within the group, subtly discouraging you from maintaining relationships outside of it. They foster a sense of belonging, knowing you crave connection, but their true intent is far more sinister. Their ultimate goal is to break down your boundaries and groom you for their own exploitation.

This tactic works well on those that are unhealed from family trauma, usually runaways or those that are introverts or hermits. People that don't have a social life because they are homebodies. Most groomers target people that don't have much of a social life because there will be no one checking on their whereabouts or safety.

Once they isolate you, they next will work on twisting your perception of reality so when you second guess what is going on around you they will make it seem like you are hallucinating or imagining things. That way you will not rely on your own instincts but become co-dependent to them and their opinions. Once you begin to rely on their opinion or trust their interpretation of reality, they can control how you move by simply disagreeing with anything you do that doesn't serve their best interest.

Attaching your loyalty to their power and control. Most groomers have a background in psychology, social work or some mental health fields, any profession in community involvement where some with their knowledge is highly respected and their methods are not questioned. Other types of groomers are former victims whose minds have been polluted to believe sexual molestation is actually okay, because it happened to them. Which of course is incorrect thinking.

A groomer often comes across as charming, helpful, and kind at first. It can be easy to trust them and lower your guard. They will often use threats, violence, or other coercion to force you into sexual activity you don't want once they have manipulated you into trusting them. A groomer will attach your loyalty to their power and control. So be careful not to allow anyone to twist your perception of reality. You saw what you saw, and you heard what you heard even if they deny it.

Any time someone makes you feel or tries to convince you that you are going crazy by making you question your sense of reality leave that place immediately or politely excuse yourself if in private and you want to get out safely without alerting them that you suspect that something is wrong. Arguing with a manipulator is useless, because they are liars, and are programmed to never give into exposing themselves even if they are caught red handed. They will still do whatever they can to keep you believing that it's you and not them. Groomers must be forced to give up their cover or exposed by witnesses outside of the group or toxic circle they have welcomed you into.

Abuse can be divided into several categories. Mental or psychological abuse is targeted to the mind of the individual preyed upon to confound or confuse said subject.

Anyone who cannot make choices for themselves without the need for affirmation from others is a sitting duck. That's the first thing every manipulator looks for—someone that needs the approval of others to feel whole. These people are an easy catch with the right bait. That is why authenticity is important because you cannot be drawn into the herd mentality when you are an original. You have your own mind, you are not easily persuaded to go with the flow.

Physical abuse is the most talked about because it's the only one you can make sense of. It leaves behind some kind of physical proof. Unlike mental abuse that is mostly invisible mind games. The scars left behind from physical abuse are visible to the naked eye, there is visual proof that a crime has been committed. Bruises, black eyes, and wounds can take weeks to heal, and they still leave a scar as a reminder. An abuser will try to get you to believe that pain is a form of punishment that is admirable, leaving you with the responsibility to live up to the gruesome expectation of others. And if you are not careful, you will allow someone to judge you unjustly. There are people out there who love to see the pain in your eyes when they are mistreating you, abusers and bullies thrive off seeing you afraid. So, you must be serious about your healing.

No matter the avenue for the abuse, mind manipulation plays a huge part in the preparation of the grooming. Sexual abuse is a real mind game. It's mostly perpetrated against children. The term rape is primarily used in the case of adult forced sexual abuse. Sexual child abuse or molestation also goes against what you feel and not just what you think. You are taught that your feelings are a lie and to deny that your feelings are reality! The touch that makes you cringe, you must endure suffering through it as a sign of strength that is impressive, bragging on your ability to withstand pain like it's a good thing. Making you process confusing emotions and feeling sick in your stomach as if you are weak for not being able to endure as to prove your commitment to them.

We grow up believing something is true because we have confidence in the adults who tell us, only to become an adult and learn that being an adult is complicated. Sadly, children grow up learning that most adults are liars, little white lies or flat out bold-faced liars. I am under the belief, we need more role models because they have somehow run out of style in this era.

That's why it's essential to know your truth and stand by it. Detoxing from people is just as critical as detoxing from alcohol or any other substance/ coping mechanism. A person that has been gaslite questions their sense of perception and logical reasoning, so detoxing from the groups and situations that played a role in your trauma is crucial to your recovery. Having a clear mind is essential to changing your perception, and you don't need to consider other points of view while establishing your own self-perception. The world will have you believing anything. You know the saying if you don't stand for something, you will fall for anything? It's true. Most of the time, we make ourselves sitting ducks for manipulators just by not believing evil people exist, evil does exist so it's okay to question everything around you to make sure you are in a safe and healthy environment. Anyone that is not understanding or patient with you while you embrace your journey to heal is not worth your time or attention because you've been there and done that.

If you don't know who you are, manipulators will bait you into believing things about yourself that are not true so they can make you rely on them for affirmation. Adults and children get bamboozled by the best of them. Manipulators don't care who the victim is. They are just happy to have an audience.

The grooming and gaslighting process is a must to overcome. You should have control over your own thinking, that's why God gave you a brain. Stress from battling with reality in the mind is the reason most people are sick in their bodies. All the mind games cause some to be hypochondriacs, and or worse throw you into a temporary psychosis- a disconnect from reality and the world around you, and you don't want that.

The best way to rise above your trauma is to do the hard thing and put yourself first. Think of your safety first. If you are the one being abused, report the abuse and keep reporting it until someone does something. Find a safe place to live, even a tiny studio apartment, with a family member or group of friends who understand what you've been through and don't mind helping you process your pain. Remove yourself from toxic environments and friend groups, better yet fake friend groups because real friends have your back. Finally, secure yourself a good therapist, a safe space to unlock your inner feelings. The dormant feelings you cover up when you pretend everything is okay.

If there are children involved, please monitor their behavior carefully to see how they are coping with the trauma and make sure they are not re-exposed in their new environment. Stay single until you heal. Unhealed trauma attracts unhealthy relationships. Ensure you recognize unhealthy red flags before deciding who to spend time with, including friendships, churches or social circles.

Now that we better understand what's going on, let us move on to healing! The past doesn't matter so much anymore. What matters is that we use our experiences as a skill set for growth. It helps if you get past the abused child syndrome. If you are an adult survivor of child sexual abuse the blessing is that you survived when a lot of children didn't, find the silver lining in your story. It's easy to explain once you look at the root of the problem. You can be 60 years old and still have a mind like a 10-year-old with daddy issues, if you don't work on your healing. Whatever came first, the gaslighting or the grooming, was the big life-changing moment that changed your perception of the truth, so find your truth. Stop believing everything people tell you, do your own research and be observant and form your own opinions.

Self-care is the best recovery. Put yourself first for once. Start saying no. You can discern if the people around you are concerned with your best interest when you set boundaries and take back your power to make decisions and come to your logical conclusions. Even if you're not always right, make decisions from the heart, so even when you're wrong, at least you tried and are willing to face the truth within yourself.

Seek professional help. You need reasonable counsellor from a professional who understands life is situational and bad moments don't make bad days. We all have a story that makes us who we are, and a story has a beginning, middle, and end. Don't allow anyone to write your story, and once you turn the page don't look back and return to a chapter that almost broke you. Go forward.

"Finally, brethren, whatsoever things are true, whatsoever things are honest, whatsoever things are just, whatsoever things are pure, whatsoever things are lovely, whatsoever things are of good report; if there be any virtue, and if there be any praise, think on these things."
Philippians 4:8

I've learned that focusing on the good things in your life and not allowing negativity to flood your thoughts is good mental self-care. Abusers gain power from you being paranoid of the past repeating itself, and that only happens when you constantly replay the trauma in your head.

Free yourself by freeing your mind. Stay away from people who remind you of your past! Stay away from the do-you-remember-when conversations. Leave those alone. Appreciate time spent with yourself. Don't be afraid to be alone. Alone is not loneliness—it's time you can just get away from it all and regroup. Find out who you are away from the trauma triggers, and understand what peace really feels and looks like. It's an opportunity to make your own decisions and trust your own thoughts!

Asserting Authority
Misusing Scripture, traditions, or cultural norms to impose gender roles that are abusive or coercive, to assert abusive authority, to reinforce privilege, to encourage you to submit to abuse, to give commands, or to punish you.

Prolonging Abusive Relationships
Misusing Scripture, traditions, or cultural norms to encourage you to forgive abuse, to prolong an abusive relationship, to excuse or minimize the abuse, to remain silent, or to accept suffering and abuse.

Controlling Sexuality and Reproduction
Misusing Scripture, traditions, or cultural norms to force you to have sex or unprotected sex, to deny or force family planning, to participate in polygamous marriage or genital mutilation, to have sex or be married at a young age, to be in a coerced or forced marriage.

Isolation
Isolating you from your faith community by not allowing you to participate in services or events, by silencing you when you are there, by moving the family from congregation to congregation, or by forcing you to attend services in a different faith community.

Spiritual and Religious Abuse
Misusing Scripture, Traditions, and Cultural Norms to Assert Power and Control

Using Children
Misusing Scripture, traditions, or cultural norms to coerce or force marriage for teens, to value male over female children, to use girls as commodities for bride price or dowry, to sell young girls as commodities, to force you to raise children in another faith or no faith.

Using Community Coercion
Working through clergy or lay leader, or friends or family from your faith community, to put pressure on you to stay in the relationship or to put up with abuse. Coercion may include letters or phone calls on the abuser's behalf, comments in social settings and on social media.

Restricting Access to or Use of Health Care
Misusing Scripture, traditions, or cultural norms to force you to forego regular check ups and medical care, family planning, medications, emergency medical care, or to neglect medical care for your children.

Blaming the Victim
Misusing Scripture, traditions, or cultural norms to blame you and justify abuse because you are sinful, estranged from God, not created in God's image, created to be a servant or slave, unclean, polluted, or defiled.

Using Coercion And Threats
Makes and/or carries out threats to hurt me; Threatens to commit suicide; Threatens to report/embarrass/out me to an agency or others; Threatens to leave me; Pressures me to commit illegal actions.

Using Intimidation
Makes me feel afraid or unsafe with actions, gestures, looks; Throws things; Breaks things; Damages my property; Abuses your pets; Displays weapons.

Using Emotional Abuse
Puts me down; Makes me feel bad about myself; Calls me names; Makes me think I am crazy, misinterpreting or over-reacting; Plays mind games; Humiliates me; Makes me feel guilty or ashamed.

Using Economic Abuse
Prevents me from getting or keeping a job; Makes me ask for money; Gives me an allowance; Takes my money; Refuses to let me know about or have access to shared income.

POWER AND CONTROL

Using Isolation
Controls what I do, who I see, what I read, where I go and who I talk to; Limits my volunteer, religious or outside activities; Monitors my behavior and communication; Uses jealousy to justify actions.

Using Privilege
Treats me like a servant; Acts like the "head of the household"; Makes all the big decisions; Defines each person's role in the relationship; Uses gender, race, class, etc. stereotypes against me.

Using Children
Makes me feel guilty about the children; Uses the children to relay messages; Uses visitation to harass me; Threatens to take the children away.

Minimizing, Denying and Blaming
Makes light of the abuse; Doesn't take my concerns seriously; Denies abuse ever happened; Shifts blame for the abuse to me by saying I caused it.

Chapter 5

Mind Games

———— ▬ ————

The Power and Control Wheel gives us visuals of what abuse and manipulation look like on paper. Mind games that specifically use psychological manipulation as its primary weapon.

What comes to mind when you think of mind games as the practice of it relates to human interactions? This world is played on a chess board, a monopoly board, a basketball court, a court of law, a poker table, or in a church sanctuary. The world has become so deceitful that we cover up the deception by labeling those who understand this truth as crazy or overthinkers.

These wheels give you the techniques that most manipulators use. The deadly combination of entitled privilege and victim mentality. As long as you operate in a victim mentality you will always fall for the trap of entitled privilege. A victim mentality is a negative viewpoint that blames others for your misfortune and feels helpless to change. The harm to having a victim mentality is it blinds you to the light of the path to get out of the helplessness to change.

Privilege and entitlement are related concepts, but they have distinct meanings: Privilege refers to unearned advantages or benefits based on social, economic, or cultural status. Entitlement refers to believing oneself to be inherently deserving of privileges or special treatment. Some people in this world feel entitled to have special treatment for whatever the reason, that they enforce that at the expense of others. Special treatment due to race is the basis of white supremacy because God is the creator of equality.

The topic can be racism, sexism, classism, religion, diversity or anyone that enforces to be treated with special consideration above others due to entitlement. This is the model for Power and Control, a superior mind-set that believes they are entitled to treat others without respect to gain respect and privilege. In my opinion based on a survivor's perspective! Which is why as a survivor, you must release the victim mentality because to a narcissist you're a walking advertisement for them to see if they can rent space in your head.

Looking at toxic relationships and communities from the two models provided, you will see a pattern evolve once you learn to overcome your trauma, that can help you defeat the mind games. Drawing a line in the sand to future dysfunction.

Physical, Sexual, and Emotional gateways are all avenues to which mind games have the quickest entry point. Your mind is the gateway into your heart and soul because your mind controls your thoughts, which controls your emotions that eventually control you!

This is why Jesus says in Matthew 22; 37 *"…thou shalt love the Lord thy God with all thy heart, and with all thy soul, and with all thy mind."* This scripture gives us the keys to keep your heart and mind covered with the love of God. That way when hate tries to enter into these 3 areas of your personal space, you can oppose the hate and negativity because you know God is love and you can swipe left and ignore negative thoughts.

You must also know bullying and physical abuse is preventable when we use our discernment to distance ourselves from pressurized environments, by pressurized I mean hostile. Whenever you are choosing a circle to hang out with or an individual to share your life with, be sure to check for certain characteristics to see if they are prone to favor aggression and if so, use caution. Like short tempered and hostile characteristics. A short tempered hostile person is less likely to choose peace as a resolve. They use aggression as a trigger to feed their anger issues, they need to find a reason to explode when they are not given a reason, due to the lack of conflict in the peaceful environment.

If you are on a healing journey and a peaceful environment helps you heal, like a clean hospital environment helps a sick person heal. Then you meet someone that is short tempered or hostile, they are not likely to discipline themselves to help you grow because they are like junkies needing the endorphin rush of drama. They are not familiar with peace and need to stir up trouble to get their fix. They are not a safe space for someone that is healing, because they are still chasing the high instead of taking part in the healing.

Each person is on their own journey and if there is no transparency in the beginning everyone in the new environment will have to figure out the hard way, who suffers from what, post -trigger. The goal is to prevent the triggers by taking part in each other's healing, this is called unity for a peaceful resolve. This is only possible when the individuals within the group are working on themselves and taking accountability for their actions.

In a toxic group setting where no one is taking accountability of their actions, instead of transparency in the group or relationship you have an environment that thrives off lies, deceit, psychological manipulation and avoidance. This keeps you locked in a toxic cycle and without the proper coping mechanisms to escape the cycle, that cycle repeats itself daily and now this becomes a routine that turns into a lifestyle. Then you ask the question, how did I get here?

You can get so deep in the web of lies from the mind games that you don't see the finish line or the starting line. You don't know how you even got involved because it's something that happened to you, not something you initiated. I was born into an abusive childhood. I did not know that I was born into it, I knew I was born because I have a birthdate, which tells me one day I was not, then after being given a birthdate, I suddenly was, having no control over where I landed.

I did not choose my parents. I was a gift that they didn't know how to properly receive, so they did what came naturally to them—and the result of what came to them naturally was how they treated me. When I got older and ran away it's because I chose differently for myself. I broke out of the web of deceit and childhood trauma. I grew up carrying that burden on my back that it made me a target because I didn't know how to resolve the trauma because it wasn't my game. It was my father's game, my mother's game of survival because they grew up in the game and they were still playing it. I did not desire to continue in the game, so I walked away choosing to leave that life behind.

I wore my trauma like a name tag. Hello, my name is Childhood Sexual Abuse. My father had sex with me, and my mother pushed me down a flight of stairs and tried to kill me. Hello, my name is Runaway. Can you spare some change? Hello, my name is Broken and Confused with nowhere safe to call home. Exposing myself as a pawn in the game, unknowingly.

All mind games stem from the narcissists' desire to gain complete control by using the most intimate parts of human attachment to bait you in! And your victim mentality is their entry point. When your emotions lead you, it leaves no room for logic. That is what hindsight is. Logical is the rationale that the math ain't mathing! You will not see the imbalance because you are not looking for it due to your need to be accepted and affirmed.

Abusers use the word love as the mask in which they conceal their intentions. If you can be drawn into something by your need for touch, arousal, or emotional support, then you are an easy target for those people who need someone to control in order to thrive.

Two bullies don't beat up on each other. One is the aggressor, and the other is the pacifist, but bullies grow up to be adults. Most don't outgrow bullying. They just become better at it. Usually, the pacifist is just as passive as an adult, because that is the role they were given. Most people believe you have to become the bully to defeat the bully. This is the foundation of nearly 90% of household abuse, the story where the bully marries the pacifist. A person needing to control another person, will never be in a relationship with someone who speaks up for themselves, because they don't want your opinion, they want your obedience. Which is silent and submissive, not outspoken and bold.

Friendships can fall into the narcissist category too, an imbalance of co-dependency paired up with an enabler, non-sexual power and control. Many co-dependent individuals are also people-pleasers. The two disabilities combined make for a pattern of lifelong servitude to someone who lives off the fear of others. Bullies like to see fear in your eyes. They are people who are deficient in self-esteem, and they feed on the negative energy of the fears of their victims. They believe themselves to be somebody when others fear them, and they hold the power, the fix I spoke of previously.

Historically, we've seen that type of twisted dynamic in the area of white supremacy and religious abuse. The two are even more dangerous because those blinded by religious abuse, compare the authority of their oppressor to having the same authoritative power that God has. The minister is not God, they are an instructor of the Word of God and if the instructor while operating in the office as someone chosen by God, if they behave contrary to the character of God can be replaced. You are you and no one is a replacement for you, which means the journey belongs to you all others either assist in the elevation of your understanding or the stagnation of it.

You were running so well. Who has obstructed you from obeying the truth? You were running a good race. Who cut in on you to keep you from obeying the truth? You were running the race so well. Who has held you back from following the truth? You were running well.
Galatians 5:7

As I write this book, we find ourselves in the midst of a pivotal election—a clash between the old, patriarchal, narcissistic, and white supremacist mindset and a new wave of intellectual, democratic ideals. Many believe that healing from the entrenched patriarchal narcissism is essential—an ideology rooted in the fears of those our forefathers once enslaved. This mindset battle pits those clinging to outdated notions of white supremacy against those who reject victimhood and embrace progress. As a society, we can no longer tolerate backward steps. A clear line must be drawn in the sand to protect the progress we've made, and ensure we continue moving forward.

The new wave of intellectuals within democracy seeks to foster growth and restore a sense of brotherly love in a nation that has endured deep-seated trauma. This collective pain has left the country grappling with the effects of what feels like national PTSD. Even our Caucasian brothers and sisters face inner conflict, often torn between loyalty to broken traditions and the opportunity to heal from a system they were born into—a system akin to an un-winnable game. The truth of our situation isn't black and white. It exists in shades of gray.

On one side, we see Republican leaders clinging to outdated traditions, often using the Bible to justify their biases. After enduring the devastating impact of Covid-19, a deadly pandemic that claimed millions of lives under the Trump administration in 2019, the nation began to recover under President Biden's leadership in 2020. Access to healthcare through the Affordable Care Act, economic stabilization, and the reopening of businesses gave survivors a chance to return to work and regain their footing. For a moment, balance was restored, and healing began.

Now, in the 2024 presidential race, former President Trump appears to show little regard for maintaining the delicate recovery process. Homeostasis—a self-regulating system that ensures stability—is essential for the health of any society. President Joe Biden and Vice President Kamala Harris have done commendable work in fostering that balance, helping the nation heal and find stability after a period of upheaval.

As a citizen of the United States, I am protected under the First Amendment, which grants me the right to express my views on matters that directly impact my life. Politics in the U.S. profoundly influence not only my present but also the legacy of thought passed down by prior generations. Just as the politics of my parents' beliefs shaped me as a child, the politics of today shape the future we leave for generations to come.

I am a person—a human being recognized as capable of possessing rights and being held accountable for duties. According to *Black's Law Dictionary, 2nd Edition*, a "person" is defined as "a human being considered as capable of having rights and of being charged with duties," while a "thing" is merely an object over which rights may be exercised. The key phrase here is considered as capable of having rights. My rights.

We are faced with an election where two parties represent two different mentalities, one toxic and counterproductive and the other progressive and hopeful. I say toxic and counterproductive because we have come too far in history to resort back to hate as a viable solution to the world's problems.

The shift takes place in the brain of either a healthy or an unhealthy mind, you will have whatever is in the condition of your mind. Like the examples of the two power and control models it all depends on if we hold those accountable for their wrongdoings when we can clearly see their motives are coming from a damaging hurtful place. Don't forget that hurting people hurt people, and healed people become healers. Jesus and his disciples help others heal in brotherly love. Those that have not healed will thrive better in a society that feeds their ego and narcissism.

Yet we know this and still continue to argue over what is best for the country in 2024, a healed person would say, a healthy democracy where we continue to heal together is what is best. An unhealed person would say a toxic narcissistic rule fueled by hate and division is best because we do not want to lose power and control of our entitlement to use people as pawns in our game. It doesn't matter the politics over the cost of gas going up or down a few pennies! And we won't even discuss the fact Kamala Harris is already a qualified Vice President woman running for president in that same patriarchal society that still thinks they have the right to define a woman's place in our society, as if her place is not imperative for social balance and emotional healing.

There are more female CEO's as entrepreneurs now than there are women baking cookies in a kitchen and why not? God used mighty women in the bible too, not just mighty men. If the female candidate is healthy, do we disregard our own safety to follow tradition? I would think not especially when women did a phenomenal job running the world when the men went off to war in 1939-1945 during World War II.

I believe it would be great to have a nurturing culture of brotherly love under a female President that cares for all the people, like Jesus died for all the people. However, my disclaimer is that she is not Jesus, although it is safe to credit her character more in alignment to someone that actually cares for humanity. A proper trait in a leader over a nation.

If we shall know a tree by its fruit, then when the two options are love vs hate. Why would you choose to drink poison if you choose to drink the antidote? The solution seems clear unless power and control is at play. It is all mind games. It doesn't matter if the topic is politics, religion, education or economics, healthy is always a wise resolution.

Unconditional love is always good. But you can't put a price tag on it because it is invaluable. And we unfortunately were gaslighted to thrive off our concern for a stable economy more than the needs for a stable humanity.

It's no coincidence that the majority of the time, a person who has been abused finds themselves in a repeated cycle of violence because they can't seem to figure out the pattern of how it repeats itself. It usually starts when you care about someone and try to prove your worth to impress, so the narcissist therefore has an in, a reason for you to look to them to find value in yourself, the need for affirmation from outside sources. When you have a history of never feeling valued, by those that have said they love you, usually causes you to fall for the shallow flattery of a manipulator.

You believe you need to prove yourself because that's what the gaslighting taught you and what your groomer expected of you. Leading us to think this is acceptable behavior. Only the roles never change—they just keep being the one in charge, and you keep playing the part of the victim. And the predator will keep you busy doing things to prove your worth to them because they know you like to hear well done!

Busy work keeps you in the mind of looking for a pat on the back to feel accomplished, but a person that has self-esteem and doesn't need outside affirmation does not make for useful prey, they move on quickly when they see trouble. A true friend will just tell you that there is no need to try to prove yourself, they already love you.

A kind and considerate person would usually reciprocate the gesture, making the exchange mutual and creating a safe space where no one is abused or controlled. These are called "healthy relationships." Only a very low percentage of humanity lives in a mutually beneficial, supportive environment in unconditional love.

A manipulator with control tendencies will eat you alive if you have low self esteem, before you even know it. The game begins with them earning your trust. They will do things initially to make you feel safe enough to let your guard down. That way, your interactions with them will be more open, and you will throw caution to the wind, exposing your vulnerability in what you believe is a safe space.

They now have you right where they want you when they think they have you in a "safe space." You never even realize it's a trap. These red flags are usually only seen in hindsight, people who play mind games are very crafty.

Now the serpent was more crafty than any of the wild animals the LORD God had made. He said to the woman, "Did God really say, 'You must not eat from any tree in the garden'?"
Genesis 3:1

Satan is the author of confusion, and this is proof. A person playing mind games will make you doubt your own sanity to make you second guess your ability to make sound decisions. So, you will become dependent on their perception of reality, unaware that they are implanting a false narrative in your head making it easier for them to control the narrative for you. Eventually making it easier for them to control you. Watch out for these people, the one that will lean into you to agree with them making everything one sided, their side!

Once you open up and share things about your life with them, they process that information by compartmentalizing a mental database with your strengths and weaknesses recorded in a small little library card catalog, a handy mental note when they need them to trigger you. Triggers mainly set you up for a flight or fight response and sometimes freeze, it's fight, flight or freeze. Freeze is when you do nothing, you don't speak up which would be a fight, and you don't run and leave. I froze when my father would close the toilet lid to sit down and watch me take a bath. I froze because I just laid in the water covered with a bath towel, watching him watch me. It was devastating. The trigger for that moment would be to "go take a bath". A trigger sort of works this way, someone does or says something that brings back a familiar memory of a traumatic event to your mind and it interrupts whatever you are doing at the time, like a bell that goes off in your head for you to do a visual check of your surroundings to see if you are safe. Once you do a safety check you can countdown from your shock of the trigger and go on with your day.

Problems arise when you don't know when someone has stored your triggers in one of their mental catalogs and they know that if they slam the car door and drive off, it takes you back to the alley with daddy. They want the unhealed version of you to feel scared and alone at 30 years old. When this happens that you are faced with someone that is playing mind games with you, don't be the little girl in the alley alone and afraid, be the 30 year old that sees she is better off alone than with someone that reminds her of her abusive father. That is what I had to do. It doesn't matter if someone does it on accident or on purpose. You don't give your triggers a chance to control you. That is how you free yourself from the victim mentality, a slammed door is just a door that was shut abruptly, when you're healed, and it has no meaning other than that.

If you do fall into a trigger trap, once triggered, a manipulator will bend your perception of reality and make you feel trapped in a place that no longer exists. They know when you are afraid because they learned your triggers and the unhealed version of you needs help getting out of the alley. Offering themselves as the voice of reason drawing you into their reality, where they play the role of God. This is how a lot of hurt people are tricked into becoming part of religious cults, they've studied you and know your subtle triggers that target you to show your vulnerabilities. Like when you get sad during a particular song, so now they play the song coincidentally as far as you know and like clockwork you cry and need a hug and now, they've got you.

People don't have that effect on someone that has done the work to heal because a healed person has control over themselves to examine their own emotions to know the timing of a proper place to show vulnerabilities or when to excuse yourself from the situation. Never allow a person to take the place of God. God is not seen visually with the human eye God is in your heart and soul.

When you elevate a person to the status of God in this place, their word is supreme over yours because your reasoning can't be trusted due to your inability to overcome your triggers from post-traumatic stress at an earlier time of your life. That is what they tell you and you believe it because you believe they know you better than they know you. Not paying any attention to the fact that they have studied you.

They can only recite your memories back to you because of a moment in time when you shared something from a safe place, they remembered, but they bring that memory up in the present, where it becomes a valuable tool to manipulate your thoughts concerning your reasoning skills. Because they learned your triggers! No one knows you better than you and you know if someone presents an idea to you that is outside of your character you don't have to do it, if you know you've been lied to, do your research, find the truth and stand on it. A bully can't bully a person that is not intimidated!

Once they gaslight you and make you doubt your ability to make sound decisions, the mind game to get you to second-guess every decision in an almost paranoid fashion. Going back and forth with yourself about every little decision. As you negotiate with yourself, unsure of what to do next, the subconscious thought lingers that maybe you're not in the right mindset to make the best choices! Now you don't know and it's because you don't know why you don't know, why you are all of a sudden second guessing yourself.

While you're focused on love or living in some little fantasy world where you want people to like you, your manipulator is manipulating you by spoon feeding you a fantasy, sometimes its love bombing. They create opportunities for themselves to shift gears and make you a passenger in your own life!

The shift happens so smoothly that you don't realize it until after it's taken place. When you were making yourself friendly, letting your guard down in hopes of making a friend, they allowed you to do so fully, knowing they had no good intentions for you. The kicker is they know they don't have good intentions, and they play the mind game to make you think they're intentions are good, keeping the secret of the mind game to themselves!

Mind games are a series of deliberate actions or responses planned for a particular outcome of psychological effect on you, typically for the amusement of competitive advantage. It also means they have come into agreement with themselves to plan an attack on you strictly on the opinion that you are gullible prey.

The first time this happened to me was probably at a stage in my life when I lived in an environment where that was the norm, even acceptable. Like for example children born in a toxic family environment don't know this is not normal. This is what we call survival skills, when you grow up in a toxic environment, you learn to survive them. You take a hell of a hit as a kid, surviving but if you survive, is "the miracle". And you know there is a God somewhere. The problem is we have a low supply and demand for superheroes nowadays, even role models are out of stock. We need more of those.

Many people are coerced into things they wouldn't normally go along with because they put their trust in the people involved to be transparent by giving them all the information upfront. Information they can't find on their own and a manipulator's ruse is to deceive, most times if they can lead you into deceiving yourself, you do the job for them. And that way you put so much trust in them you stop asking questions and go along! Which is in total control. Not understanding compromise will never offer you anything of substance and with someone else at the wheel of your life, some will really take you for a ride.

Children suffer most from this. Their guard is always down, and they don't know any better; easy prey for a person who doesn't feel bad about hurting a child. You commit a crime of the soul when you take an innocent child and carry them off into the darkness to be introduced to the devil himself. It does something to their sense of safety, where they may never be safe again, and grow up to become adults with trust issues and defensive demeanor.

The worst-case scenario is an adult who can't contain the need to revisit those painful moments and incite the riot all over again. That is the reason most people become drug addicts, most of those in the LGBTQ+ community have so many horrible stories of childhood memories that are so painful, they can't even look in the mirror and see the same person. They want to transform their face to hide the pain, the very reason you can't judge a book by its cover. When you've been hurt, the mask becomes your coping mechanism. It's easier to put on a hat then fix your hair.

I had to work very hard to choose to be heterosexual when I finally decided to face myself in the mirror. I was on the run from me, the "hurt me," avoiding the pain of accepting the truth about my life. Step 6 in the AA path is focused on acceptance, which involves accepting character defects exactly as they are and then being willing to let them go. You have to face in the mirror the emotional scars you were left with in your escape.

For example, I had to heal and learn to be social because I was safer in isolation in survival mode. Now having a healthy life, I understand it's okay to go hang with people that have no intent on harming you. So I get out of the house more, not a lot but more than I used to, because I have a safe partner, my husband that I hang with and a social circle that for as much as we can as humans, they live for Christ and we keep one another accountable.

A healthy person under a compound level of stress can grow up running from place to place, trying to escape the unhealed version of your inner child, looking for a new start far away from the madness. A person stuck in the cycle sees the boogeyman tucked deep in your memories when you close your eyes, unable to look ahead with the chains of yesterday tugging at your heels. My experience is to stop being afraid.

It's like when you grow up and you're not afraid of the dark anymore, and you don't need a night light because you're not afraid of the dark. That's when the boogeyman goes away, he doesn't scare you anymore so there is no place left for him in your mind, and he goes away. And everyday after that celebrate who you see in the mirror.

I chose to be heterosexual because of my belief in Christ and for me because I know I wasn't born that way it came from trauma. I always knew it was a temporary emotional decision that never lasted past the need for me to feel comforted. I had such a hard time feeling comfortable sexually with a man, I had bad memories of being sexually assaulted over my life that even being married didn't help if my husband was not caring enough. Thankfully, I've outgrown that stage of my healing and it is no longer an issue. When you deal with sexual assault triggers your lover must be kind and understanding because we've objectified sex to the point, we forget that sex is emotional as well. Not all women want a man that is a tough guy in the bedroom, you guys watch too much porn if you think that, it's called making love for a reason.

I had to keep trying to live out the Word of God trusting that God is real and he will help me figure it all out. I was doing horribly on my own, leaning on myself and after being let down by so many people, I said God I'm still here after all that bad history, so you must have a purpose for keeping me alive, show me! That was my prayer. Lord, show me what you have for me, my purpose.

Our society is saturated with sexual abuse because it associates love with perversion, as if sex is a business and get what you can out of it. We are taught to believe that sex is the result of having a loving bond, well what is not love, is the process of being sexually degraded, like an initiation ritual, like a group of teens think it's cool to see who can lose their virginity first?

Most people don't know the difference between sex and making love, and it is the reason for all the misconceptions that lead us to think love is physical. Love is not physical. God in Heaven we pray to everyday and without seeing his face or feeling his embrace, know that the trees are growing, the sun is shining, and all God is good.

You must know true love when you find it. It will not gaslight you, it won't ever sell you out and it won't take your heart for granted. True love will be gentle, true love is male and female, men need to be treated tenderly just as the woman does. I'm all about hugging my husband throughout the day, I don't wait for him to approach me for affection, I show it because it's not a secret that he means the world to me. That has also helped him see that a man should be appreciated for just being a good man like he is.

I was in my late forties when I understood that truth. God is love, and I'm a sucker for Jesus because I believe in the kind of love that you will die for. Sin took something that was supposed to be felt on the inside, such as love, and associated it with the sensation you feel externally when your genitals are aroused, which is a huge distortion of perception and misleading as to "what love is", not what it feels like.

We have visuals that contributed to the false ideologies of sex. Porn comes into play and feeds our bored minds with the idea that sex is entertainment. No bonding, just fun. Something that is for external enjoyment, separate from the soul, no relationship needed. They lied to us. Women live stream either on their own trying to make a buck or sex traffickers set up online accounts to put girls to work. There are very degrading images of treating women like trash less than humans and you take all of those visual images and try to fit them into our definition of love. See how crazy it sounds when you say it out loud?

To an adult, sex becomes scripted. The wonder is gone because they have been overly stimulated externally and empty from the absence of love to capture the heart, just empty memories of unfulfilling sex. Leaving most adults dead on the inside. Tipping them into a more violent sexual scenes like S&M to experience the thrill they lost to casual sex. They need to feel something because the heart is numb. If we keep feeding this insatiable monster that leads us further and further away from love, we have loveless adults trying to feel love through sexual acts, we can't become that, just another toxic cycle. Like clothes in a dryer that you have to spin twice because it didn't dry enough the first time.

Not every lesson needs to be learned twice. We need to value second chances more, to get it right, not to do it again. Leave the victim mentality behind with the lesson, don't live with regrets, accept your wins and losses. Don't leave anything for a manipulator to use against you, they can only trigger you when you haven't come to terms with your trauma.

We only fail to bond with a healthy person because of our unhealed wounds. Our lack of understanding about love burnt us out and turned sex into a mind game, a game where power and control are the ultimate high reward to the ego of the oppressor. Fear, physical pain, bondage, rape, in some instances gang rape, and ritualistic orgies are just feeding a beast that lives off our pain and emptiness. The pursuit of real love through a sexual experience is like running on a treadmill trying actually to get somewhere but you never do, which is a perfect visual for the wise to see the futility of it. Sex can also be used as a mind game if your partner shows disapproval of you during the day and in an attempt to isolate you from affection, they withhold sex to get to you in line. Because if you want affection, you will "act right"!

It doesn't even have to be a serious relationship between two lovers. Just sex is being used as a bartering system between aggressor and pacifist. Like sex for food, sex for shelter, sex for approval. It's a billion dollar industry that must be dismantled for us to heal as a culture. Cleaning the lenses of our glasses, how we see the truth.

Physical abuse takes on a more aggressive approach of manipulation, when you don't agree with or submit in the way they ask, then the abuser feels they have the right to force you into subjection through physical violence. Hoping you don't fight back, bullies won't usually take a chance on someone that will fight back.

The perpetrator makes their argument so convincing the mind believes it, especially for the people who have experienced trauma in their past. The majority of people who grew up in healthy family environments are not going to fall for the banana in the tailpipe when it comes to physical violence. You can have been born in a healthy family and still experience all these things, the difference is that those incidences are few because you grew up in a healthy household so you see the red flags sooner.

Child abuse victims, on the other hand, have already been programmed to believe physical punishment is the penalty they have to pay for disobedience. Therefore, the cycle is easily perpetuated into adulthood. Some people wholeheartedly believe they do not deserve to be treated with respect, as if they were born lesser than everyone else.

This is an example of learned behavior. We are not born with feelings of inferiority. It's an idea that develops over time after repeatedly being treated less than by someone you believe is superior to you. It's usually someone you look up to, someone you esteem and honor, and you feed their ego without knowing it. Be careful not to put anyone on a pedestal, for this reason.

The mind games will have you believing lies before you know it, you will find yourself in a situation where you are no longer in control of your own life. Constantly feeling the need to get approval from the person you believe knows it all.

Anytime a person resorts to violence on any level, run! It is better to remove yourself from the situation than to take the risk of losing your life or, worse, taking a life. You do have a right to defend yourself against your abuser. It's called self defense. Self-defense is the protection of one's person or property against injury attempted by another.

You must dispel the myth that you can't attack your attackers. In order for a self defense to apply, the defendant must have believed that he or she was in imminent danger of harm and that the use and degree of force that he or she used was reasonably necessary to protect his or her safety or that of a third person. Legally it is okay to fight back. You do not have to just lay there. Like I was taught, my father didn't always stop when I asked so I didn't think to grab a lamp and swing at him, I just thought this is my father I'm not allowed to fight back. It's okay to resist. Even in the bible it's okay to flee from anyone that makes you feel uncomfortable, even leadership.

> *And though she spoke to Joseph day after day, he refused to go to bed with her or even be with her. One day he went into the house to attend to his duties, and none of the household servants was inside. She caught him by his cloak and said, "Come to bed with me!" But he left his cloak in her hand and ran out of the house.*
> **Genesis 39:10-13**

Some abusers start by gradually testing your boundaries to see just how much you can take, studying your tolerance to see where your breaking point is. How far will they get beyond your trigger point before you fold or explode? That's when things get real because you have to refute what someone thinks they know about you to use it against you.

If your temperament seems to be able to tolerate or put up with negative behaviors or comments, then they can see that your self-esteem is already low enough that it won't take much convincing that you are worthless. Next, they will become more aggressive in their demands, seeming impatient with you. Asking you to do things and putting a time limit on them creates panic attacks or other fear-based reactions if you miss the mark. This sets the stage for the victim to work harder, having to prove one's loyalty to make up for the lack of on-demand performance. Not paying attention to the fact that they are setting unrealistic expectations on purpose, to make you try harder to be accepted and prove yourself.

Demands that are impossible or unrealistic for one person, therefore never even coming close to meeting the goal.

Since they don't expect you to be honest and say no, completely backing out of the situation. Do just that and say no. Saying no to unrealistic requests, you learn who loves you for real, when it's not about what you can do but about who you are, and then honoring that! You have the right to be honest about how something makes you feel and in a healthy environment we solve the problem together. Love doesn't lead to violence.

In a problem decorated in red flags, you persist in the cat-and-mouse game, hoping to gain approval from your circle. A deadly move that puts you right where your abuser wants you. The mind game is this: if they create a situation where you have to stand up for yourself, and you don't, then they know you are weak and will bow down in the face of conflict. However, if they create a situation and you buck against it, they know you are not an excellent candidate to manipulate and will most likely move on.

It's unfair that we are taught to be kind to unkind people and love our enemies. It made it easier to manipulate kind people, people who don't even speak up when being done wrong. And if you don't speak up, you likely won't fight back. It's important to teach boundaries and personal space when teaching kindness.

Physical abuse and sexual abuse go hand in hand. If someone doesn't mind sexually assaulting you, they won't have any reservations about putting you down physically. For many people, this roller coaster is normal, so much so that they cease to function without drama in their day-to-day lives.

When toxicity is all you know, breaking the cycle is almost impossible because change must occur in the mind first. Since the game is being played on the mind, that is our first line of defense for survival, get your head in the game to find the way out! Harriet Tubman had to become a free slave to know how to free slaves.

The first thing we are going to do is separate ourselves from situations that make us feel less than. Abusers feed off your need for validation. Self-esteem is the only way to combat the need for validation from others.

One true way to ruin yourself is to put someone else in the driver's seat of your life. You can't trust someone you barely know and have not proven themselves, why don't you put that trust into yourself? Believe in yourself, trust yourself.

When you believe in yourself, you change the game and regain your power. Believing in yourself means trusting your gut. That feeling called intuition is personal. It means you know what's best for you, even if you stand out like a sore thumb in the midst of non-believers—knowing that everyone doesn't have to believe in you or the decisions you make for yourself. Honestly, they have their own lives to tend to. Your power is your freedom to choose. We were born with a free will.

Stand fast therefore in the liberty wherewith Christ hath made us free and be not entangled again with the yoke of bondage.
Galatians 5:1

You have the right under heaven to choose for yourself. That's how you take your power back. Even if that means you walk alone until you can be united with a circle of people who commend you for walking in your freedom rather than condemn you for finding your own path. To the good all and the harm of none.

People who appreciate authenticity will appreciate you for being you. And those that oppose, they are free to walk away. Let them because God made you, they didn't, and they need to see that you can still make it. You need to know that you are better off without them. That's true freedom, and freedom is power.

We've talked about sexual abuse and physical abuse, but let's not leave out emotional/verbal abuse from our discussion. Emotional and verbal abuse is more challenging to admit because it comes down to personality vs. intent. Some people you meet are good people with not-so-great bedside manners. Which means they have a good heart but no filter.

They can be rude or smart asses, but tolerable human beings that wouldn't hurt a fly. That comes down to a matter of opinion. Everybody has one friend who is a little feisty, which is no big deal. When we focus on the subtle indicators of emotional /verbal abuse, it is more about intent. Did they intend to hurt your feelings?

Someone who sets out a plan and puts forth the effort to intentionally harm you by hurting your feelings, is emotional abuse. Emotional abuse is not visible. It can only be heard and felt, usually through some form of negative communication, such as verbal abuse accompanied by offensive body language. When emotional boundaries are trampled over, slowly chipping away at your self-perception. In an attempt to distort how you see yourself.

If you are told you're stupid and believe it, then when it's time for you to make decisions, you will not think you can make sound decisions. The only reason that someone tells you something negative about yourself knowing that it isn't true, is to take away your confidence to the point you second-guess yourself.

A person who tells you a hurtful truth and apologizes is perfectly understandable. They are trying to help you. A big part of healing is hearing uncomfortable truths. When done unintentionally or without thinking, a considerate person will make sure not to act out in a way that could be emotionally damaging to you. The difference in an abusive person is that they will disrespect you as long as they can get away with it.

As long as you stay in the same environment as the abuser, they will always believe they have a chance, a constant power struggle in the works. A manipulator is always working strategically to get the upper hand. They only know you are serious when you set up boundaries that no longer give them access to anything personal concerning you.

Haters will try to sabotage your success. Success means an opportunity for happiness without them, and that is what they don't want you to realize. When you realize happiness is a decision, you must cut ties with your oppressors. It's a matter of courage after that. You decide when enough is enough and regain your freedom. Build your own self esteem up with positive daily affirmations, speak kindly to yourself.

If you look back at the Power and Control Wheel shown earlier in the chapter, you will see many examples of behaviors considered red flags and should be avoided. Learning to recognize toxic behaviors in the early stages of any friendship or relationship is beneficial to your mental health. The enemy comes to steal, kill, and destroy. Where the mind goes first, the body will follow. Staying grounded, trusting your instincts, and learning from earlier experiences will help you pull away sooner rather than later from a toxic situation. Before living in survival mode, you must take drastic measures to regain your freedom.

The best way to overcome the cycle of abuse is to heal! Get to a place in your journey where triggers do not control you, get counseling if necessary, and focus on what's essential for you to get started on your journey to recovery. Truthfully, if you grew up in an environment like I did, constantly second guessing yourself, it may take a while to heal because you were taught that overthinking is crazy and believing what you are told is better. However, it's more about being observant of your environment that you begin to notice toxicity. Overthinking is only harmful when you don't have facts and are guessing all the time.

If what you see and hear don't match up, that's a red flag and someone is lying to you. Once you are aware of the lies, you see people around you telling you one thing, but doing another. They are not living up to the same standards they have mandated you to follow. If a rule is made that only you have to follow, then a trap is set to keep you in line or bondage.

For example, when a parent tells a child, "Do as I say, not as I do," that is a sign of a toxic parenting dynamic. Similarly, in a relationship, if one partner allows themselves the freedom to have friends of the opposite sex and freely interact with others, yet imposes strict rules on the other partner—banning them from having similar friendships and monitoring their phone calls and interactions—that behavior is toxic and manipulative. The controlling partner enjoys unrestricted freedom while binding the other with rules and ultimatums.

This imbalance in the relationship creates feelings of fear for one person while the other feels free. That is a red flag. An honest person practices what they preach and is transparent when they are wrong.

Suppose you attend a church where a pastor preaches against fornication but has adulterous affairs with other members in the church. Making everyone but themselves appear accountable to God for their actions, the flock is accountable to the leader and the leader is accountable to no one is a cult. Accountability is a healthy leadership quality, it's a good trait in a role model.

Without accountable leadership that church is a toxic church, and you should find a new church immediately, if church is your thing, however self discipline and healing is a must regardless. Hypocrisy is manipulation. That means instead of practicing what they preach they are setting the standard to do as I say, not as I do. Not living by what you preach manipulates the members to be a part of an occult mentality, the mind game in this scenario is to make the congregation think the preacher is above reproach. God will forgive the pastor like he does the congregation, but no one is above reproach.

The gaslighting preacher is a wolf in sheep's clothing because he uses manipulation to keep the sheep for himself, just as Jim Jones did in Jonestown. His followers drank the poisoned punch at their South American commune in 1978. Run from that kind of place. You combat this by recognizing the truth for what it is and being your own voice of reason. It is okay to be the only one in a crowd who says, "This is not right," and follow through with separating yourself when you feel in danger. Pray and let God know, Lord I do not feel safe here can you please lead me to a healthy more positive place of worship.

When you are renewing your mind from the patterns of unhealthy learned behavior and toxic thinking, a good counselor or support system is the best course of action. God gave us all a brain for a reason—it's so you can think for yourself. Read self-help books that support positive mental health. Be around healthy people who listen to what you have to say and care about how you feel. They don't always have to agree, but caring is important. These are people who support your individuality and respect your opinion. They love you without you having to jump through hoops to impress them or keep their respect.

When I started to see my way out of manipulation, I took my power back. Saying no when I disagree. I don't have to listen to things that make me feel bad about myself. I realized my world didn't fall apart when I walked away from situations and people who didn't respect me personally as a good woman who deserved respect. That was my first step towards becoming free in my own skin, loving the skin I'm in. Never again thinking less of myself.

Chapter 6

Wake Up!

———————■———————

Since you died with Christ to the elemental spiritual forces
of this world, why, as though you still belonged to the world,
do you submit to its rules.

Colossians 2:20

There is a period in every person's life when they come to the truth of what it means to be in this world and not of it. If you are chosen to be one of the people God reveals himself to, you will understand why the earthly and spiritual bodies are so very different. We are created in the image of God, but what does that look like if God is invisible?

We don't know because we can't imagine God without structuring him in a body. We read made in his image we imagine appearance, but what if we were created in his essence. His character! The character of God is very different from the character of evil or the devil, if you read your bible, you will clearly see that evil takes on a veiled personality. So, if we were looking for God without a body, we would be looking for his personality. I believe that being created in his image means having his personality.

Which is why he tells us not to worship graven images, graven is defined as an excavation for burial of a body broadly: a burial place. If he is a God that rose from the dead he doesn't have a grave. There is no one on a cross anymore. God left us the character of his personality in the form of Jesus the man, a man with no grave! Think about that for a minute.

We must wake up to the fact that God projects all that is good, such as treating others with the same good graces as Jesus treated us while he walked on the Earth. Of all the information that can be acquired about God in all the bibles and religious theologies the truth is God himself chose Jesus to be his example on the reflection of his character.

There are rules pertaining to love, then there are rules pertaining to flesh. We are known by our love and by our love we are known by God. Or known by our lack of love therefore we lack God. The condition of being awake is to love, woke means wake up to the differences of love vs evil.

In the Bible, evil is described as anything that is bad, deficient, harmful, or wicked. Evil defiles what is good, bringing chaos, distress, cursing, and death. The Lord hates haughty eyes, a lying tongue, hands that shed innocent blood, a heart that devises wicked plans, feet that make haste to run to evil, a false witness who breathes out lies, and one who sows discord among brothers.

Evil can involve human action (moral evil), environmental factors (natural evil), and contextual elements (structural evil) which structural is another term for leadership!

So now that I have given you tangible examples of intangible things such as love vs evil. You can't say you don't know what I mean when I say to wake up is to be woke. Woke is the truth, sleep is continuing to believe the lie, disregarding truth. Woke is knowing Jesus was brown and with melanin, sleep is believing that the color of your skin is even important to God.

They say a hard head makes a soft behind. The Urban Dictionary explains it as someone who insists on making mistakes rather than listening to wisdom. As much as we think we know, the more we understand, the more we should be able to admit that we don't know anything in comparison to the span of time that God existed before us before man. He created us, we did not create him. We have merely existed for a moment.

Even if we give humanity credit for imagining God and attempting to recreate His image, we still fall short—we can't create water from H_2O, nor can we hold the sun in our hands.

There comes a time in every person's life when they experience a profound awakening. For some, it happens on their deathbeds. For others, the revelation comes sooner, allowing them to reap the benefits of being "Woke in Christ" while still on Earth. As a human being, you may have an epiphany—a moment that shakes your core and makes you question everything you've ever been taught. It can be a startling, even overwhelming experience.

Often, this awakening is triggered by a major life event that forces you to reevaluate yourself and your choices. You start reflecting on your life from a "where did I go wrong" perspective, revisiting the past to see what you could have done differently. But time doesn't move backward, and most of us can't go back to fix our mistakes. Even if time travel were possible, there's no guarantee we wouldn't make things worse by trying to rewrite the past.

The truth is, most people wouldn't choose to go back, even if they could. I'm one of those people—I move forward every single day.

The only honest answer when your woke moment comes is to be truthful with yourself and wake up to the facts. The human design is too intricate of a design to be man made. Therefore, we are the creation not the creator and we can only exemplify his likeness when we walk in love. Since you know God is love, choose love over hate every opportunity. If you know God hates a heart that devises wicked schemes, you must not submit to vengeance in your heart when you feel wronged. Vengeance is the Lord's not ours to take. When you have been wronged or assaulted, report it, stay away from those people and pray, you will see naturally God solve the problem of evil without us returning evil for evil.

The Serenity Prayer says: God, Grant me the serenity to accept the things I cannot change, the courage to change the things I can, and the wisdom to know the difference. The woke moment comes when you let go of control and allow yourself to see your hurt as small trials that came to develop your character. It's the moment you choose to save yourself over sacrificing yourself for the benefit of others. I've tried it and it works. When my father molested me, I reported it, stayed away and didn't repay evil for evil. When he died, he had a closed casket funeral because he was unrecognizable, he did not die a peaceful death. I did not go to the funeral because I did not have a peaceful childhood, yet without him I have peace. I do not know if he ever really stopped being an abuser, I don't know if he repented before he died. I do know it was too gruesome to open the casket. God controls both good and evil and the choices with their consequences are yours to make. Choose wisely!

As a people pleaser, you give far beyond what is socially acceptable at some point when you have no boundaries to show others when enough is enough. There is a time and a place for everything. A people pleaser does not have healthy boundaries related to personal space and can go overboard, "doing the most," appearing attention-seeking or dramatic. Not understanding when you are in the company of individuals with a healthy mindset, they don't expect anything from you. Shocking right?

You are going overboard to be helpful, and they are wondering why you feel the need to do anything at all. It becomes clear by the room's atmosphere that no one needed or expected you to be helpful, so you ask yourself, "What am I doing?" You are operating from a conditional mindset that believes people will like more, the more you do for them. You believe it is by works that you are loved.

This is the moment where you realize you are so mentally and emotionally stuck in a victim mindset thinking that's what was required of you. Because you have survived narcissism and you don't realise whenever you operate in the mindset of doing it out of works, instead of love, you are in the company of a narcissist but haven't realized it yet! You are just asleep to your trigger being pulled, an unhealed people pleaser in the presence of a narcissist will start going out of their way to do things not asked of them.

For example, a guest with narcissistic tendencies comes into your home unannounced. They sit down and say, "you have clean towels on the couch, I would have put those away already." A people pleaser would fold and put the towels away just because they mentioned it. A healed person would say, "yes, I'm doing laundry."

There is a saying that goes, "What's understood doesn't need to be explained." Well, if the understanding is that we are the designated to help one another then we together will do what needs tending to, you will swing into action without a second thought, together. A user will make you carry the weight of the assignment alone. All because your circle has you programmed, so much so that you never even consider taking a moment's rest, not even dare to. For you, it is your responsibility at all times, whether you are tired or not!

When your life has shifted from an unhealthy place to a healthy place, and the requirements are no longer a requirement. What do you do now?

Now that you don't have to sacrifice yourself for once, because you have a friend that comes by unannounced and says, "Wow you must be busy, your couch is covered in clean laundry, let me help you while I am here!" The reality of that moment is priceless. You realize how much time you've wasted being the flunky for narcissistic people that never cared about how bothered you were, just what they could get out of you.

Woke is not a foul word, it just means, I once was blind but now I can see through the BS. When you realize you only did certain things because you thought you had to, it was so deeply embedded in you that most people around you just let you play the role, and that was less they had to do.

If you want to break your neck being the undesignated room monitor, then go ahead and get stuck playing a part only because you believed you had to. The difference is good people won't watch you do it alone, they will help, because good people have enough love in their hearts to help the next person with no strings attached and no reward.

Half of our struggles come from not seeing ourselves more positively. When you perceive yourself as more than a conqueror, everything around you must shift to match your energy! You have the power to change your circumstances. You only need to wake up from the lie that you are less than and believe you are so much more.

Woke is just coming to the truth of who YOU are. In essence, the seed comes out of the ground to blossom, and nature reveals God's creation. You are God's creation. You have to see your life as just more than the street you grew up on back in the day or be defined by the circle you associate with.

I recently visited my childhood home, the place of my torment, and to my surprise, it was gone, not even a trace of the concrete that formed the foundation remained. The house was demolished, and the land was covered in fresh green grass as if nothing ever stood there. Amazingly, I heard the voice in my head say, "It's gone. The cause of your misery has been destroyed without a trace." At that moment, I realized that the childhood I had dreaded for many years was gone. My husband Kenn took a picture of me standing in the spot crying, happy tears. My baby sister and I would often joke about buying the old house just to tear it down. She was there with us, and we said God tore it down for us.

After my mother finally moved out with my brother, the house was abandoned for many years. It looked unlivable, with boarded-up windows, a faded porch, broken lattice, and overgrown weeds. It was creepy, for lack of a better word. The evil that was in that house wasn't meant to be followed by another family.

> *Whoever sows to please their flesh, from the flesh will reap destruction;*
> *whoever sows to please the Spirit, from the Spirit will reap eternal life.*
> **Galatians 6:8**

Generational Curses are a high priority on the list of breaking things. Another woke state begins with the understanding that breaking anything has to be done by first breaking those habits that cause you to be stuck in a cycle of reaping the seeds of sin.

Each generation down the family has struggled with the same thing, believing the same thing because they all learned the same way. Family pride can bring everyone together or tear it all apart. If you do not break out of the cycles of behaviors that caused you to become stuck in the ways of those that came before you, you will constantly be held back in the same way.

Finding out what is best for you and putting those things into practice, separate from any other of the traditions or ideals of the society around you, is where you begin. Harriett Tubman had to become free to free others, it works that way. You must be free to free your family if they too choose to wake up.

Begin by trusting yourself! It's not such a bad thing to be the odd-ball out. Going along with the crowd gives you the same experiences and understanding as everyone else. Why would you want that? Jesus never followed the crowd!

If you've been made the master designer of your life, feel it from within and trust the still, small voice that guides you through life. We should expect the best results when we put our best foot forward for the good of all and harm to none. If your family has a pattern of living off public assistance and never owning a home, there is a poverty mentality that has been a curse to your family.

Public assistance is no laughing matter. It's been around for decades and has helped a lot of families. It was not designed to be a lifelong source of income, it was intended to assist. Needing assistance generation after generation shows the need to be educated about finances, about starting a business, taking whatever resources available to you legally and growing your income, being more responsible over your spending habits. Assistance is designed for those that have fallen temporarily on hard times and need help to get back on their feet. For the elderly that have worked and need a check from the government because they are too old to work anymore, it's for veterans that have come home from the war or homeless, orphans, the handicapped. Not for lazy people that manipulate the system to just sit around and be lazy.

My great-grandparents and grandparents were the only ones from our direct family who owned a home. Out of 20 people, only three have ever owned their own home. That is a poverty mentality that says "I'd rather just let someone else pay for it than work on it myself." They tax it: free housing, free maintenance, grocery allowance, and easy sailing for the most part. Until you realize it keeps you from imagining what you could be, a free ride is just that, a ride! If you don't stand for something, you will fall for anything. Because there is a stipulation that says if they give you this money you are not allowed to make any other money anywhere else above a certain limit. I own my home and my husband and I teach our children to be owners as well to continue to break the cycle generationally. So, at some point you must consciously choose failure or success based on whether or not you can let go of the old way of doing things.

You must think differently because the true battle is fought in the mind. This isn't just a game—it's about reclaiming our identity. Our identity in Christ, as God's children, born again and free from the law of sin. It's about seeing ourselves as more than we ever thought possible, and that realization is not something to take lightly.

When you become the first in your family to accomplish something that has never been done before, you shift the energy of your bloodline—from poverty to prosperity, from limitation to possibility. For example, graduating high school may seem ordinary to some, but for a family where generations worked on farms from a young age, it's monumental progress. Many children in such families didn't go to school beyond the age of 7. Being the first to earn a diploma isn't just a personal success. It's a victory for the entire family line, a symbol of forward movement.

Recognizing and operating in that success—that's what it means to be truly "woke" or "awake." It's the art of noticing the shift within yourself, moving from unhealthy to healthy, from darkness to light. This is where the phrase "born again" comes to life. You can't physically be born twice, but something transformative happens inside of you. It's a spiritual awakening, a new way of seeing yourself. It feels as if your soul has been plugged into an external power source—like flipping on a light switch and suddenly illuminating everything.

The heaviness of having to carry the weight of the world on our shoulders is what it feels like. When we connect with our higher self, we release the weight of the world, darkness, and gloom in exchange for access to the source of Love. For God is love, now we can walk in love towards others because we have been saved by love.

A source that helps you to see yourself as something other than just a human, living a time-centered experience, going to school, working, and then retiring at an age so old the only thing we might have any time to do is die gracefully. Hopefully not, but no one knows. And that is what we give up, the belief system that the only thing we will ever experience in this movie we call life is birth, joy, pain, trauma, and death. There is more we have access to eternal life! Releasing our limited view of life.

"Faith is the substance of things hoped for,
the evidence of things not seen."
Hebrews 11:1

Waking up means understanding there's more to life—even when you can't see it right in front of you. When we say we are "woke," we're not rejecting belief in an Almighty God. Instead, we're seeing Him in a deeper, more personal way—beyond what the traditional religious institutions have taught. Being "woke" means diving deeper into our existence, letting go of the need for outside gratification from things that were never meant to serve us but to harm us.

Every day, we must put on our invisible armor—the garment of walking in love. Why? Because we are learning to break free from the unhealthy habits tied to the darker sides of life: hate, sexual assault, racism, sexism, greed, ego, lust, poverty, and darkness. These are the chains we fight to break.

Psalm 23 says, "Yea, though I walk through the valley of the shadow of death, I will fear no evil, for thou art with me." That valley—*The Valley of the Shadow of Death*—is not just a metaphor but a spiritual and emotional place. It represents the generational curses and twisted behaviors passed down through family lines. It's the low point where the cares of this world hover like a dark cloud, waiting for an opportunity to overwhelm you.

In life, the valley feels like a hollow, a depression—a place of humiliation, where you're weighed down by the burdens of what your parents and ancestors endured and passed on to you. It's as though life has forced you into a never-ending ritual of struggle, stuck in the same social class and hardships, simply because of your bloodline.

But Jesus is the door to elevation, the way out of the valley and into the light. He shows us how to walk through the rite of passage without getting stuck in the darkness. His resurrection is a reminder that there is life on the other side of healing. It's not just about escaping the shadow—it's about stepping into a new life, free from the chains of the past, and embracing the light of transformation.

The wages of sin is death, death is the result of being stuck in the cycle of darkness, a life void of light. I will use the example of my baby cousin whose mother was a drug addict, and she was born addicted to crack cocaine. After having an epiphany of who she was, that baby girl crawled from the darkness to the light and now she is a pharmacy technician at a hospital working her way through nursing school. Her mother, my aunt, is still stuck in the cycle of a living death cycle because she can't release her addiction to living in the light. While her daughter conquered her darkness and used it as a tool for elevation.

If you're not willing to apply self-discipline to your life, you will remain stuck in *The Valley*. Why? Because *The Shadow* lives in *The Valley*—that's where its name comes from. Psalm 23 speaks to living in darkness, weighed down by a sense of hopelessness.

Life often throws us curveballs, and things don't always turn out the way we imagined. For example, as a little girl, I believed my mother should have protected me from my father. For a long time, I carried anger because no one came to my rescue or stopped him. That experience became my own *Valley of the Shadow of Death*, a painful memory I replayed over and over.

Every time I felt unprotected in life, that memory would surface, and I would fall into a victim mentality. It made me feel hopeless, even as an adult—a grown woman with the means and the power to make changes in my own life. It wasn't until I realized the weight of that memory and chose to break free from it that I began to climb out of *The Valley*. Self-discipline is the first step toward choosing freedom and healing.

Overlooking the truth right before me, I survived despite whoever didn't come to my rescue. I had to realize that living in the past, in my mind, was the shadow, and if I stayed in that memory, that would have been the death of me as a grown woman. As a grown woman I have the power to rescue myself and walk out of any room I didn't feel comfortable in. That's my right!

That's how "misery loves company" comes to life. Instead of freeing yourself from the mental state of darkness, hurt people hurt people because they'd rather invite people to the pity party than get out. The enemy hovers over the Earth, the Prince of Darkness. The darkness in this reference speaks of his shadow. It's got to be a fact. Why else would a father molest his own daughter? My only guess is that he lived in the shadow and pulled me in with him and I had to claw past the trauma and the ptsd triggers into the light bringing my children with me.

> *But I am afraid that just as Eve was deceived by the serpent's cunning, your minds may somehow be led astray from your sincere and pure devotion to Christ. For if someone comes to you and preaches a Jesus other than the Jesus we preached, or if you receive a different spirit from the Spirit you received, or a different gospel from the one you accepted, you put up with it easily enough.*
> **2 Corinthians 11:3-4**

> *For such people are false apostles, deceitful workers, masquerading as apostles of Christ.*
> **2 Corinthians 11:13**

No wonder, for Satan himself masquerades as an angel of light. It is not surprising, then, if his servants also masquerade as servants of righteousness. Their end will be what their actions deserve.

People who live in the shadows hide from the light by masking themselves as light, but without truth. They have studied what is socially acceptable behavior and have learned it enough to know what the crowd wants to see and what the crowd wants to hear. They mimic the light, and the next thing you know, you let them into your personal space, becoming close to what appears to be friends.

I say "appears to be friends" because the term friend is generalized more than it is personalized. The dictionary defines it as a person who is not an enemy or who is on the same side: a person who acts as a supporter of a cause, organization, or country by giving financial or other help.

Friend means more than just being friendly to my face. I stopped calling everyone my friend just because we have similar daily encounters like shopping at the same grocery store, or attending the same church, working in the same office. Rotating in similar social circles does not make a friend. By its definition we can see it as much more than shallow surface interactions. The O'Jays made a song entitled Back Stabbers, the lyrics say "their smiling in your face all the time they want to take your place, the back stabbers".

What else should we expect from deceit? A deceitful person will hide their intent while they bait you into their web. It's the same tactic that a domestic abuser will use to get his victims to marry him. They will bait their targeted victim by showing them the appearance of a loving, kind person, acting as if they are genuinely interested in what's important to you. Hanging out with you, watching you so you won't stray from them. They are gaslighting you through subtlety.

That's what we call naive; you never see it coming. When you get comfortable with them believing the facade is the real person, you don't realize it's just a mask they wear around you, that's when the energy shifts in the relationships, from what they can do for you to what you can do for them. That's when they slowly start to drain you by confusing you psychologically and inject you with their agenda, putting their ideas in your head so you can follow their lead. This is the mind game you must wake up from, you have to stop being naive and start to see the pattern of manipulation they are using against you. You must see the facade for what it is. The facade is the wizard behind the curtain in the Wizard of Oz, just a man with a microphone and a sound system that has no real power over you.

The world is exposing itself now more than ever. Everyone gets to be exactly who they want to be with no apologies. The twisting of society is like a sponge being wrung out until every ounce of God is gone. To the good of all and the harm of none, we have the liberty in Christ as God's children to choose who we want to be, which, for the most part, is liberating until your liberty costs someone their life.

It used to be "Thy shalt not kill," but now it's kill first or worse, setting someone up for a downfall. Like setting a person up for a humiliation ritual to embarrass or destroy their character because you won't play the mind game.

The competition to be the best is overrated, when you come to understand we are all running our race because you learn the only person you are running against is yourself. And in that race, you are either running towards or away from God. Transforming into a new person by breaking generational curses or staying stagnant in the cycle of darkness and evil behaviors.

In a religious sense, it's easy to confuse God with the institution of the church, thinking the church itself represents the Kingdom of God. But the truth is, the church is not the Kingdom of God unless it operates through Godly principles rooted in the power of love.

Here's the reminder: *you* are the Kingdom of God—whether or not you're inside a building—when you live as a witness to Jesus Christ, the way out of the darkness. As believers, we are the church collectively, across the world, and God is present everywhere.

If your church doesn't embody the purity of God's love in its actions and teachings, take caution—it may not be a church at all but a cult in disguise.

I mean, the story of Jesus dying on the cross is not exclusive to a building because Jesus didn't die in a building, and he made himself the sacrifice which means no church ritual is ordained by the living God. He died for you to know that you are fearfully and wonderfully made as a human being in God's image. Belief is the requirement. Not some sexual rituals or right of passage. If you desire transformation in Christ, you must read the bible for yourself, get a dictionary and study it like a handbook for life.

For God so loved the world, that he gave his only begotten Son, that whosoever believeth in him should not perish, but have everlasting life.
John 3:16

If you confess with your mouth that Jesus is Lord and believe in your heart that God raised him from the dead, you will be saved. For one believes with the heart and so is justified, and one confesses with the mouth, and so is saved.
Romans 10:9-10

Saved from what? A narcissistic society that mandates we are to remain enslaved mentally and emotionally to concepts and ideas that will not produce the best version of ourselves.

I speak of God and Jesus so much because when I was alone in my worst moments as a child, I prayed to an invisible being that I only knew then as the "Man upstairs" back then. And here I am alive and writing this book instead of caught up in an old victim mentality, strung out on drugs or degrading myself in some scandal.

It has happened to the best of humanity because they chose evil instead of good. It's that simply do good whenever possible and when you are healing from trauma and toxic triggers, just be honest and get some help.

I read in the pages of my Bible that he died for me to be free of the pain of the sexual, physical, and mental abuse my parents put me through. I kept praying as an adult and prayed my way through to even write this book. I'm not a religious fanatic who believes in a building or denomination. I'm just telling you that God gave me the strength to write and finish this book. By the power of the Word of God, I believe! I believe the same

God that helped me can help you and us all live a healthy life in harmony together.

To wake up means to take God off the leash as if He is reserved exclusively for the church from 8:30 am to 2:30 pm on a Sunday and Wednesday night bible study. We need to stop making such a big deal about the building and make a big deal about being the building.

When you do a walk-through at an open house, you don't credit the house to the realtor. They are just selling it. No office or title holds a position higher than the Creator himself. We can't get caught up with the golden calf.

These are the things that make our society function on a level where we put the things of the Earth above the Creator of the Earth, the Pastor before God, and the laws of the government above the Word of God. And knowing this is called "Woke". To be woke is not illegal. The adversary will try to make you feel as such, if you play the mind game.

Wake up, sleepy head, and get out of bed. God has a Promise to be fulfilled within you. Stop living your life based on the idols you subject yourself to every day, through unhealthy learned behaviors. Get up, look in the mirror, and know the blessing is you! You are the one Jesus died for, Yahweh, Yahshua in Hebrew origin.

God so loved the world that he gave Jesus to you as a gift to reflect His love towards you. Nowhere in the bible will you ever read about Jesus plotting destruction on anyone. If you are not reflecting the love of God, you become more of a problem to the world than you are a solution. My problem was that I was sleeping on myself!

Fake love broke me several times, and I never understood why! I kept trying and trying to find it or earn it. I didn't understand that by needing love I was showing my vulnerabilities to the wrong people. A famous saying is "don't hate the player, hate the game" and because I never played the game, I didn't know the do's and don'ts, now that I do. I am sharing what I learned with you to help you win!

The best way I can sum this up is that "YHWH is Love" and that phrase caused me to search out what that truly meant! My findings showed me that the fake love I had been receiving was not from God. The Bible defines love as patient and kind! My abusers were impatient and very unkind, and I thought it was me. I thought I was to blame when I was married and I had husbands I could never please, I didn't know they were taking me down the rabbit hole.

I used to have so many unanswered questions as to what it was that I was experiencing at the hands of people who said they loved me, because this is not what I was living out. Let me be clear, I never wanted to play the game, I just needed love. I wanted to be loved. That was my trigger, and I didn't know it because I was offering love in exchange. You can't be that transparent with evil people.

Evil is a term used to describe something or someone that is morally reprehensible, sinful, wicked, or cruel. It refers to actions or behavior that cause unnecessary pain and suffering and is often seen as the opposite of good. How do you stay out of the way of the wicked? My answer is in Proverbs 4:23-27 that says guard your heart.

When we redefine religion from an artificial institution of laws, in the way that we persist to enforce a bunch of does and don'ts. To a practice or belief system that helps us understand how to treat one another in a plutonic, nonsexual way, that produces the fruit of love, we grow in a better understanding of what love is because our Creator left us a handbook for living life in the best possible way. In which no one feels the need to hurt their neighbor. I learned of a nonabusive God, different from the people who even told me about him! They were hypocrites because they didn't practice what they preached. Honest christians will tell you they are not perfect and are subject to falling off the wagon just like you, but they don't go backwards once they have healed from certain traumas and their triggers, they wake up and stay woke. You can trust transparency.

Transformation is unexplainable until you feel the Love of Jesus in your heart for yourself. Until you see how peace surrounds you through the Power of His Holy Spirit keeping you from toxic environments by helping you recognize red flags. When I read about how God is love and saw in the scriptures how he fights for me to have a better life against unseen forces, it seems almost unreal but deep down I know it is real and I walk out that belief daily.

The fact that I was left in the dark alone with my father was the most scared I'd ever been growing up and to be faced with the same fear in the dark alone with my first husband the day I left him. I realized as impossible as it seemed to believe in an invisible God, I learned the hard way without my belief in Christ and his Holy angels fighting unseen battles on my behalf, I could have died multiple times.

It was the reality that I trusted the wrong people every time, thinking it was love. The scripture reminded me that love is not abuse, and by walking out on my abusers I was actually learning how to love myself. When I started loving myself, I could stay out of situations that did not reciprocate love back to me. True love is a give and take win win, we help each other. If I didn't know that, I would have believed abuse was love because it was all I had known. Some of my family and old friends smiled in my face, saying I love you, only to use the word as a knife in my back.

If it had not been for Jesus, I may still be the fool in my own story. Now, I have the victory over my abuse and abusers because I learned the hard way what love was not. That may not be your story, but it's mine, and I'm sticking to it because here I am, by the Grace of God, alive and healed.

Chapter 7

The Purge – Letting Go!

——————

Cleanse me with hyssop, and I will be clean;
wash me, and I will be whiter than snow.
Let me hear joy and gladness;
let the bones you have crushed rejoice.
Hide your face from my sins
and blot out all my iniquity.

Create in me a pure heart, O God,
and renew a steadfast spirit within me.
Do not cast me from your presence
or take your Holy Spirit from me.
Restore to me the joy of your salvation
and grant me a willing spirit, to sustain me.
Psalm 51:7-12

What a powerful statement! The poetry of the Bible is like jazz for the soul, resonating deeply with the human experience. In this passage, David confesses his sin and prays for forgiveness after committing a grievous act—killing Uriah and marrying Bathsheba.

David, a man after God's own heart and a devoted servant of the Lord, fell into lust and sought to cover his sin through murder.

This psalm reflects the raw and tragic confession of David's heart. He acknowledges his sins of adultery, murder, and the stubbornness that initially kept him from repentance. It wasn't until Nathan the Prophet boldly confronted him that David was shaken from his hardened state. Once confronted, David came before God with complete honesty and brokenness, praying as we all do when we desperately need God's mercy.

And God forgave him. However, David's sin had lasting consequences. Though he deeply desired to build a temple for the Lord, God did not allow him to fulfill that dream. Yet, in His mercy, God permitted David's son, Solomon, to carry out that vision. Back then, it was a physical temple. Today, we might call it a church. David's story reminds us of the power of repentance, God's mercy, and the beauty of redemption, even in the aftermath of failure.

David uses the word *"purge"* as a powerful and intentional plea. The word means to rid someone or something of an unwanted quality, condition, or feeling. When David says, *"Purge me,"* it's deeply personal—and likely painful—because it speaks to the cleansing of his *"secret heart."*

We all have a secret heart—a place where we hide our deepest secrets and feelings, things we're too ashamed or afraid to admit, even to ourselves. David felt the weight of his guilt so heavily that he was moved to examine his heart, confronting the uncleanliness within. This moment of introspection was vital because, without such honest self-reflection, change is impossible.

David's prayer was one of genuine repentance. He recognized his error, turned away from it, and resolved to be better. And the Bible never records him repeating the sins of adultery and murder. His story reminds us that true repentance begins with looking inward and asking God to cleanse us, no matter how uncomfortable that process may be.

Salvation (also called deliverance or redemption) is the saving of human beings from sin and its consequences—which include death and separation from God—by Christ's death and resurrection at the cross, that is the whole purpose of this Christian faith. When we look deep inside ourselves and see the truth of our flaws, introspection "should" cause us to change the will of our hearts to do right, not to judge ourselves but instead to help us see the truth about who we are. It doesn't excuse bad behavior. Nevertheless, only to reveal it to ourselves and confess to God above our shortcomings and take accountability.

The reason we often repeat the same mistakes over and over can stem from several factors. Sometimes, it's a lack of accountability—we only stop when we're caught, much like David, who needed the prophet Nathan to confront him with God's truth. Other times, it's because we shift the blame onto others rather than examining ourselves.

True change begins with introspection, the act of looking inward and honestly examining one's own thoughts and feelings. Until you take that step, like David did in his heartfelt prayer in Psalm 51, you'll remain trapped in a toxic cycle. Your potential to live your best life will continue to be overshadowed by your inability to master yourself.

This is where self-discipline comes in. It's the key to breaking the cycle, taking ownership of your actions, and walking the path toward growth and transformation. Without it, the same patterns will keep repeating, and true freedom will remain out of reach.

At some point, it's time to not just "act" like a grown up, but to be a grown up, somebody has to be the role model. We often wonder what's wrong with the youth today while the youth is wondering what's wrong with the grownups. Everybody can't be on TikTok acting a fool, put your clothes on ladies and gentlemen on Instagram. The kids are doing what the adults are doing, period! But why? We somehow leaped into an era of grown ups that don't want to grow up. Let it go!

What are we letting go of? The old you! You have to mentally let go of all the lies you were told about yourself. You must let go of the people that don't want to see you get any better. The naysayers and the people who criticize, object to, or opposes you and your growth. Those are the people that every time you have a brilliant idea to make your life better, they try to talk you out of it.

They are the saboteurs—the ones who can't stand to see someone trying to better themselves and, out of spite, will do everything in their power to derail those efforts. You know the type—a clique or group that thrives on tearing others down instead of lifting them up.

Take, for example, a man who decides to turn his life around and do right by his wife after years of being a womanizer. Most people would applaud him for making the right choice. But no, we live in a world where many adults still operate with a high school mentality. Instead of supporting his decision to change, they'll try to sabotage his progress. Some might attempt to tempt him with offers of sexual favors or one-night stands, not out of genuine interest but purely to disrupt a good marriage.

Then there are co-workers or even family members who fuel the sabotage by gossiping to small social circles. They might paint him as "whipped" or joke about him being "no fun anymore" because he doesn't have a side relationship. Rather than celebrate his growth, they undermine it, exposing their own insecurities and toxic mindsets in the process. If that man is not strong, if he can't let go of those people for the sake of his marriage, he will potentially lose a good marriage to bad friends because of the lack of support and encouragement.

It sheds light on how some people devalue the covenant of marriage, treating it as if true companionship is not the ultimate goal—when deep down, everyone knows it is. Take, for instance, a woman who chooses to stay home to be a present and nurturing mother. Instead of being respected for her dedication, she's often labeled as lazy or accused of "doing nothing all day," simply because she spends her time creating art with her children using coloring books or finding meaningful ways to engage with them.

These are the women who recognize the challenges of raising children in today's world and prioritize healthy pastimes over letting social media do the parenting. And yet, society often dismisses them, calling them boring or homebodies. I know this all too well because I was one of them.

I was the mom everyone thought was "stupid" (to put it bluntly), the one people talked about as if I weren't even in the room. But I endured the criticism because I valued showing love to my children more than earning acceptance from a social circle that didn't align with my priorities. In the end, I chose to invest in what truly mattered—my family.

People treated me as if I was dumb for not taking advantage of being a cool adult and doing whatever I wanted too, because I stayed home all the time with my children. However, my adult children today know beyond a shadow of doubt that their mama loves them and always has their back.

The same people who didn't love or accept me back then still don't now—but my children do, and for 20 years, that was the point of being a homebody. I chose to focus on raising my boys and building a foundation of love and stability for them. Now, I'm free to pursue my dreams as a successful entrepreneur alongside my husband, become an author, and build the career I set aside for two decades to prioritize my children. Now, we have a thriving construction company where we build beautiful custom built homes. My husband is an amazing builder and together we make dreams come true, along with making music as my husband is a singer/songwriter/producer and manages all of my podcast and book deals. I did not give up any thing that the Lord did not give me back in due season.

I had to let go of societal expectations to give my children the attention they deserved. While others were chasing social acceptance, I was on the couch watching the entire *VeggieTales* series with my boys. Do you know how many times we watched the "angry eyebrows" episode? Too many to count—but that's where I wanted to be. Nothing was more important to me than being present for my children, all their lives.

I didn't aspire to climb the social ladder or chase superficial validation by attending every ladies' luncheon or gathering. My first husband, however, thrived on that attention. He loved the admiration and feeling of acceptance he got from being part of that social scene. For the 10 years we were married, he would come home just long enough to eat, change clothes, and leave again. When we divorced, I didn't miss him because, in truth, he was never really there.

Meanwhile, I stayed home with my boys—tucking them into bed myself rather than leaving that responsibility to a stranger so I could gain social brownie points. I didn't care about being missed at gatherings full of empty small talk and gossip. My priority was always clear: my children.

Now, the past is forgiven, and my boys have a healthy relationship with their father, even though we took different paths in life. We've managed to co-parent respectfully, which I'm proud of. He thrived in the local limelight, enjoying his moments of small-town fame, while I focused on being the best wife and mother I could be at that time.

You have to let go of the things that aren't healthy for you in order to truly heal. My marriages weren't absolutely horrible if I compare them to what I saw growing up with my parents. But the truth is, neither of my husbands actually cared about me. Marrying a woman just to have someone to cook your meals and do your laundry is miserable—for her. And marrying a man just to have someone to pay your bills is equally miserable—for him. We live in a time when services like Angie's List allow you to hire help for those things. If marriage is reduced to a transactional exchange, it's bound to fail.

A man should feel free to ask for help, and if he takes on the financial responsibility in the household, it's only fair that his partner respects that effort and avoids unnecessary waste. On the flip side, relationships shouldn't just mirror social expectations of "keeping up with the Joneses." Marriage, at its core, is about love—and where love doesn't exist, God isn't present. A loveless marriage cannot thrive because it lacks the foundational element of God's love in the couple's hearts.

If you didn't marry for love, the truth will eventually come out, and you'll have to confront it—more often than not, through divorce. But when love is at the heart of a union, it blossoms into something beautiful. A loving couple lights up a room with their connection, people can see it and say, "Wow, they truly love each other."

My point is this: to have a successful adult life, you have to let go of the high school mentality. Purge the mindset that keeps you stuck in adolescence, chasing superficial validation or popularity. Marriage is about honoring your spouse and your shared commitment. Adam and Eve depended on each other in the garden—God created them to be partners, not to share that bond with anyone else. Threesomes—whether literal or metaphorical—don't belong in a marriage.

If marriage isn't for you, then honor yourself by refusing to live just to be someone else's "good time." My second husband was the kind of person who thrived on being the center of attention—he was famous in high school and never seemed to outgrow that mentality. Honestly, he should've stayed single. He was never faithful, and in the end, I degraded myself to match his insatiable sexual appetite. I thought I was doing it to hold the marriage together, but in reality, I was losing myself. He believed he deserved to be a star, and I allowed myself to be a fool, ignoring all the people who tried to warn me.

I stayed because I didn't want to be labeled a "twice-divorced woman," but eventually, I had to choose my children over the toxic home life. His infidelity became so blatant that he stopped even trying to hide it. He suggested we live as "roommates" in an open marriage until we figured things out. I told him that wasn't a marriage—and I was done with the games. My children had started noticing my slow decline during this period, and I couldn't let them continue to see me like that.

I left him to focus on building a better life for myself. The first man didn't treat me well, and the second made even bigger promises but didn't keep his vows. I compromised myself in ways no one should ever have to, all in an effort to make the relationship work. In the end, I walked away, leaving him with everything we worked for, which he turned into his "love shack." He dragged my name through the mud with false accusations and lies, but I refused to engage in the same behavior.

Years later, I met his second wife, who divorced him not long after they married. She hugged me and said she didn't know how I had managed to stay with him as long as I did because he wasn't the man he pretended to be. She seemed like a kind woman, and I didn't ask questions or elaborate—I simply said, "God is good," and moved on.

At one point, I started to feel crazy. All I had ever wanted was love, but it felt like I kept missing it. Over time, though, I realized that the love I was chasing wasn't the kind of love God intended for me. Healing meant letting go of toxic cycles and trusting that real love would come in God's time.

It wasn't until I moved into my apartment after my second divorce that I experienced my true "come to Jesus" moment. For three years, I had to work on purging my heart of the feelings of unworthiness and teach myself how to love again—starting with loving myself.

Let me tell you, learning to love myself wasn't easy. It was humbling and, at times, humiliating. I had to stand in front of the mirror and face my own mistakes. I had to own up to the things I had done wrong, and it left me feeling utterly alone and baffled. How had I mae so many poor choices? Choices that could have been avoided had I been more focused on loving myself instead of chasing love from others. Taking accountability for that—acknowledging that I hadn't prioritized self-love sooner— was one of the hardest things I've ever had to do.

But that wasn't the only hard lesson I had to learn. Just six years ago, I had an experience that completely changed my perception of life. As I stated earlier when, I went out one night with a woman I trusted, only to find out she wasn't my friend at all. I was set up—roofied and raped. That night broke me. I was too trusting, too naïve, and the aftermath only added to the trauma.

That same night, the police stopped me and arrested me for reasons I still can't comprehend. They assaulted me on the side of the road and threw me in a freezing jail cell for 18 hours, ignoring my requests for medical assistance. Despite having no prior charges, they refused to let me press charges for what had been done to me. I was humiliated, confused, and abandoned by the very system that was supposed to protect me. In the end, I had to accept that it was a miracle I even survived.

After that, I decided to focus on the fact that I was still alive. My children still had their mother, and for that, I was grateful. But the reality was harsh: someone had tried to take my life, and many others turned a blind eye to the truth. I know I'm not alone in this. There are countless sexual assault survivors who never receive justice. Many of us are left with the miracle of survival as our only resolution, forced to move forward without closure.

To anyone reading this who has experienced the same—who has had to endure victim-blaming or been denied justice—you are not alone. I see you, and I stand with you. It's time to demand accountability. It's time for a new movement that holds law enforcement and the judicial system accountable for properly protecting sexual assault survivors. Justice shouldn't be a privilege. It should be a guarantee.

But here's what I've learned: no one can take my life because it belongs to God. My days are recorded in Heaven, and I will not leave this earth until my purpose is fulfilled. I believe I died that night in June 2018, but the Lord spared me. He brought me back because He knew I didn't sign up for that. He knew I went out with good intentions—I was just blind to the fact that the woman I trusted was not my friend.

Instead of holding onto anger or chasing answers, I have chosen to let it go. It's not my job to dig into the rabbit hole of who, what, or why. Letting go freed me to focus on healing, valuing myself, and building the life I have today. I'm here because God spared me, and I trust His plan.

Do not take revenge, my dear friends, but leave room for God's wrath, for it is written: "It is mine to avenge; I will repay," says the Lord.
Romans 12:19

I had to make drastic changes in my life to ensure I would never be in that kind of situation again. I came to realize that being the "nice lady" was rooted in my own ignorance. People only call you a "bitch" when they can't take advantage of you, and they'll call you "stupid" when they can. The key is finding a balance between being kind and knowing when to draw a firm line in the sand.

After spending 15 years at home raising my children, I was eager to be accepted by my peers and to rejoin the social world. What I didn't realize was just how naive my outlook on life had become. I kept holding onto hope for the best in people, but instead, I was met with the harsh and ugly side of humanity. The hardest reality I had to face was this: my downfall was that I was *too nice.*

That wake-up call forced me to take off my rose-colored glasses and see life for what it really was. For the next six months, I dealt with the fallout of that night. The police had "accused" me of being drunk and charged me with a DUI, even though I had never been in trouble before. I kept insisting I was roofied and raped, but they wouldn't allow me to open a rape case. Instead, they added a charge of resisting arrest because, in my drugged and panicked state, I struggled when they tried to handcuff me.

The DUI charge was eventually dropped after I wouldn't stop speaking up about what really happened, but the damage was done. My driving privileges were suspended for six months. During that time, I had to depend on others to get me back and forth to work and church. The boys' father stepped in when he could to help make sure they didn't miss school.

It was a humbling experience, but it taught me a valuable lesson: being kind doesn't mean letting people walk all over you. I had to stop trying to create a perfect picture of life and start protecting myself and my peace.

In September of that same year, Kenn and I became good friends, and he turned out to be a true blessing in disguise. Our friendship helped me start to love myself again—he was the first person to ever tell me to focus on *me.*

At first, I was hesitant to let him into my space. I was so broken and embarrassed by everything that had happened in my life, and I didn't feel worthy of a friend like him. I didn't even want him to know the details of my struggles because I was ashamed. But Kenn didn't push—he just kept calling to check on me, telling me that God had put me on his mind and that he wanted to be my friend because he thought I was a good woman. He reminded me of the person I had always been and told me I needed someone "cool" in my corner.

I couldn't believe he saw me as beautiful or worth being around after everything I had been through, but when I finally told him about my experiences, he was understanding and compassionate. By this time, we'd known each other for years, and I realized how comforting it was to have someone in my life who didn't want anything from me except my company. Kenn was a breath of fresh air during a time when I was navigating so much chaos—he simply wanted to make sure I was okay.

He understood my circumstances: I was a single mother, and at the time he was a single father, working tirelessly to provide for my boys, starting over from scratch after giving up everything in my divorce just for the chance to be left alone. He knew I was a loner, and he admired that even though life had knocked me down—multiple times—I refused to stay there.

I remember him saying to me, "If you'll be my friend, I'll be yours." He was honest and upfront, telling me, "Jerri, I don't know what will happen with us. I just got divorced, and so did you. I'm raising my son, and you're raising your sons. Let's just help each other when we can." He didn't make big promises, but he did promise to be a good friend because he could see I needed one—and he admitted he did, too.

He told me, "Even if we're just friends, I'll make sure you're never taken advantage of again. This world isn't the happy-go-lucky place you think it is, but I can help you navigate it. I know you're hurting but let me help you."

Those words hit me deeply—no one had ever spoken such honest and genuine truth into my life. Even if it was only once or twice a week, Kenn would call to check in, ask if I needed anything, or simply see how I was doing. It felt amazing, for the first time, to have a man in my life who didn't want anything from me but my friendship and truly enjoyed my company.

On the other hand, the work to heal was ultimately mine to do—no one could do it for me. I had six months of downtime to clear away the old parts of me that had allowed others to treat me like a doormat. The first step in healing and purging was forgiving my abusers, and there were many. I had to forgive without any apologies, even though no one ever came forward to say, "Jerri, I'm sorry." I had spent so much time waiting for the truth to be revealed, but instead, all I got was silence.

I had to rebuild myself, especially because I still had sons who needed their mother, and I was determined to show up for them. I didn't have much left holding me together—just a 900-square-foot apartment, barely furnished, and a 9-5 job at a local hospital. But God worked a miracle with my "two fish and five loaves of bread" situation and built me a new life from the ground up, starting from rock bottom.

Everything is meant to be purged at some point. Just like the changing seasons, we need to rid ourselves of the toxins—both inside and outside—that contribute to the chaos around us. We get trapped in habits and patterns that keep us bound to past mistakes, repeating cycles until something, often tragic, happens to jolt us into a wake-up call.

"As a man thinketh so is he,"
Proverbs 23:7

The renewal of our minds helps purge us of toxic learned behaviors, transforming us into a new creation. We evaluate our old thoughts one by one, weeding out the bad seeds. Our thoughts—good or bad—are what we manifest, so those bad seeds represent the harmful beliefs we've absorbed from the selfish environments in which we were raised. Often, we're gaslighted into believing things about ourselves that never should have been our truth. And we don't realize that we're unknowingly playing a dangerous game with evil, having no knowledge of the rules. These are lessons you learn the hard way, through falling and getting back up, refusing to stay down. Mistakes become tools for victory when you learn from them and adjust your approach. It all starts with positive thinking, because positive thoughts lead to positive actions.

Bad company corrupts good morals just by being around you. Can you imagine the transfer of negative energy if you're not careful about the people you spend time with?

In the beginning of my journey, I didn't fully grasp what it meant to have a true relationship with God. But there was a drawing within me toward the things of God, and I followed the call.

Everything we need is in our Bible. We just have to believe in God, understand He is our Creator, and walk in the ways of Jesus to reconnect with our true identity as His children. It's not about corporate religion. It's about individual relationship. The key is looking inward, not outward. People can be a good support system, but no one can help you overcome what's inside you except you. You know yourself better than anyone else

> *"Come to me, all you who are weary and burdened, and I will give you rest. Take my yoke upon you and learn from me, for I am gentle and humble in heart, and you will find rest for your souls. For my yoke is easy and my burden is light."*
> **Matthew 11:28-30**

The truth is, I was exhausted when I gave my life to Christ. I can't paint some perfect picture of how I found God by living a good life, going to church every Sunday, and doing everything right. No, I was a mess. I was lost and alone. I ran away from home and kept running, doing whatever I could to survive and stay out of sight from the evil I knew existed in this world. I didn't make the right decisions. I stumbled many times and did things I'm not proud of just to get by. It was either run and survive, or stay and become a sacrifice to my father, who I believed had given himself over to evil. For most of my life, all I had was me.

My father was a cruel man, and my mother was his victim long before I ever was. I knew I had to leave when I was about 10 years old. I was in the car with him, and though I don't remember where we were going, I will never forget the look on his face when he said to me, "You're beautiful. Just wait until you get older." The way he said it made my stomach twist. I didn't know what he meant, but I couldn't bear to wait to find out. That moment stayed with me, and six years later, I finally had the courage to leave home for good. It wasn't easy. In those six years, I tried to protect my younger siblings from the same pain I had endured. My mother was deeply affected by all the abuse she had suffered, and I became the responsible one, the caregiver in the family. I did what I thought was right because the last thing I wanted was for anyone to experience the same horrors I had.

I may never fully understand how it all began, but one thing I knew for sure—I was not going to spend my life in an incestuous relationship with my father. Nor was I going to continue being my mother's emotional punching bag because of the wounds she couldn't undo from her own past.

There were some good days, and there were many bad ones. We managed to survive, by the grace of God. Now, with my father gone, I can close the chapter on my childhood. I pray that, before he passed, he made peace with God. We stopped talking for good reasons, and I can only hope that in his final moments, he turned to Christ. As I work to purge the last remnants of unforgiveness from my heart, I do so with gratitude to God, my heavenly Father, for keeping me alive and protecting me from the enemy's plans.

I didn't meet God in a church. I met Him as a child, alone in a dark alley, abandoned by my biological father. That night, God was all I had—but He was enough. For 49 years, my testimony has been that through it all, God is real!

This is what the LORD says: "Heaven is my throne,
and the earth is my footstool. Where is the house you will build for me?
Where will my resting place be?
Isaiah 66:1

To answer the question, God lives in my heart and will always have a place there. Each day, I strive to become a better person—not perfect, for only one lived a perfect life, and that was Jesus, who died for me. My heart's desire is to tell you that He died for you too, and if you choose, today you can receive the gift of Salvation. Just by reading this book, this is your sign, just like the moment in the alley was mine.

I won't mislead you. I'll be honest—realigning your life with God will take effort. But it will be worth it, for your greater good. Start your journey as soon as possible. This is not about religion, this is an opportunity to come as I did with all your baggage to God and find rest for your weary soul.

The enemy's main goal is to stop you from becoming who God created you to be. If he can use your past against you, he will chain you to it and make you live out the role of a victim for as long as you let him. Take the story of the man with the legion of demons, for instance. The people were content to leave him chained to the tombs by the seashore as a display for crowds to gawk at. This man wrestled with demons day and night—caught in a constant battle, a place of flight or fight, a struggle within himself. Yet, it was in that very place of torment that God healed him. Let that sink in.

The location of his miracle could very well have been where the generational curse began. It was the role that was thrust upon him. He was so overtaken by demons that when asked his name, they responded, "Legion." His true calling and identity were buried under an army of fallen angels, suppressing who he truly was. When deliverance came, the demons needed a herd of pigs to enter into, and according to some accounts, as many as 2,000 pigs ran into the sea and perished. Can you imagine one man carrying that many evil spirits, tormenting him day and night? He was so overwhelmed that he resorted to cutting his own skin. The Bible records in Mark 5:5 that he would cry out and cut himself with stones, night and day, among the tombs and hills. This is a powerful reminder that we don't always know the depth of pain others are experiencing, the weight of generational curses, or how desperately they may need help but don't know how to ask.

Can you imagine being stuck in a state of psychological torment, unable to pull yourself together enough to find your way out? The scriptures we have don't offer us the full backstory of this man's life, and we don't know what led to his manic state, but what we do know is that Jesus healed him anyway—even without the man asking for help. That speaks volumes about the nature of God. We don't have to wait until Sunday or a church service for God to move in our lives. God knows exactly where we are, and He already knows what we need. This is called Omniscience.

Omniscience, or the all-knowing nature of God, refers to the "I am, that I am" and His ability to know absolutely everything. Whether God exists outside of time or as part of time, I believe God exists within every living thing, as the very Atom—the nucleus of all life. But I'll leave that thought for another time.

Thank God Jesus stopped by! When Jesus comes, He doesn't just visit—He comes to cleanse. The demonic entities that operate under the spirit of darkness will attempt to inhabit your body, and once they do, they aim to stay for as long as they can. They cannot function in this realm without a vessel. That's the truth. So, don't deceive yourself into thinking you are more important to Satan than you are to God. The audacity to think you can manipulate the situation is foolish. You will either yield your body to darkness or to light.

"For we wrestle not against flesh and blood but against principalities, against powers, against the rulers of the darkness of this world, against spiritual wickedness in high places."
Ephesians 6:12

But one who prophesies speaks to men for edification and exhortation and consolation.
1 Corinthians 14:3

We often use the Word of God to condemn others, but we rarely look inward for self-reflection and evaluation. The truth is, many times our problem lies in our desire to be right, and this drive to be correct can blind us to our own flaws. You'll never free yourself from yourself until you admit that you have a problem. Life is more complex than simply enjoying a hot dog at a football game, shouting with joy in a stadium full of fans.

That's just the surface. While you're at the game, trying to relax and enjoy the moment, there are unseen forces at work, scheming to kill your purpose, steal your joy, and destroy your life. In that very space, just a few feet away from you, are alcohol addiction, prostitution, domestic violence, poverty, child abuse, robbery, envy, jealousy... and the list goes on. How do I know this? Because when it says we wrestle not against flesh and blood but against principalities, it's referring to the forces behind "human beings."

Humanity is the flesh we see and interact with, but it is the spirit inside that yields to the manifestation of the flesh's sinful works. These include sexual immorality, idolatry, sorcery, jealousy, strife, fits of rage, dissension, drunkenness, and so much more. The human part is what we see and experience through our five senses—taste, touch, sight, sound, and smell.

This is where the purging happens. Let me break it down. When you're feeling sadness or depression, many people turn to substances like drugs or alcohol to numb the pain. But this numbing process puts your subconscious mind to sleep, just like when someone overdoses and becomes unconscious to their actions. It's similar to when a woman is roofied and doesn't remember what happened, or when someone is under surgical anesthesia—the soul and spirit are in that same place. Instead of numbing your pain with temporary distractions, you need to go within and confront the emotions that cause your sorrow.

> *"From the fruit of his mouth a man's belly is filled; with the harvest from his lips, he is satisfied. Life and death are in the power of the tongue, and those who love it will eat its fruit."*
> **Proverbs 18:20-21**

Even though it's painful, you must speak life into yourself. Speak to your pain. Tell it, "You are not real, go away!" Positive affirmations are powerful in purging the old you. No one truly wants their life in ruins or to fake their way through it.

Step one is realizing that you are not your body—you are your soul. When you take the time to cleanse your soul of childhood trauma, you begin to live in the present, not the past. You break free from generational curses that have stolen your joy, hope, and future. You release yourself from addictions, from seeking love outside of yourself. When God lives in your heart, evil has no place there.

The latter is much like being lost—it describes anyone who has yet to recognize Jesus and accept the gift of salvation. Each represents a homeless soul, a drifter with no clear path into the promised land. This is why salvation is so crucial: it is the soul's redemption, restoring you to the promise of God.

Salvation is like a filtering process for the soul. It reminds me of the game Operation, where you have to carefully remove and replace pieces without setting off the buzzer. We remove old, learned behaviors and replace them with something new. It's a kind of soul surgery—taking out the toxic traits formed by past traumas and triggers. This is the transformation of becoming a New Creature in Christ. To me, the word "creature" in this context refers to you becoming an upgraded version of yourself.

When we receive the salvation of Christ, that's where the work begins. All those scriptures about yielding your vessel to Christ point us to the need to lean into God and submit to the only power capable of providing our way out of the confusion and chaos of life.

"Therefore, if anyone is in Christ, he is a new creation:
the old has gone, the new is here!"
2 Corinthians 5:17

As you move forward, it's important to confront the truths behind the things that held you back in the first place. You have the power to reprogram yourself and shed the labels that were unfairly placed on you. When I was a little girl, people would say things like, "Wow, you're so pretty; you're probably going to end up just like your mom, pregnant at 14." That was such an inappropriate thing to say to an innocent child who had no understanding of what they were talking about. I ended up fighting a battle that wasn't even mine because someone projected my mother's struggles onto me. A child is not responsible for the circumstances they're born into and should never bear the weight of those consequences. I remember giving birth to my first child at 30, and I couldn't help but thank God for not letting the lies of those labels define me.

Chapter 8

Transformation

———————

*God saw all that he had made, and it was very good. And there was
evening, and there was morning—the sixth day.*

Genesis 1:31

This statement reinforces that God's creation was aligned with His
original purpose and design to reflect His nature, power, and goodness. It serves as the foundation for us to start unlearning the false
identities placed on us.

We are good because God said so. Since God is love, and we are made
in His image, we too are products of His love. It's time to remove the
labels and look within ourselves and in the mirror to embrace who we
truly are — a beautiful creation of a great, loving Creator. We cannot let
hate define us, nor can we allow labels to shape our identity. Instead, we
are called to recognize our worth and share in the joy of being exactly who
God created us to be.

We can't allow labels to define us because, just like the caterpillar's
inevitable transformation into a butterfly, change is part of our purpose.
I once watched a video of a caterpillar's metamorphosis, and I encourage
you to watch it too. You can witness with your own eyes how the creature

that once crawled on the ground undergoes a miraculous transformation and gains wings. I saw myself in that caterpillar, crawling through life in a lower state, collecting crumbs and barely surviving. I was dodging predators that were bigger and stronger than me, hiding in the safety of the greenery, trying to blend in and protect myself from the dangers of the world. I dreamed of the day I could fly.

I endured the storms, the wind, the rain, and the constant threat of being taken away, either by the dangers that soared above me or by those that lurked beneath the surface, threatening to pull me under. But in the end, I was transformed. We share a deep spiritual connection with nature, and it's more than just a backdrop to our lives—it's proof that God is real. I know this because, like the caterpillar, I became the butterfly. I earned my wings once I freed myself from the skin that once bound me. That skin wasn't just my past struggles. It was the generational curse that had held my family captive for generations. I believe my ancestors made a pact with the devil out of fear and lack of faith in God.

This might sound far-fetched but think about the celebrity rumors where people exchange a common life for fame and riches, often at the cost of their future generations. But Jesus became the ultimate sacrifice to break that cycle and set me free. My salvation in Christ means everything to me because it was the exchange that allowed me to be freed from the service of evil. Just like the caterpillar becomes a butterfly, I too was transformed when I chose freedom in Christ.

In this world, it may seem like you need to play by its rules to rise above, but that's a shortcut that leads nowhere good. If you stick to what's right, eventually right will come to you. That's the law of the universe—when we study God's Word and align ourselves with it, we naturally evolve. We move from the caterpillar to the butterfly. Here are two natural laws that help explain this evolution:

The Law of Divine Oneness teaches that everything in the universe is interconnected. This means our thoughts, actions, and beliefs have an impact not only on ourselves but on the entire world. Imagine a spider's web: when one part moves, it sends a ripple throughout the entire web.

We are all connected, and separation is just an illusion. When we do good, it affects the whole of creation. When we do evil, it harms the whole. The truth is that everything we do, good or bad, ripples outward.

The Law of Correspondence explains that patterns repeat at different scales. What happens in the physical world mirrors what happens in the spiritual realm. This is why we say, "What you reap, you will sow." It's the boomerang effect—what you put into the world, through your words or actions, always comes back to you.

The phrase "As above, so below" reflects the principle that the same rules apply at all levels of existence, just on different scales. What is above represents the good or heavenly, as seen in Colossians 3:2, which says, "Set your minds on things above, not on earthly things." This teaches us that positive, good energy is constantly at work, shaping the world to be a better place. When we align ourselves with this higher energy, we contribute to a more loving and harmonious environment.

On the other hand, negative energy is described in Philippians 3:19-20: "Their end is destruction, their god is their belly, and their glory is in their shame. Their minds are set on earthly things. But our citizenship is in heaven, and we eagerly await a Savior from there, the Lord Jesus Christ." This scripture warns that focusing on negative energy through words and actions leads to destruction.

I was able to break free from the evil in my life and bloodline because I made it a priority to focus on the good. By staying in alignment with positive energy, I've worked on becoming a better person—drawing from the teachings of Christ and practicing God's goodness. In doing so, good has returned to me, and this has been my personal transformation.

If you declare with your mouth, "Jesus is Lord," and believe in your heart that God raised him from the dead, you will be saved. For it is with your heart that you believe and are justified, and it is with your mouth that you profess your faith and are saved.

Romans 10:9-10

God will accept you and save you if you truly believe! This means you don't need to clean up your life before coming to Him for salvation. You can come to God just as you are—a caterpillar—and it's inevitable that you'll transform into a butterfly, without having to sacrifice your wings! Real talk! This is powerful stuff, and I hope you're catching what I'm saying!

The Holy Spirit is best understood as the presence of a divine conscience that guides us back to our Heavenly Creator, embodying goodness. We are spirits living in a body with a soul. The Holy Spirit is an invisible partner who keeps our thoughts aligned with the goodness of who we are and who God is. It helps us discover our true identity in God, not in our circumstances.

God existed long before the "discovery" of religion—just like how Columbus "discovered" America, even though it was already here. Religion didn't invent God. It just renamed Him. The goodness of God was always here, before King James labeled it as religion and called it the Bible. However, he left out some key points, which is why it's essential to do your own research and get to know the Creator of all things for yourself.

However, as it is written:

"What no eye has seen,
what no ear has heard,
and what no human mind has conceived"—
the things God has prepared for those who love him—
1st Corinthians 2:9

There is neither Jew nor Gentile, neither slave nor free, nor is there male and female, for you are all one in Christ Jesus.
Galatians 3:28

Most churches claim to be the authorities on God, but I've come to realize this isn't entirely true. The Bible is part of a universal truth that offers us a glimpse of who God is. But how can anyone claim to be an expert on something they haven't fully seen, heard, or even felt in their hearts? We can't. This is where the religious gaslighting stops. We are all capable of studying God for ourselves—not to prove something to others, but to embody goodness. It's about being a person who doesn't judge, who recognizes we're all connected in the same fabric of life. It's about practicing kindness and empathy, knowing that what we sow comes back to us, whether good or bad. If we choose to sow evil, we should understand that the consequences can return in ways we least expect, and it won't be a pleasant surprise.

We are all part of one body, interconnected in this shared universe, breathing the same air. Polluting that air for others is deceiving ourselves. When we understand these truths, we begin to elevate—to transform into a higher, freer version of ourselves. Choosing evil over good keeps us trapped in the lower vibrations of the caterpillar. If the caterpillar refuses to transform, it dies without ever experiencing the joy of flight. How tragic!

We all face death but imagine dying having chosen to trade in your wings for fleeting things like money or status. There's nothing beautiful about a caterpillar living on 22's when it could have been soaring like a Boeing 747. Transformation is about seeing things as they are and deciding whether we will stay stuck in our old ways or take the leap to become something greater.

Too often, we exclude others from Jesus' love because they don't look, act, or speak like us. We become self-appointed gatekeepers, standing in the way of others' access to the beauty and goodness that is their birthright as children of God. But God will move those gatekeepers out of the way when you elevate yourself through your words and actions. You can't succeed by bringing others down—down is not up.

If God is love, and we keep people from Jesus based on our own biases, we must humbly admit that we are not living in love, nor are we living godly lives. We don't need to conform to religion to be spiritually grounded in Christ. Anyone who professes Christ as their Savior can experience transformation through grace, guided by the Holy Spirit's personal touch. Just as Satan represents evil, the Holy Spirit represents good.

True transformation happens when we are not conformed by the world, but instead come into a deeper knowledge of ourselves. Many of my Christian peers misunderstand others because they only see their way as the only way. But the truth is, just as 2+2=4, so does 3+1. There are many paths to the same truth.

I find beauty in nature, enjoy yoga, and am drawn to the healing energy of Amethyst, my birthstone. I also love reading books about the body and aligning my chakras.

Chakra means "wheel," referring to the energy centers in the body. These spinning disks of energy should remain open and aligned because they correspond to key bundles of nerves, major organs, and parts of our energetic body, influencing both our emotional and physical health. This spiritual aspect of being human is completely natural, and I believe it helps us stay in harmony with God, much like a musician and their instrument.

Some of my church peers might argue that applying science to help us understand God better isn't the true path to Him, but how else do we explain Genesis 1 without delving into the science of how God created the heavens and the earth? This is something that needs to be addressed in our churches. Without it, we remain in a caterpillar state, stuck in a space and time meant for us to spread our wings and fly.

Unfortunately, these truths aren't often shared in our church buildings because some individuals with power and control shape how we view God. As a result, much of the deeper truth about God has been left out of the Bible. We don't know the full story until we step beyond tradition and religion and connect with Him on a deeper, internal level. We've been taught to see things as simply good or bad, black or white, when the truth about who we are as human beings is far more complex than that.

This shows that there are both traditional and nontraditional ways to reach God. As His unique creations, our diversity makes the world a special place. This is why Christ died for everyone—so each of us can have the opportunity to come to Him, find love in His word, and transform into the butterfly we were always meant to be.

Jesus is in the church building for those who seek fellowship with fellow believers, but He is also out on the boat with the fishermen, just like He was with Peter, or sitting by the well with the Samaritan woman, talking about water.

We can't truly say we know all of God if we shut others out, pretending to be experts on Him. How can God—the Father of all—be so universal, and yet we exclude others in order to feed the "god" complex of false narratives rooted in colonization and white supremacy? We are all part of a greater picture, and it should never be our place to judge or control when someone steps outside the traditional box to seek a deeper level of worship in Christ. Our focus should always be on the good of all, causing harm to none.

You, dear children, are from God and have overcome them, because the one who is in you is greater than the one who is in the world.
1 John 4:4

To maintain good mental health, I must tap into the vibration of the Creator within. The greater is He that is in you reminds me that I have already overcome the world by connecting with the greater abundance of my unique self. It's similar to how a doctor, when you have stomach pain, will look beyond the visible symptoms. You might point to where it hurts, but the doctor will use tools like an X-ray to understand what's happening internally in order to resolve the external pain. This is key to spiritual awakening as well.

In order to manage the health of my body, I must be mindful of what I put into it—eating foods that suit my body type and learning how to conserve and manage my energy. To maintain a healthy mind, I must also feed it positive affirmations, keeping my thoughts in alignment with my physical well-being. Balance is essential.

I do many things to keep this balance: I meditate, ride my bike, exercise outdoors, read books on topics I've never explored before, and delve into Eastern philosophy, which is where Jesus' teachings originated. The story of civilization is not the same as the colonized, westernized way we study religion today. The "I Am that I Am" is the God of all, not just of churchgoers.

If we can study openly and learn about different ways of knowing God—seeking the good of all and the harm of none—why wouldn't it benefit us to get to know someone before we condemn them? I'd love to travel the world, learning how people from various cultures express their love for God.

For those who may not yet understand or embrace the gift of salvation, it's better to listen to their reasons and engage in open conversation, hoping to win them over to the love of a kind and compassionate God. We can heal humanity and protect this beautiful Earth we all share if we find common ground between religion and spirituality.

If our bodies are the temple of the Holy Spirit, then we were always meant to house something greater. Holiness is a gift that keeps us from living in a low vibrational state. And by holiness, I don't mean a pious, hypocritical display of virtue. I mean maintaining hearts free from evil, with minds focused on the goodness of humanity.

The Holy Spirit is our guide and helper. God knows that we can't do it alone, and thankfully, He doesn't expect us to. The Holy Spirit is a beautiful gift of love from God, sent to support and strengthen us on our Christian journey.

Do you not know that your bodies are temples of the Holy Spirit, who is in you, whom you have received from God? You are not your own.
1 Corinthians 6:19

You are not your own, and it's in that realization that true transformation begins. When you understand that transformation, you'll find a home in God's presence, bearing the fruit of the Spirit. This offers you a permanent foundation rooted in love, joy, peace, patience, kindness, goodness, faith, gentleness, and self-control.

This positive change will help you walk in the newness of the Spirit, leaving behind the works of the flesh. One choice at a time, you will become a new person, gradually stepping into the future version of yourself. I'm not promising that this journey will be without challenges, but my goal is to help you start strong, understanding how to take the necessary steps toward making better decisions. You will be tempted to quit or change your mind when things get tough, but that's just self-sabotage in disguise.

Even Jesus was tested in the wilderness, proving that staying focused on your mission is key. He rebuked temptation each time, showing us that we must remain mission-minded, not allowing life's ups and downs to hinder our growth.

I've come to believe that the Bible is just the beginning of our understanding of who we are as humans. It's our life handbook—much like a car manual that helps you understand your vehicle. But we cannot stop there. To fully understand the Bible's teachings, we must dive deeper into history, geography, science, and the culture where Jesus lived. Jesus wasn't born in America, and for a long time, his name wasn't even "Jesus." It evolved over time, from Yehoshua to Yeshua, Iēsous, IESVS, Iesu, and finally, Jesus. We have over 2,000 years of study ahead of us to truly comprehend what it means to follow Christ.

That said, receiving Christ and the gift of salvation happens in an instant. I am transformed because I refused to give up on the dream of living a life pleasing to the Savior who died for me. By not giving up, I am divinely protected and assured that history won't repeat itself.

Being a new creation in Christ means that your spirit has been renewed. The old nature is gone, replaced by a new one made in the image of God. This is echoed in God's covenant with Noah in Genesis 9:1-17, where He promised to never again destroy the earth with a flood, offering us stability and the opportunity to turn to Him.

Just as a caterpillar becomes a butterfly, I've been promised a life full of transformation and the beauty of a new beginning. I don't look back. I press forward, eager to learn all that I can about God and the abundant life He promised. My purpose is to be a living witness to His love and His reality.

Chapter 9

New Beginnings

———————

Now faith is the substance of things hoped for,
the evidence of things not seen.

For by it the elders obtained a good report.

Through faith we understand that the worlds were framed
by the word of God, so that things which are seen were not
made of things which do appear.
Hebrews 11:1-3

By faith, we understand that the worlds were created by the word of God, so that the things we see were made from what is unseen. This is the moment when our eyes open, and we begin to see the beauty of love and choose it.

Choose to see God in the birds, in the flowers, and in the Earth around you. Appreciate the gift of life and what it truly means to be alive. This is our time to clear the darkness from our path and let our light shine as brightly as possible—just like Rihanna says, "Shine bright like a diamond!"

This is your chance to move forward and not look back. For example, I recently gave up drinking, not because I had a problem, but because whenever I drank, I found myself crying—crying about all the painful things that had happened to me and realizing that I was just focusing on past hurts. I knew I had to respect myself enough to remove the source of pain from my life. Drinking no longer brought joy. It only brought more heartache. I started to see that many commercials glorified drinking as part of having a good time, but in my experience, it never ended well. So, I decided to take control and stop drinking.

One of my new beginnings is choosing to live sober because I realized I don't need alcohol to have a good time. The idea that I couldn't enjoy life without it was a lie I'd been fed. I can have an amazing time, stay sober, and love my sobriety. I don't live by the law an occasionally enjoy a glass of wine or champagne but I absolutely do not indulge in using anything as a problem solving coping mechanism, as I did before.

These are the "mini new beginnings" that lead us to an overflowing life of blessings. Blessings that come again and again, forever, because I serve an eternal God.

In my new beginning, I'm living a life full of unfolding transformations, embracing each new chapter with the love of my life by my side. We are free from darkness, awakened and sober, fully in our right minds, and loving the skin we're in. I'm writing my first book, making it a bestseller, and building my career as a female entrepreneur with a construction company my husband and I run together as business partners. Oh, and let's not forget—I'm also a soccer mom! Can you feel me?

Every day, I walk in forgiveness because I know that Judas was a necessary part of my resurrection. So, not only am I living in my resurrected life, but I'm free from the weight of carrying the past as if it's a punishment. Life is a blessing, baby, and I embrace it fully.

Life is defined as any system capable of performing functions like eating, metabolizing, breathing, moving, growing, reproducing, and responding to stimuli. Genesis 2:7 tells us, "Then the Lord God formed a man from the dust of the ground and breathed into his nostrils the breath of life, and the man became a living being." That's proof—we are living beings, created by the Creator, with bodies designed to live out God's promise on Earth. Let the Earth rejoice in Jesus' name!

As Solomon said, we can see evidence of God's creation in nature, just like Matthew 6:26 reminds us: "Look at the birds of the air: They do not sow or reap or gather into barns—and yet your heavenly Father feeds them. Are you not much more valuable than they?" But the proof of God is not just out there in the world—it's woven into every fiber of our being, as close to us as the breath we breathe. As you purify and transform, you'll feel that breath of life flowing through your lungs, reminding you that you are fearfully and wonderfully made.

You are not just a body that dies when the body does. No, never that. Every grain of sand that made you is infused with God's essence. You are that grain of sand, a living part of the body of Christ. It's your choice to be transformed from clay to sand, from sand to stone. And may you be the rock upon which God builds His church, just as He said to Peter in Matthew 16:18: "Now I say to you that you are Peter (which means 'rock'), and upon this rock I will build my church, and all the powers of hell will not conquer it."

It's "meant to be" when you transform from darkness to light and become the resurrected body of Christ, the very cornerstone that the builders rejected. Your old foundation crumbles, just as Jesus said, "In three days, this building will fall." He wasn't talking about bricks and mortar, but His body, the vessel He inhabited—sand, not stone.

When you purge from your old life, it may feel like everything around you is falling apart—but I say *seems* because it's all part of the transformation. Toxic family members start to fall away, frenemies reveal themselves, and the trauma bonds dissolve. Your habits shift, your choices change, and soon enough, even your financial situation aligns with your new path. That's the old body Jesus was referring to—the body of the past that no longer serves you.

When He went to hell and took life back, He rose again to offer that same gift of life to us through God's son. We are His body, His Bride—predestined to have a seat at the table.

One question I've always had is: why isn't this being preached? Are religious teachings being manipulated by a class of narcissistic, male-dominated, sexist fanatics, to the point that women's roles in the Bible are downplayed or erased? Have they hidden the truth to diminish the influence of women, even the Lord's Bride? I hope not. After all, only a fool says in his heart that there is no God.

I pray we're not being led by a bunch of political "pathological liars"—people who compulsively tell lies, often tied to mental health conditions or trauma. I believe narcissistic men in positions of power have used the Fall to their advantage to maintain superiority over women. But a wise man knows when God said, "For woman, your desire will be for your husband, and he will rule over you" (Genesis 3:16), He meant it for protection, not dominance. If someone is responsible for something, they protect and care for it, not keep it underfoot. A man is meant to be the umbrella in the storm, the warm blanket in the cold, the cool water on a hot day. He is meant to cherish.

Do they still use the word "cherish" in their wedding vows? The problem, I believe, is that vows are hard to keep when we say things we don't fully understand. To truly keep a vow, we must be able to define it. "Cherish" means to protect, honor, and value, not to treat someone as property. Both men and women are creations of God, and though He made woman as a gift to Adam because He saw it wasn't good for man to be alone, who among us would despise such a gift? Especially when it's given freely, with God's favor.

A woman is a gift, and in our transformed new beginnings, we are the Bride of Christ—God's precious gift to His Son. We are promised a mansion! I have the promise of that mansion if I allow myself to be transformed, shedding the old and walking in the new—walking in the right to be who I was meant to be: great and beautiful.

As for me, I'm not trying to be the hero in anyone else's story—that place is reserved for you, because the choice is yours to make. But as for me, I'm free every day—living without fear, as a mother, wife, business mogul, bestselling author, philanthropist, and so much more. And this is just the beginning.

Because I don't bring my past with me. As a woman born into trauma, it feels amazing to have a husband who doesn't rule over me but is protective and responsible for me. That's the kind of love and partnership that transforms everything.

We nurture each other, which means my husband waters me just as it's described in Ephesians 5:25: "Husbands, love your wives, just as Christ loved the church and gave Himself up for her to sanctify her, cleansing her by the washing with water through the word, and to present her to Himself as a glorious church, without stain or wrinkle or any such blemish, but holy and blameless." Y'all, I can truly feel the love. And the best part about my husband is his sense of humor—he's hilarious and loves to laugh. It's the complete opposite of what I've experienced in toxic relationships, where laughter is often used to belittle you, making you the punchline of condescending jokes, and then getting offended when you speak up for yourself or refuse to laugh. I've been there before, but not anymore. Now, we laugh together, sometimes even cry together—he's the best!

I'm sharing this to remind other women that there are still good men out there. And to give a special shout-out to good Black men and Black love. It's taken such a beating in the media, but may Black love be romantic again! May it be portrayed in its original beauty, as created by God. May Black children feel at peace embracing their natural hair, free from the pressures of wigs, perms, or short haircuts. My husband and sons have beautiful, natural, woolly hair, and I love helping them care for it, watching them live authentically. As for me, I style my hair in various ways—sometimes straight, but most often in its natural, curly state. I love seeing Black women embrace their natural hair, whether it's braids, afros, or styled and groomed with pride.

I just want to give a shout-out to my Black family, who are long over-due for their recognition. You've kept your chin up and your hope alive, and we will be free from the oppression of colonization. We will live as citizens of Heaven on Earth, in our authentic selves. Most cultures live in the essence of their ancestry, embracing their grace, style, and traditions, yet it seems the Black race in America is the only one whose heritage has been stolen. It's time for our heritage to be restored—immediately, in Jesus' name.

Loose us and set us free—not just all women, but especially Black women, who have always played a powerful role in the creation of life and deserve to be honored. It's our time to shine. I speak as a woman who was once repressed but is now free, and it's my time to embrace that freedom. I can't speak for anyone else, but I urge you to believe in your own power.

A woman is a gift, and in our transformed new beginning, we are the Bride of Christ—God's precious gift to His Son. We are promised to live in a mansion! I see a new life unfolding right before my eyes, and my heart overflows with tears of joy.

The truth is that living in your highest self transcends sex, money, or external gains. It's about the example Jesus showed His disciples after His resurrection: He got up! At Jesus' first appearance to His disciples after the resurrection, He greets them with "Peace be with you." Living a res-urrected life represents a life of peace—not that everything will be easy, but a life that fosters a healthy environment for healing. A healed life is one that brings mental clarity for problem-solving when challenges arise. It creates a loving space where unconditional love can thrive, benefiting both the giver and the receiver.

When I say He "got up," I mean He rose from the grave, a place where broken or discarded things are left behind. For some of us, unresolved trauma can make life feel like we're broken or discarded—*feeling* broken, because once we overcome those feelings, we climb out of that grave, roll up our sleeves, and conquer the emotional grave.

Now, to tie this all together—this applies to us, mankind. Even if we don't fully understand the spiritual warfare between God and Satan, or the depth of Jesus' sacrifice to reunite us with God's presence, our birthright is to live the good life on Earth, just as it is in Heaven. We may be misinformed or blinded to the truth, but understanding this is vital. The devil tries to torment us for no other reason than to steal our birthright. But I reclaim mine today!

Webster's dictionary defines "reclaim" as to rescue from an undesirable state, to restore to a previous "natural state," or to make available for human use by changing natural conditions. Changing those natural conditions—allowing God to move on your behalf to restore your birthright—is how we reclaim our place in the Kingdom of God, here on Earth as it is in Heaven.

The saying goes, "I once was blind, but now I see." Your ability to see things for exactly what they are, and to take the necessary steps to resolve and heal from your trauma, is key to aligning your vision with God's power. This alignment is what enables you to live in your resurrected state.

We understand the concept of yin and yang, but when we say that good always conquers evil, it's not just a coincidence. There's a spiritual battle taking place above us, beyond our comprehension as humans. And we come to realize that we were meant for more than just existing—we were meant to thrive, to soar, not just reaching for the stars, but actually achieving them!

If we choose to walk in the favor and footsteps of Christ, His sacrifice on the cross makes it possible for us to be protected from the evil that exists. Some call it hell, some call it the matrix, purgatory, or unlucky living in darkness. Call it whatever you like, but just know there is a way out. It all begins when you look in the mirror and recognize that you were meant for more, for greatness!

Now, I am clear-headed, undistracted, and fully aware that I have a purpose in this life, a purpose that extends into the future. I've traded sorrow for joy, and it's not just some conspiracy theory—it was a carefully crafted plot by the devil to steal my birthright, just like he did with Adam and Eve in the garden. It's good vs. evil. But now, the NEW Bridegroom is Jesus, and we, the Bride of Christ, are His! I hope you feel that truth because this isn't just a test—Jesus is real, and I've seen the light!

We are the body of Christ, and with all due respect, you are invited to come as you are.

I hope I've shed some light on the truth for you. I chose to believe in a higher power than myself because, when I was alone, something protected me from the fear that sought to devour me—from the hands that wanted to sift me like wheat, using me as a sacrifice for evil to steal my birthright.

Please believe me when I say, Jesus is real. It's not just religion as the churches have presented it—it's the truth, hidden in plain sight. I encourage you to memorize Psalms 23 and 91 for protection and guidance, and put on the Armor of God, as outlined in Ephesians 6:10-18.

Praying the Lord's Prayer, as found in Matthew 6:8-13, is a powerful part of the journey of transformation.

Each day, you rise and pray:

"Our Father which art in Heaven, Hallowed be thy name. Thy kingdom come, Thy will be done on Earth, as it is in Heaven. Give us this day our daily bread. And forgive us our debts, as we forgive our debtors. And lead us not into temptation, but deliver us from evil: For thine is the kingdom, and the power, and the glory, forever. Amen."

As you pray, you walk into your new life, and just as God changed Jacob's name to Israel in Genesis 32:28—*"Your name will no longer be Jacob, but Israel, because you have struggled with God and with humans and have overcome"*—you too are stepping into your transformation

May the blessings of Abraham, Isaac, and Jacob flow over me today, and may I walk in the promise of forever! I am a daughter of Abraham!

Now, the choice is yours. I can't be the hero of your story, but the power to change is in your hands.

My point is simple: Your new you is not just for you. When we all strive to become our best selves, everyone benefits, and no one is harmed in the process.

Mankind, in its slumber, often lacks the wisdom to see beyond what's immediately before us. But with the help of a Higher Source, we can choose better for ourselves, living by faith—not by sight. And all it takes is faith as small as a mustard seed.

I can't tell you exactly what your journey looks like because it's unique to each person. No two lives or purposes are the same. We're all crossing paths, searching for ways to heal the wounds from the past, the trauma that shaped who we are today.

If you read my story and think, "Wow, it's a miracle she's still alive," I'll tell you that God is the author and finisher of my existence. It was only through His power, in Jesus's name, that I was able to walk through the darkness of my subconscious, what felt like hell, and find my way back into the light.

This new life—free from the generational trauma that once plagued my bloodline—is a gift I will never take for granted. I once was blind, but now I see, and I won't look back. I choose the future that's waiting for me, here on Earth as it is in Heaven.

In my present, I'm promised a husband who genuinely loves and respects me for who I am—my personality, my purpose—and walks alongside me in Christ. My children and their children will be blessed. I see a beautiful new home, a thriving business, a best-selling book, and more pouring into my life.

I claim excellent health and a vision for the future—all before I leave this Earth and enter Heaven. This book is my testimony to the greatness of God, the Big G—not the little "g" gods.

My soul trusts in Jesus because He answered my prayers and shielded me from unseen evil. I could have died without ever truly living if it weren't for His divine protection. Now, I hope to inspire you to believe in and receive a gift that keeps on giving: Salvation!

Matthew 4 is a powerful illustration of this truth. In this passage, Jesus, after being baptized, is led into the wilderness by the Spirit to be tempted by the devil. He fasts for 40 days and nights—imagine the exhaustion He must have felt, having no food or nourishment for so long. Fasting, in the physical sense, means abstaining from food, leaving the body deprived of its usual fuel.

Spiritually, fasting breaks strongholds, frees us, and enables us to experience God's power in our lives. When the body has nothing left, the only strength we have is divine. Jesus faced the devil head-on in the wilderness after this fast, but He had two key elements we all need in any spiritual battle: the Holy Spirit leading Him and a disciplined body to unlock Heaven's power.

Then, the tempter enters, trying to trip Jesus up. He says, "If you are the Son of God, tell these stones to become bread." Right here, we see the immense power Jesus held—the ability to speak and turn inanimate objects into whatever He wished. Imagine having that kind of power! But Jesus didn't succumb to greed or temptation. He didn't even entertain the devil's suggestion. Instead, He replied, "It is written, 'Man shall not live by bread alone, but by every word that comes from the mouth of God.'" He cut off the conversation right there, knowing the danger of engaging with distractions. We too must learn when to shut down the enemy's conversations and stay focused on God's plan.

Next, the devil tries again, using flattery to manipulate Jesus, tempting Him to jump off a cliff. He manipulates the situation by reminding Jesus that God has commanded His angels to protect Him. This is the trap of ego—the devil trying to make Jesus prove Himself, fall into self-sabotage, and act out of pride. Jesus doesn't fall for it. He understands His mission and stays focused on defeating Satan.

Like Jesus, we must resist the temptation to act on ego or to prove ourselves unnecessarily. When our ego feels wounded, we must remind ourselves of our true purpose and let go of others' opinions. We have to stand firm in our identity and walk confidently into new beginnings.

Thank God for the Holy Spirit, our comforter and reminder of God's love, especially in times of weakness. The Holy Spirit empowers us to stand firm every day, living from our higher self. Now that we know the truth, the truth sets us free.

With this knowledge, we destroy our narcissistic enemy, the devil, establishing our victory from the start. Our birthright was secured before the battle even began, and we must walk in that truth. It's not just about reciting scripture—it's about living it out, embodying the Word in our daily walk. By carrying God's Spirit with us, we are never alone, and we carry the power of Heaven with us always.

And my God will meet all your needs according to
the riches of his glory in Christ Jesus.
Philippians 4:19

Lastly, in your new beginning, don't trade your truth for lies. The Lord will provide for all your needs. This passage reminds us that God will meet both our spiritual and physical needs from His endless riches. The devil can never outgive God, and I need you to know that your soul is not for sale.

The world may say, "The world is your oyster," or "YOLO," but your salvation is your greatest blessing, and you don't have to lower your standards or dim your light for anyone! In Matthew 4:8-9, during Jesus' final temptation, the devil offers him all the kingdoms of the world and their splendor, saying, "All this I will give you, if you will bow down and worship me." Isn't it interesting how when someone can no longer make you self-sabotage, they try to win you over with false promises, pretending to be your friend? The devil does the same thing, trying to distract you from his real agenda: to kill, steal, and destroy your abundant life.

It doesn't matter who switches up on you. Narcissists have no loyalty to anyone but themselves. Whether man or woman, the narcissist will only relent when faced with the Word of the Lord. Jesus understood this process and took our place on the cross, defeating evil for us. If only we could always see the enemy's schemes right in front of us. In reality, no one will warn you that you'll be tempted by the devil today, but when you do face him, resist.

Narcissists will use anyone to try and pull you away from your promise. Misery loves company, and a narcissist who has lost their own inheritance will try to trap you in their misery. But the joke's on them because God knows how to protect His own. Evil will never triumph over good. The battle is simply to expose the Judas in the midst, and God's plan is always to checkmate evil!

Our inheritance is the Kingdom of Heaven if we hold fast to the promises of God. And the Kingdom of Darkness will reap what it sows. So, what's next? Freedom!

Chapter 10

What's Next? Freedom!

It is for freedom that Christ has set us free. Stand firm, then, and do not let yourselves be burdened again by a yoke of slavery.

Galatians 5:1

What comes after all the purging and realizations? After you're left standing face to face with your truth? Notice I said, "your truth," because that's all that remains once the curtain is pulled back. We can't control anyone else's life or circumstances. All we can do is be accountable for ourselves. So, what's next after all is said and done? Don't recontaminate yourself. Do the necessary work to discipline your emotions so you don't fall prey to old triggers—those toxic soul ties and past wounds that once kept you oppressed.

Responding to old wounds pulls you backwards, mentally and emotionally, trying to reattach feelings of unworthiness to your self-esteem with the goal of destroying your newfound confidence. Stay in your freedom and refuse to be bound by the lies of the false identity you once wore, the role you were taught to play.

Instead, always be the main character in your own story. When you fully love yourself, embracing both the good and the not-so-good parts

199

unconditionally, you'll understand how to love others in the same way—and why that's so vital. Don't settle for less than that love from yourself or those around you.

Take the time to uncover who you truly are beneath the lies and false generational patterns. Dig deep into your DNA, much like the Old Testament traces family lineages. I did my own ancestry research and uncovered some fascinating things in my bloodline. You might just find that you come from a royal priesthood. If you're reading this book and made it to Chapter 10, the question becomes: What's next for you?

What's next is understanding that I finally stood up to the generational trauma in my family and said, "No more!" I turned over the tables of injustice in my life, rejecting the unhealthy patterns that were passed down. No more mental fog clouding my judgment or being afraid to trust my own voice. For me I plan on taking the world by storm with my amazing counterpart, we have so many plans of the future that the past is nowhere in sight only eyes front for me, because I have a new lease on life, a better understanding of what love is and no regrets! Building a life for our children and children's children, one that is built on a foundation and belief system of healthy behaviors.

Once I recognized the gaslighting tactics, I knew to distance myself from those who operated in that energy. It was then that I could finally stand up to the psychological mind games that had me constantly questioning my reality, doubting my own abilities and purpose. I freed myself from the unhealthy, codependent fake friendships and toxic family dynamics that I once tolerated, believing it made me kind. As if it was my duty to endure pain with a smile, to serve without complaint.

There's a saying people often repeat, "Blood is thicker than water." But that's not true. It's the family we choose along the way that truly matters. There is blood family, and then there's a spiritual family—your soul tribe. When you find your soul tribe, it doesn't matter if you share blood or not, because both are essential. Don't let everything else out there define you. Learn to attract what's meant for you and let the rest go.

I learned the importance of distance over disrespect with everyone, no exceptions. Not everyone has the best intentions for you.

I also had to learn how to love the parts of me I once felt ashamed of. I had to remind myself that I couldn't control the free will of others, especially when they used it to harm me. The only thing I could control was the courage to get back up, no matter what. Reflecting on the little girl who felt she had no choice but to leave home and live on the streets, relying on the kindness of strangers, it blows my mind. Now, as an adult, I realize that if I hadn't left, I wouldn't be where I am today.

Looking ahead, I had to forgive myself for the choices I made, thinking they were the only way to break free. I had to stop apologizing for choosing myself. The day I ran away, I made a promise to myself: I was never going back, no matter what.

Now, I visit my family with peace in my heart. Since my father's passing, I feel a sense of ease, knowing that he was a major source of the struggles. I love my siblings deeply and am proud of their survival. When I visit, we celebrate life together, and that brings me joy.

By the grace of God and through many prayers, I'm doing well, 20 years later, and looking toward the future. Jeremiah 29:11 reminds me: *"For I know the plans I have for you, declares the Lord, plans to prosper you and not to harm you, plans to give you a hope and a future."* I stand on that promise every day, trusting that the best is yet to come.

Leaving behind the guilt of my shame that I felt, the days that I felt worthless are over, no longer feeling like someone that people used and threw away. I began to move in a way that I gave myself over to God to shed the darkness off me, like a butterfly emerging from the chrysalis.

Once I felt unlovable, but now I know that I am loved. I've become for myself what I never had: a role model. I've chosen to clothe myself in positive character, embodying the qualities of a loving mother, and vowing to give my sons what I wished I had as a child. I now strive to be the example of what I needed to become in order to grow into more. Compassionate and understanding, I give my children choices, and I work to create and maintain a safe, peaceful environment for them to thrive in.

I no longer stay in unhealthy relationships that could have broken me. I learned from the mistakes I saw my parents make.

I woke up and turned on the light within me, pushing the darkness out of my way. I took the time to work on myself, going through the stages of grief to become "Born Again," bidding farewell to the old me. The old me, to me, was someone who saw life as a series of random events, just moving through existence. But being born again means realizing that I am a spirit having a human experience.

With that in mind, here's my personal interpretation of the stages of grief that helped me heal and ultimately realize that I am enough:

Denial – I stopped believing I could do it all on my own and no longer allowed my triggers to define me.

Anger – I let go of the anger over what I thought was love, and when I learned what it truly was, I overcame the victim mentality.

Bargaining – I stopped telling myself that running away from my problems was the right solution. Instead, I learned to stand firm and deal with life in a realistic way.

Depression – I improved my reaction time, learning to recover from setbacks and feelings of defeat. When a tragic event tried to leave me feeling depressed, I made myself get out of bed, get in the shower (where I had my best prayer time), get dressed, put on a smile, and keep moving forward.

Acceptance – I learned to be proud of myself, celebrating the small victories. I stopped counting myself out, stood in my truth, and embraced who I am in the present—both the good and the ugly—while striving to become more. I repeated these steps over and over again until I became mentally and emotionally stronger than my past, stronger than all the people who hurt me. Eventually, I could look my past abusers in the face, smile genuinely, and know that my life was proof they didn't stop me from living or believing in the future.

One thing I did was learn from the mistakes of others. I observed the traits and behaviors around me that I found unappealing or unimpressive, and I made a conscious decision to do the opposite, ensuring I didn't fall into the same traps. I realized that just "going along" with the flow wasn't a reliable way to navigate life's most complex challenges. Discipline, especially, kept me out of the wrong circles.

The next step was to carefully study the positive traits of people who reflected the qualities I admired. I practiced these qualities, even if it meant appearing indecisive or inconsistent to others. It didn't matter to me what they thought, because I knew they didn't see the work I was putting in to rebuild myself. I was aligning with God and the Holy Spirit, staying committed to walking in my newness.

Joshua 24 says, "Choose ye this day whom you will serve." When you make that choice, it's important to align with Source in every decision, choosing the best version of yourself to serve and be an example of Christ on Earth. For me, Christ is the answer. He helped me understand I was loved when I thought no one cared. I read that He loved me enough to take my place on the cross, offering Himself as a sacrifice for me when no one else had ever done anything for me. Learning about the miracle of a new life became everything to me because it keeps you in the light, no longer in the shadows, protected under God's grace.

Waking up every day, I say, "Thank you, Lord, for all You've done," knowing what that truly means—protection from all things, seen and unseen, that might harm me. Provisions are being made for me, like manna from heaven. Angels are interceding on my behalf. If you think that's strange, you must not read your Bible, where countless stories recount how angels intervene to protect mankind from unseen evils.

The angel of the Lord encamps around those who fear him,
and he delivers them.

> *Taste and see that the Lord is good;*
> *blessed is the one who takes refuge in him.*
> *Fear the Lord, you his holy people,*
> *for those who fear him lack nothing.*
> **Psalm 34:7-9**

I believe angels are encamped around me, and it's not just a statement of faith—it's a living truth. It's more than simply confessing Jesus as your Lord and Savior or waiting for a distant promise that He'll one day come to get you. No, Jesus desires to live within you, in your heart.

After you've confessed Him, you must cultivate a set of habits that reflect the light of love in your life. You must believe in the light within you, allowing it to shine outward onto everyone you meet. It's God's source living inside of you, guiding you every day!

Today, Jesus is knocking on the door of your heart. I've already let Him in, and I'm walking in my freedom. I invite you to consider doing the same. Rise again, like Lazarus, and shed those grave clothes—this is the new life waiting for you.

Once you've confessed your salvation and Jesus has lifted you from your past struggles, bringing you from darkness into light, it's time to put into practice the habits that allow you to walk in love and reflect that light. But know this: not everyone around you will be happy for your transformation—and that's okay. When you are no longer dependent on others' approval, you can stand proudly in the freedom of your own growth.

As this new life unfolds, be cautious not to return to the same environments or situations that led you to seek God's rescue. Put on the mind of Christ, think with wisdom, and use discernment. Recognize the difference between those trying to manipulate you and those who genuinely need your help but don't yet know how to ask.

My truth is simple: I was in the wrong place at the wrong time, ignoring the inner voice that desperately tried to warn me and keep me safe. I kept putting myself back into situations that God had delivered me from, staying connected to people and circumstances that only led me to more harm. I didn't realize at the time that cutting ties with those tied to my trauma was the key to my deliverance, my freedom, and my mental sobriety. By setting healthy boundaries, I've finally broken free.

There's a way to separate peacefully, with respect and closure. In the past, when I was afraid to stand up for myself, I would simply ghost people. My mindset was that if someone showed they didn't want me around, I should just leave without a word, thinking that if I had to fight to prove my worth, I wasn't in the right place to thrive.

But as I grew and learned to walk in forgiveness, I realized that some people don't know they're hurting you unless you tell them. These are the people you give second chances to—the ones you try to make things right with, or at least give the opportunity for resolution before taking drastic steps. If healthy communication can resolve the issue, then unconditional love should be on the table.

I've learned that when you walk in your own healing, you become an example for others to heal too. When you heal together with your circle, the whole circle gets better.

There will be times in life when walking in your authentic truth leads you to have a small circle of trusted friends, and in those moments, you must learn to be content with your truth. The reality is, many people are sleepwalking through life, simply following along without ever tapping into their inner selves. As you walk in your truth, you become an example to those same people of how to wake up and start living authentically too.

I wish I could tell you that the challenges won't come, but people will sometimes use your vulnerabilities against you as weapons to harm you. Without you even knowing, your good intentions may be tested because of an emotional decision you made without full discernment.

Even as Christ experienced ups and downs, we too will face our struggles. But knowing that darkness will never overpower light is all the reassurance you need to move forward with faith.

You must put on the mind of Christ, thinking with wisdom and discernment. Learn to tell the difference between someone trying to manipulate you and someone who genuinely needs help but doesn't know how to ask. When it comes to people, there will be times when your path requires you to stand alone, and in those moments, you must learn to be "complete" in your own company.

It's crucial to remember to trust God, even if the phrase sounds overused. Many people turn to prayer only as a last resort, after all other options have failed. But praying first, no matter how big or small the situation, shifts you from the back of the line to the front. This is how you learn to walk in the Spirit. God doesn't operate on the same level as we do as humans, and to align with His will, you must prioritize prayer. Matthew 20:16 says, "So the last will be first, and the first will be last."

To trust God, you must believe in what His Word says and stand firm in His promises. You must study His Word, as it's the bread of life, not just religious jargon. It's the key to understanding the depth of the gift of salvation.

I once had a friend whose father would tell her, "Look at the goal and make the next best step," whenever she had to make a decision. So, ask yourself, what is the next best step toward a better future? Start walking in faith, not by sight, speaking new life into every situation. When we all take our best steps forward in Christ, we win together!

No one can truly know what's next for you except God. With the guidance of the Holy Spirit, you can't go wrong. So, don't seek external validation to discover your purpose—just pray and build a personal relationship with God. He will send His heavenly hosts of angels to protect you as you journey toward truth.

Remember, you are never alone! The Holy Spirit is here to help. As John 14:26 says, "But the Helper, the Holy Spirit, whom the Father will send in My name, He will teach you all things and remind you of everything I have said to you." Trust in this divine assistance and guidance as you walk your path.

I had an epiphany today while scrolling through my TikTok feed. I noticed how many different perspectives on life are out there, just floating around for anyone to grab, each one offering only a 60-second snapshot of someone's viewpoint—often without deeper understanding. While

TikTok is an amazing platform, I couldn't help but reflect on how much information is out there, and how important it is to look beyond the surface.

I came across some political videos, and it hit me: This election is monumental, perhaps one of the most important since Obama was president. Kamala Harris, a qualified bi-racial minority woman, is running for president, and I thought, "We need this." That thought lingered, especially considering that the last chapter of this book is titled "What's Next." I began to imagine if I could personally pick the next President of the United States and all I had to do was vote—I would vote for Kamala Harris. We've come so far, and we're not going back.

It made me think about a new world, one where everyone can thrive, and it filled me with hope. I wouldn't be alone in my pursuit of inner truth and self-improvement—the entire world could join me. A girl can dream, right?

We need to dismantle the systems that suppress women from stepping into their God-given roles, standing alongside men with equal dominion on this Earth. It's incredibly frustrating to see the opposition in this race, especially when you consider the background and the alleged criminal activity of one of the candidates. We have a qualified woman running for president, and yet her opponent, who faces 91 felony counts, is still a contender. This dynamic is deeply unfair.

Why are we still struggling with the truth when we know what it is? These criminal cases, which might take years to unfold, shouldn't even be a topic of debate. We should be prioritizing role models, leaders who inspire, not those who are mired in scandal. If it were on the ballot, I'd vote for bringing positive role models back into style!

Too many organizations use trickery and propaganda to control people's choices for their own financial gain and world domination. Why are criminals at the top while good, hardworking people are left struggling? That shouldn't be the way it is. We need change, and we need it now.

But I digress. It's not my place to make decisions, but to be a vessel, allowing the will of God to flow through me. I am but a vessel, much like the ones Jesus used when he turned water into wine at the wedding in Cana, as described in John 2:1-12. At that wedding, Jesus performed the miracle of turning water into wine, demonstrating his divine power. This transformation symbolizes abundance, provision, and the arrival of a new covenant. It also foreshadows the sacrament of communion, where wine represents the blood of Jesus, which saves humanity from sin. If God can turn water into wine, surely, He can transform someone, even a former president, and cause them to fall on their knees and confess that Jesus is Lord, embracing a new mindset and living in alignment with God's divine purpose.

God is above politics, and He made Jesus the ultimate authority. Wouldn't it be miraculous if someone with a history like that of an alleged insurrectionist, or someone with 34 felony convictions, were to give their life to the true and living God? We serve a God of miracles, and politics is not God. If both Republicans and Democrats were to sincerely give their lives to the Lord, as their corporate logos suggest, we as a people could take flight. Remember, the left wing and the right wing are both part of the same bird. And yes, even those in the MAGA movement, who are simply part of the political ride, would need to repent and get right with God.

I say "repent" because of self-righteousness, as only the Lord has the right to separate the wheat from the tares, as mentioned in Matthew 13:28. When the servants asked Jesus if they should gather the tares, He responded, "An enemy has done this." He said, "Let them both grow together until the harvest. At that time, I will tell the reapers, 'First gather the tares and bind them in bundles to burn them but gather the wheat into my barn.'" Only God knows the ultimate plan, and it's not for us to make assumptions when lives are at stake.

The Bible teaches us in Romans 3:23 that "all have sinned and fall short of the glory of God." No one is righteous enough to judge others—only Jesus Christ himself has that authority. No human being, regardless of status or position, is supreme over the majesty of God in Heaven.

When the righteous are in authority, the people rejoice: but when the
wicked beareth rule, the people mourn.
Proverbs 29:2

Church and politics should never be intertwined, as they serve different purposes. The government's role is to serve the people—*all* people—without bias, favoritism, or partiality. We are the great melting pot, a nation built on diversity, and it's time to celebrate this fact. We must acknowledge that no one is truly righteous until they align themselves with the true and living God, and even that alignment is a daily process. The greatest miracle we could witness would be for our next president to be aligned with the Lord, so that the entire world could rejoice in God's goodness. This would defeat the enemy's plan to destroy countless lives and would bring us all closer to a future where peace, love, and unity reign.

Let's ask ourselves honestly: why would we continue to create causes for war, knowing it only brings trauma and suffering to us all? Who benefits from murder and division, and why are they still in power? There's a better plan, a divine plan that calls for love, peace, and reconciliation. Matthew 5:44-45 reminds us: "Love your enemies and pray for those who persecute you, that you may be sons of your Father in heaven. He causes His sun to rise on the evil and the good and sends rain on the righteous and the unrighteous." From a government perspective, if anyone were to ask me, I would say it is our responsibility as a nation to ensure that everyone is cared for and that our leaders exemplify the love of Christ to all. Isn't that what we stand for? "In God We Trust"? If we truly believe that, then let us live by it. We are the land of the free and the home of the brave.

As the Body of Christ, all denominations of the Church must make room for everyone to find a home in the house of the Lord, without fear of rejection or being cast out. It should be a place of healing, where individuals can come to know their true selves, give glory to God, and respond to His call. It is the Lord who leads us to righteousness, not by power or might, but by His Spirit (Zechariah 4:6). We must leave no one behind in this move of God. We are vessels of His love, walking in His light, calling all of God's children home.

This is how I see it, and since no one asked me, I decided to write about it. It is my heart's desire that everyone has the opportunity to experience the same comfort and peace in Christ that I have found.

My story is just one of many, most untold. If I've suffered, then in some way, we've all suffered. Because when I believe in Jesus Yeshua, the Christ, I'm called to love my neighbor as myself—no matter how different they may be from me. As long as we can learn to walk in a love that transcends all boundaries, we can live in harmony.

We need leaders who cares about the well-being of the entire world. If America is truly a superpower, then America must reflect the love of Jesus, who died for all people, regardless of race, status, or nationality. The words "In God We Trust" are engraved on everything that represents America—it's about time we trust in that, not just use it as a slogan.

Over the past few months, I've watched as we've fought over who is right or wrong, left-wing or right-wing. But isn't it all the same bird? If we tear the bird in half, it won't fly anymore—it will die, and then no one will soar. Now is not the time for division. It's time to come together. Jesus died for all—races, genders, economic statuses, and sexual orientations, the broken-hearted, and even those who are still unsure of who they are in God's eyes. He died for the lost remnant. The new Church must be a place for all people.

He died for the oppressed, the broken-hearted, and for those still fighting for freedom—whether from the legacy of slavery or from the chains of modern-day mental enslavement. We are called to be free, not just from physical bondage, but from negative perceptions and influences. This is more than just an exodus—it's a crossing over into the promised land.

Jesus died for Republicans and Democrats alike and Liberals. He even flipped over tables when He saw the commercialization of God. We can't afford to keep fighting over who's right, because no one is truly right when we're fighting. The only right thing is to love one another, to walk in pure brotherly love so we can heal together. We've all suffered in some way—

nobody escapes without scars. Scars are the proof that we've fought and survived. Even Jesus bore nail marks in His hands at the Resurrection.

If Jesus were president, He would want everyone to live a good life, to eat good food. That brings me to a crucial question: why are we eating food that's poisoned? Why are we allowed to buy food approved by government agencies like the FDA, when they knowingly allow harmful substances to be sold to us? It's the government's responsibility to ensure that our food is fresh and nourishing, not toxic. God created nature to provide us with healing—lab-grown food doesn't have the same power. Our food should be free of harmful chemicals, nourishing us and assisting the body's natural ability to heal itself. With all the technology we have today, we shouldn't have to live with sickness or disease. Our bodies were created to heal, and our food should support that process.

If our national motto is "In God We Trust," then it's time to really trust God for more. We need to ban all ungodly and unjust treatment of people. No group should be treated better than another based on any ideology, including white supremacy. God is supreme, not any human ideology or race. It's time for us to align with God's truth and love for all people. Let's trust in God, not in systems built on division or hate.

What's next is a new beginning for everyone. Too many people are afraid to face the past, reliving traumas and nightmares that should have never happened. There should never be sexual, physical, or mental abuse of any kind, because we are not animals—we are better than that. We are meant to treat each other with dignity and respect. As the saying goes, "treat others as you want to be treated." If we're honest with ourselves, we can admit that we all need love and safety. We must especially learn how to take personal responsibility for ensuring our children are always protected and accounted for.

Husbands should love their wives fully, keeping their commitment to her and honoring the covenant they've made. Wives should love their husbands, appreciating the protector and provider he is, and supporting him as the helpmeet he needs. When couples work together, finding what works best for both, they are stronger because they are unified. True power lies in understanding each other and walking in harmony, as the scriptures say.

Marriage shouldn't be burdened by a set of rigid rules. Couples should be free to live happily ever after, as long as love and respect are at the center of their relationship, free from abuse. The promise of marriage is to be partners in everything, showing the world that love is a blessing, not a burden. This love gives hope to those who are seeking it. Too many marriages fail because we try to live by someone else's example, rather than setting our own. After all, no two people are the same, and no two marriages should be either. Each marriage should be unique, built on love, understanding, and mutual respect.

In my world, what's next is ensuring that veterans have access to free government housing. They fought to protect us, often from threats we didn't even fully understand, and they absolutely deserve a safe place to call home. They also deserve prompt, quality healthcare. Additionally, I believe that everyone, everywhere, should have access to excellent mental health support. We've all faced our own battles, particularly in the battlefield of our minds, and we all need help at times. It's crucial that mental health care is available to everyone when they need it most.

In my world, what's next is transforming our foster care systems to focus on rehabilitation programs for both parents and children. We need to teach families how to love and support one another because at the core, that's what we're doing—building families, not just homes. We need to help heal families and show them how to live in harmony.

By using the Bible as a guide and leading by example, we can create a better world. We all share this planet, so it's up to us to ensure that no one is forgotten or left behind, doing our best to account for everyone.

We should also ban organizations that use deception and manipulation as tools of power, controlling people's choices for financial gain and global dominance. That kind of behavior is criminal! Why are those who deceive and harm others in power while good, hardworking people struggle? It's time to make an example of those who thrive on evil, take away their influence, and replace them with people who genuinely care about the well-being of mankind.

The pain and injustice in the world have impacted my own life—my father, a military veteran, didn't return the same way he left, mentally. And my teenage mother, struggling on welfare, had her children taken by child protective services. This is a reflection of a deeper issue: we've been treating the symptoms of our choices, not addressing the root causes. It's time to focus on healing and prevention.

When I was a little girl, I saw the world around me and felt powerless to change it. But now that I've grown up, I know I no longer have to feel helpless. I am walking in my power and will do my part to make this world a better place. It's bigger than me—I see the pain in others, and I realize it wasn't just me hurting. So many people are struggling, and it's my deepest desire that everyone has access to the same healing power that helped me.

If Jesus was the ultimate sacrifice, then there are no more excuses for us. We must walk in the new covenant, embracing the next chapter of life in His name, without needing to sacrifice ourselves just to live a healthy, blessed life. Isn't that what "In God We Trust" should truly stand for? It's time we set that standard and live by it. Anything less would be messy, and there's no room for messiness anymore. We've allowed evil to persist for far too long—it's time to do what's right!

America cannot continue to act as a bully. This country is destined for greater things. Remember when we were the great melting pot, where people from all walks of life came together to heal and grow? I live in America, but my ancestors come from Nigeria, Europe, and Ireland. And if God is love, let's start with that—because against love, there is no law.

We must be the example. Our roots may span the globe, but we all live here together now. If God is love, let's make that our foundation. The fruit of the Spirit is love, joy, peace, forbearance, kindness, goodness, faithfulness, gentleness, and self-control. Let's embody that and show the world what it looks like to truly take care of one another.

Hebrews highlights that Jesus' sacrificial death is how God established the new covenant, offering abundant mercy to all people, as described in Jeremiah 31:31-43. Through His sacrifice, which is the ultimate offering for sin, no further sacrifices are necessary.

For me, I am not just a Christian who attends church. I am an Ambassador of the Most High God, called to share His message with the world. Jesus died for everyone, so we can live together in harmony and learn how to walk in love with one another.

We can never truly know someone's story unless we take the time to listen. Life shouldn't just be about where we are born, where we work, what we acquire, or when we eventually die. If we can't pause and honestly look at ourselves in the mirror, then who are we really? We need to look inward and find what can't be obtained from the outside world. Without this, we miss out on living a full, abundant life and walking in our own truth.

Another point I want to address is how absurd it is that multi-racial children are often forced to choose sides between their black or white families, or whichever blend of backgrounds they come from. That's just ridiculous. I remember growing up, not being "white" enough for my white friends or "black" enough for my black friends. No one should ever be defined by their race. We come together to create life, so why can't we come together to teach our children the truth of their ancestry in love? It's something I still don't understand.

We should all be enough, just as we are, without feeling the need to fit into these narrow, socially acceptable boxes. It's time for us to be more open-minded about this. This is what makes the great melting pot so incredible.

We can't go backward. Our children are too progressive for that—they didn't grow up in the same world we did. They are far more emotionally intelligent than we were growing up.

I want my sons and my husband, men of color, to feel safe in their God-given skin, without the fear of being harassed or killed by a police officer who's been taught to be racist and shoot brown people on sight. We can't go back to that. African Americans, Native Americans, and all people of color have endured enough. They deserve kindness and respect. What society calls "minorities" are truly the majority, the ones who built this country, yet they never received the land they were promised. It's time for reparations for the cruel and inhumane treatment throughout the history of colonialism.

Reparations should start with wiping out all debt, offering free housing, and providing free college, in honor of those who fought for freedom and who died for the hope of a better future. We should also compensate for the patents and inventions created through the forced labor of slaves. The generations who prayed for the freedom of the next generation should be honored, and we have the resources to do it—plenty of money in the federal reserve or abandoned land to reallocate. I would like to have the opportunity to spread generational wealth to my children. It should be more than 1% of the population with all the wealth. I would like to see millions of dollars if not billions of dollars in my bank account for all the hard work my husband and I press through everyday! To become a philanthropist and give back to society is a great dream of mine.

We also desperately need racial harmony for the sake of our children. No more choosing sides—because we're all in this together. We are destroying humanity when we teach hate and envy or say one person is better than another.

One Nation Under God, right? If we say God is love, where is the love in promoting hate? We can't afford to be that ignorant. If God is love, then what are we waiting for to walk in it?

It should go without saying that we also need to look out for our LGBT+ community, especially given the immense trauma they have faced. Same-sex issues existed when Jesus was on the cross, and he didn't exclude anyone when he took those 39 stripes. We need to help people understand that sex, whether gay or straight, is not the answer to anything real. We can't continue living in a world where sexual pleasure is prioritized as the core of our identity.

Perversion often turns to sexual gratification as a coping mechanism, regardless of who you lay down with. We need to heal from using sex in this way, and we need everyone's cooperation to assist in that healing. We must help people understand that sex is not the answer to our deeper needs, whether they are gay or straight.

We often label people as gay simply because they don't fit neatly into a "straight box," with prescribed mannerisms and emotional reactions that society deems acceptable. Even women who were strong were called "tomboys," which is just another form of gaslighting. Some people adopt roles they don't fully identify with because religion and society have dictated gender roles, such as teaching that men can't show pain by crying. Yet, religion also told us that the Easter Bunny lays eggs—and that's clearly not true. There are many lies we've been taught that we need to unravel to get to the truth.

Before we can unravel these false narratives, we must stop demonizing each other. Didn't Jesus say that what you do to the least of these, you do to me? And I'm not calling anyone the least, but if we make someone feel that way, we are neglecting the very people God loves. We can't afford to fight over petty differences. Our ancestors died fighting for our freedoms—yes, all of our ancestors fought one another, but they also fought for a better future. Let's honor that fight by coming together, not tearing each other down.

It's time for us all to learn what real love is and not just use sex and war as a temporary coping mechanism to problems that are much deeper and soul related. We don't really know what love is and we will never know until we try to stop and understand one another.

Now faith is the substance of things hoped for,
the evidence of things not seen.
Hebrews 11:1

It's time to step into freedom, to embrace our true identity, and to take off the masks we've been wearing. It's time to face the truth and break free from the lies that have held us back. The generations before us fought and died with the hope that the next generation would be better, and now, it's our turn to live out that legacy.

There are two distinct mentalities at play: hate on one side and love on the other. These are polar opposites, and whichever one you embody reflects whether you are healed or not. One mentality is bent on destroying anyone different, while the other seeks to embrace differences and foster love. Hurt people hurt others, but healed people love, because they have experienced the pain themselves. These misconceptions divide us in our churches, neighborhoods, workplaces, families, and even governments.

There will always be those who choose love and those who choose hate, but when the moment comes for you to choose, don't choose hate. That's the real struggle when you're being hated on. The war is in our minds, and if you choose love, you've already won. When we pray, "Thy kingdom come, thy will be done," we must also learn to wait in love, working together, trusting that over time, our prayers will be answered as we grow and develop.

Lastly, in your transformation, it's important to understand that not everyone around you will celebrate your progress. As you grow, avoid putting yourself back in the same places and situations where you found yourself when God rescued you. I can recall many moments in my life when I felt like my soul was clean and ready to welcome the Holy Spirit, only to let myself fall back into old habits and patterns of deception. But not anymore—I am standing firm in my recovery with a "do not disturb" sign for anyone trying to steal my progress.

I wish I could say that the weapon won't be formed against you, but sometimes hurt people hurt people because it's all they know until they learn better. What I can tell you is that it won't prosper, and that's all the assurance you need—if you believe. Once we've learned, we can teach, and that's how we spread goodness. Learning to do good by others and showing what it means to walk in pure love, free of ulterior motives.

If you can see the whole picture in one glance, that's not faith! Faith is trusting in what you can't fully see or understand. Once you've turned your test into a testimony, how will you activate your faith? You have to choose to believe in the plan God has for you, as stated in Jeremiah 29:11—"Plans to prosper you and not harm you, plans to give you hope and a future." Hold onto that promise as your firm foundation, knowing that His plan is perfect, even if it's not fully clear yet.

Too often, we rush ahead of God's plan, thinking we know what's best for our lives. That's not healthy, nor does it allow us the space to reflect on who we truly are. But when we take the time to pray, "Thy kingdom come, thy will be done," and trust that for the good of all and the harm of none, our Father in Heaven has heard us, then we can wait with childlike faith and expectation, knowing that God's miracles will follow.

If we can come to the table, air out our differences, and allow space for healing, I believe we can live as a nation where everyone feels valued. The word "if" introduces a conditional possibility—suggesting that if we take the right actions, we can create the change we wish to see.

> *If my people, which are called by my name, shall humble themselves,*
> *and pray, and seek my face, and turn from their wicked ways; then will*
> *I hear from heaven, and will forgive their sin, and will heal their land.*
> **2 Chronicles 7:14**

This concept may seem simple and straightforward, but it becomes much more challenging when it's time to choose God over a more enticing path. Just like Adam and Eve in the garden, who thought taking that forbidden fruit would make them more like God, we often fail to trust the command we're given and, in doing so, fail to trust God.

But we don't have to walk the same path as the fallen. You can do better, you can be better!

It's crucial to remember to trust God, even though it's a phrase so overused that many people only turn to God as a last resort, after all other attempts have failed. To truly trust God, you must believe in what He has said, and His Word makes it clear. You must study it diligently, just as you would any great piece of literature, because this Word is the bread of life. You must understand that God lives within you, and in order to tap into

His wisdom, you need to pray and meditate on it to discover what that looks like.

In most biblical stories, the great figures were alone when God spoke into existence the purpose for their lives. You might question your sanity when that still, small voice calls your name, as it did with Samuel, or think you're imagining things when you stand before a burning bush like Moses, all alone with only your faith to validate what you see. But instead of doubting, meditate on this: It's your inner conscience, the voice within, guiding you on your path to your purpose.

Think of what happened after Daniel was released from the lion's den and after the three Hebrew boys emerged from the fire. The entire village turned to worship the Lord God! But it took years before the purpose behind their captivity was revealed. During that time, they were doing the inner work, and when they were finally released, they were better than when they entered.

The scripture tells us, "They that wait on the Lord shall renew their strength!" (Isaiah 40:31). So, ask yourself: What's the next best step towards a brighter future? Begin your new journey by walking in faith, not by sight. No one else can know what's next for you except you, and with the guidance of the Holy Spirit, you can't go wrong. When we all put our best foot forward in Christ, we all win together!

Let's end on a simple prayer:

Dear Lord,

Your Word says in Jeremiah 29:12-14, "Then you will call upon Me and come and pray to Me, and I will listen to you. You will seek Me and find Me when you search for Me with all your heart. I will be found by you, declares the LORD, and I will restore you from captivity and gather you from all the nations and places to which I have banished you, declares the LORD. I will restore you to the place from which I sent you into exile." We seek You with all our hearts, Lord, trusting in Your promise of restoration and guidance. Amen.

I pray that anyone reading this book is touched by my testimony, understanding that You love us all the same. I pray they have the faith to turn hopelessness into hope for the future, knowing You are no respecter of persons, and that what You did on the cross was for all humanity. I pray they come to believe they were born on purpose, with a purpose, and that they trust You, the Creator, to reveal their purpose through the good gifts You have placed inside of them—qualities meant to serve the good of all and harm none. I pray they continue seeking a personal relationship with You, amidst everything else in their lives.

In the Name of Christ Jesus Yeshua,
Amen! God Bless.

www.ingramcontent.com/pod-product-compliance
Lightning Source LLC
Chambersburg PA
CBHW051612120626
46551CB00014B/1761